555

I met you in a story
Upon an autumn eve;
We built a treetop hideout
Among the russet leaves.

I met you in a story
Upon a snowy morn;
We wreathed a deer in holly
And fed him sweet white corn.

I met you in a story
Upon a summer night;
We took your sloop exploring
Through seas of silver light.

I met you in a story
Upon a rainy day;
We rode on armored stallions
Into the battle fray.

I met you in a story—
And, friend, I do believe
I'll meet you in that treetop
Another autumn's eve.
—Eileen M. Berry

Reading 4 for Christian Schools®
Second Edition

Bob Jones University Press, Greenville, South Carolina 29614

This textbook was written by members of the faculty and staff of Bob Jones University. Standing for the "old-time religion" and the absolute authority of the Bible since 1927, Bob Jones University is the world's leading Fundamentalist Christian university. The staff of the University is devoted to educating Christian men and women to be servants of Jesus Christ in all walks of life.

Providing unparalleled academic excellence, Bob Jones University prepares its students through its offering of over one hundred majors, while its fervent spiritual emphasis prepares their minds and hearts for service and devotion to the Lord Jesus Christ.

If you would like more information about the spiritual and academic opportunities available at Bob Jones University, please call **1-800-BJ-AND-ME** (1-800-252-6363).

NOTE:

The fact that materials produced by other publishers may be referred to in this volume does not constitute an endorsement by Bob Jones University Press of the content or theological position of materials produced by such publishers. The position of the Bob Jones University Press, and the University itself, is well known. Any references and ancillary materials are listed as an aid to the student or the teacher and in an attempt to maintain the accepted academic standards of the publishing industry.

READING 4 for Christian Schools® Second Edition
I Met You in a Story

Produced in cooperation with the Bob Jones University School of Education and Bob Jones Elementary School.

for Christian Schools is a registered trademark of Bob Jones University Press.

© 2000 Bob Jones University Press
First edition © 1982
Greenville, South Carolina 29614

Printed in the United States of America
All rights reserved

ISBN 1-57924-348-7

15   14   13   12   11   10   9   8   7   6   5   4   3   2

Contents

EXPLOITS

ENCOUNTERS

QUESTS

CREATURES

POTPOURRI

HEROES

Acknowledgments

A careful effort has been made to trace the ownership of selections included in this textbook in order to secure permission to reprint copyright material and to make full acknowledgment of their use. If any error or omission has occurred, it is purely inadvertent and will be corrected in subsequent editions, provided written notification is made to the publisher.

"Abraham Lincoln Was My Friend" excerpted from *The Humorous Mr. Lincoln: A Profile in Wit, Courage, and Compassion* by Keith W. Jennison. Copyright © 1988. Reprinted with permission of the publisher. The Countryman Press/W.W. Norton & Company, Inc.

"A Narrow Fellow in the Grass." Reprinted by permission of the publishers and the Trustees of Amherst College from The Poems of Emily Dickinson, Thomas H. Johnson, ed., Cambridge, Mass.: The Belknap Press of Harvard University Press, Copyright © 1951, 1955, 1979, 1983 by the President and Fellows of Harvard College.

"Cat." Copyright estate of Mary Britton Miller. Used by permission.

"Champion Stock" by Bud Murphy. Copyright 1949 by Scholastic, Inc. Reprinted by permission of Scholastic, Inc.

"Eletelephony" from *Tirra Lirra* by Laura Richards. Copyright © 1930, 1932 by Laura E. Richards; copyright © renewed 1960 by Hamilton Richards. By permission of Little, Brown and Company.

Houghton Mifflin Company: Glossary material based on the lexical database of the *Children's Dictionary,* copyright © 1981 Houghton Mifflin Company. No part of this book may be reproduced or transmitted in any form or by any means, electronic or mechanical, including photocopying and recording, or by any information storage or retrieval system, except as may be expressly permitted by the 1976 Copyright Act or with prior written permission from both Houghton Mifflin Company and the Bob Jones University Press.

"Johnny and His Mule" by Ellis Credle, from *More Favorite Stories Old and New for Boys and Girls.* Reprinted by permission of the author.

"The Kite" from *Windy Morning* by Harry Behn. Copyright 1953 by Harry Behn. Copyright renewed 1981 by Alice Behn Goebel, Pamela Behn Adam, Prescott Behn and Peter Behn. Reprinted by permission of Marian Reiner.

"Pony Penning Day" from *Misty of Chincoteague* by Marguerite Henry, as it appears in the book *Favorite Stories Old and New,* condensed from the book *24 Horses: A Treasury of Stories,* collected by Francis and Ruth Cromer Weir, copyright 1950. Reprined by permission of Rand McNally & Co.

"Trip: San Francisco" by Langston Hughes. Reprinted by permission of Harold Ober Associates, Inc. Copyright © 1958 by Langston Hughes.

"What Is Black?" copyright © 1960 by Curtis Publishing Company. From *Hailstones and Halibut Bones* by Mary O'Neill and Leonard Weisgard, Ill. Used by permission of Doubleday, a division of Bantam Doubleday Dell Publishing Group, Inc.

"Wind Song" from *I Feel the Same Way* by Lilian Moore. Copyright © 1967, 1995 Lilian Moore. Used by permission of Marian Reiner for the author.

"Yukon Trail" by Willis Lindquist. Reprinted by permission of the author.

Photograph Credits

The following agencies and individuals have furnished materials to meet the photographic needs of this textbook. We wish to express our gratitude to them for their important contribution.

Suzanne R. Altizer
J. Bean
Bob Jones University
    Classic Players
George R. Collins
Corel Corporation
Creation Science Foundation,
    Ltd., Australia
Eastman Chemicals Division

Beverly Factor
Zoltan Gaal
Brian D. Johnson
Breck P. Kent
Sam Laterza
Library of Congress
Miriam Mitchem
NASA (National Aeronautics
    and Space Administration)

National Archives
John Nesbit
PhotoDisc, Inc.
Roper Mountain Science
    Center
Unusual Films
John Wolsieffer
www.arttoday.com

Front and Back Cover
PhotoDisc, Inc. (background)

Title Page
PhotoDisc, Inc.

Unit Openers
Exploits PhotoDisc, Inc.; **Encounters** Breck P. Kent; **Quests** George R. Collins (war men and cannon), Unusual Films (U.S. Constitution); **Creatures** Breck P. Kent; **Potpourri** Corel Corporation; **Heroes** PhotoDisc, Inc.

Unit 1
PhotoDisc, Inc. 23 (background), 48, 50; Corel Corporation 46, 47; John Wolsieffer 49

Unit 2
National Archives 90; PhotoDisc, Inc. 91; Unusual Films 133

Unit 3
Corel Corporation 168, 185; Library of Congress 194, 196; Courtesy of Zoltan Gaal 199, 202, 206 (both), 213; www.arttoday.com 200, 207, 209, 212, 215 (both); Eastman Chemicals Division 210

Unit 4
Creation Science Foundation, Ltd. Australia, photo by J. Bean 238 (moth); Miriam Mitchem 238 (butterfly); Corel Corporation 239 (both), 240 (toad), 241 (Canada goose); PhotoDisc, Inc. 240 (frog and duck), 241 (chimpanzee, monkey, and white goose); © 1996 Beverly Factor 242 (dolphin); Unusual Films 262 (both)

Unit 5
PhotoDisc, Inc. 352, 359, 360, 362 (background), 397 (both), 398-99 (background); Unusual Films 353, 356 (both); John Nesbit 355 (Jolly Roger flag); Sam Laterza 402, 404, 405, 406, 408, 409; NASA 411; Roper Mountain Science Center, photo by Suzanne R. Altizer 412; Corel Corporation 394 (background)

Unit 6
Brian D. Johnson 436, 437, 438 (both), 439, 441, 442; Unusual Films 477

Glossary
www.arttoday.com 544

EXPLOITS

Watching Wallace

Sharon Hambrick
illustrated by Mary Ann Lumm

The Agreement

Timothy jumped when Mr. Parker slapped him on the back. Not that Timothy was a scaredy-cat, nothing like that—it was just that sometimes, if something jumped out at him or if someone shouted suddenly, he would jump.

"So, Tim, my boy," Mr. Parker's voice boomed in the late September afternoon, "what about it? What about watching Wallace for me while I'm gone?"

Timothy concentrated on breathing normally so Mr. Parker wouldn't know how startled he'd been.

"Okay," Timothy said. He hoped Mr. Parker wouldn't notice how his voice shook.

"Then it's settled," Mr. Parker said. "I'll leave Monday morning, and I should be back Saturday afternoon."

Timothy nodded. Mr. Parker slapped him on the back again and tromped off to his house next door. He turned and shouted, "Ten bucks, Timmy! I'll give you ten bucks for it!"

"Ten dollars? What for?" a deep voice beside Timothy said. Timothy looked up into his dad's kind face.

"I told him I'd watch Wallace, Dad," Timothy said, not hiding the shakiness in his voice now. "For a whole week."

"Oh," said Dad. "You okay about this?"

"No," said Timothy.

Timothy lay in bed that night, wishing he hadn't agreed to watch

Wallace. Wallace was a huge mongrel dog whose tongue hung out slobbering. He never walked anywhere—he bounded. He didn't run. He galloped. He jumped. He barked.

"I will both lay me down in peace, and sleep," Timothy thought, remembering a Bible verse his mother had taught him long ago, "for thou, Lord, only makest me dwell in safety."

It didn't work. The more Timothy thought about Wallace, the more he could not sleep. He lay thinking about that other time, before, when he was seven.

Timothy had been walking home from school. He was in second grade then, and his mind was full of second-grade thoughts like adding two-digit numbers, writing in cursive, and playing first base for the city team. Timothy stopped at the edge of the empty field. Mom had told him to come home as fast as he could that day, but the field looked so inviting. He just had to crawl under the fence where it was loose. His backpack snagged for a minute on the metal chain links, but he managed to get it loose. Then it was just Timothy and the field, an open expanse of grass and weeds and dirt.

Timothy didn't see the dog until it had knocked him down and was standing over him, teeth bared, a deep growl in its throat.

"Get off," Timothy screamed. "Help!" He struggled to free himself. Timothy pulled on his backpack, and the dog—a huge beast, just like Wallace—opened its powerful jaws and bit deep into Timothy's leg. Timothy screamed, struggled to his feet, and ran home, limping and sobbing.

Even now, two years later, he remembered his mother's frightened face as she washed off his leg and the white coat of the doctor who put in the stitches.

They had to catch the dog and watch it for two weeks to see if it had rabies. When Timothy heard the word "rabies" he shuddered. Even back in second grade, he knew that people didn't always recover from being bitten by a dog that had rabies. Timothy didn't want to die when he was seven. And he didn't want to die now.

His door opened. Mom came in and sat on his bed. She stroked his hair and kissed him. "It's very brave of you," she said.

"I'm scared. What if he bites me?"

"Remember Psalm fifty-six, verse three, 'What time I am afraid, I will trust in thee.' That means that anytime you are fearful, you can trust God to help you through the difficult situation.

Wallace has had all his shots, Tim," Mom said. "And he's a good dog. You won't be in any danger."

"I know."

Mom prayed with him and sang him a song. Even though he was almost ten years old, he liked it when Mom came in and sang. It was comforting at the end of the day.

"I know how you feel," Mom said.

"You do?"

"Yes." Mom's voice got quiet. "Once," she said, "when I was about your age, I went to a fair with my family. My sister and I got in a ride that spins around flat, and then goes up steeper and steeper, until you're spinning around suspended from the earth. We were at the very top of the ride, with our backs toward the ground, when the ride stopped. It was stuck. There I was, thirty feet off the ground, holding onto the handrail with hands that got sweatier and sweatier. I was sure I was going to slip out of the car and fall to the ground. We hung there for what seemed like hours.

It was the most frightened I've ever been in my life."

"Is that why you don't go on roller coasters now?"

"That's why. I know they're safe, but they terrify me."

"Like me and Wallace."

"Tell you what, Tim," Mom said. She took a deep breath. "You watch Wallace for the week, trusting God to take care of you, and I'll go on the biggest, twistiest roller coaster you can find."

"Wow!"

Timothy knew how frightened his mom was of roller coasters. Every year at the county fair, she'd wait, sipping a soft drink, while he and Dad stood in line for the loop-the-loop rides and the huge metal roller coasters that twisted back on themselves like snakes. Often he'd said, "Come on, Mom, it's fun!" and seen her shake her head no.

But now she had promised. If Timothy would overcome his fear of caring for Wallace, Mom would ride the Tingling Terror at the county fair with him this year.

Taking Charge

Mr. Parker left Monday morning. Monday after school, Timothy did his homework. Ate dinner. Brushed his teeth.

"Don't you think it's about time to feed that dog, Son?" Dad's voice broke through his thoughts.

"Yes, sir," Timothy said. He got Mr. Parker's key off the key rack and shoved his hands into his pockets. He looked at the floor.

"Will you go with me, Dad?"

Timothy scooped out Wallace's dog food. He poured clean water into his water dish.

"Mr. Parker said Wallace likes to be played with," Dad said.

Timothy reached out and touched Wallace's coat. It was soft and deep. When Wallace turned his head suddenly, Timothy pulled his hand away.

"Try again, Tim," Dad said.

Timothy petted the top of Wallace's head and scratched his neck. He ran his hands through his thick coat.

On Tuesday, Timothy asked, "Dad, will you go with me again?"

"Go alone, Son," Dad said. "You can do it."

Timothy shuffled to Mr. Parker's house, his hands shoved deep into his pockets. He thought back over the Bible lesson he'd heard in Sunday school this week. He thought about how Jesus had stood up in the boat and had said to the wind and the waves, "Peace, be still."

"Lord," Timothy prayed, "make the wind and waves inside me be still."

Timothy's heart pounded as he turned the key in the lock.

He opened the door. "Wallace?" he called.

Out of nowhere, Wallace bounded, barking. He knocked Timothy over. Timothy's heart beat with fear. Wallace stood over him, slobbering wet drool onto his face.

"Jesus," Timothy whispered, "calm my heart. Help me not be afraid."

Wallace lowered his massive head right over Timothy's. And licked.

"Yuck, you old ugly dog," Timothy said, laughing.

He struggled up and—still shaking—scooped out Wallace's food and freshened his water.

"Good job, Son," Dad's voice startled him.

"Dad!"

"I came behind you," he said, "to make sure you were okay."

"You were here all the time?"

"Yep."

"Thanks, Dad. I was afraid."

"It's okay, Son."

On Wednesday, Timothy told Dad he would go alone. "I've prayed for a peaceful heart."

Mom stood behind Dad. "I'm not so sure I like this brave son thing," she said. Timothy smiled. He knew Mom was getting worried that she'd have to ride the Tingling Terror at the county fair. He smiled at Mom as he grabbed the key and headed out the door.

That day he watched Wallace play in the back yard. Dad watched over the fence.

On Thursday, Dad didn't watch anymore.

"Aren't you afraid of Wallace anymore, Timmy?" Mom asked at dinner Thursday night.

"No," he said. "Wallace is great. I took my Frisbee today and played catch with him. We had fun." Timothy dug into his mashed potatoes like a plow and shoveled a great load into his mouth.

"Do you think Mr. Parker would mind if I walked Wallace around the block today?"

Timothy asked on Friday. "The leash is hanging up in the pantry where he keeps the dog food."

"Why not?" Dad said.

Timothy hooked the leash to Wallace's collar and opened the door. In a bound, Wallace was off—tearing off down the sidewalk. Timothy held onto the leash for dear life.

"Wallace, slow down!" Timothy called, trying to keep up.

His hands hurt as he held tight. Still the big dog raced, Timothy stumbling after him. He headed for the big field.

"Stop, Wallace, stop!" Timothy pleaded. But it was no use.

Wallace tore the leash out of Timothy's hand and scooted under the fence that surrounded the empty field. Timothy stood on the other side of the fence, shaking.

I can't go in there, he thought. He'll bite me. He ran his hand down his leg where he knew the scar was. He looked at the fence. He looked at Wallace.

"Help me, dear Lord. Help me get the dog back."

Slowly, Timothy lifted the loose part of the fence. He crouched down and slid his body beneath the chain links.

"What time I am afraid, I will trust in thee," he said aloud.

"Come here, boy," he said. "Come here, Wallace."

Wallace ran wildly over the field. Timothy watched, feeling helpless. Wallace trotted toward him, then ran away. Timothy felt annoyed.

"Come here, Wallace!" Timothy shouted. "Come here!"

Wallace stopped, turned, and ran over.

Maybe he needs me to sound forceful, like Mr. Parker does, he thought.

"Sit!" Timothy said, as loudly and forcefully as he could. Wallace sat.

Timothy laughed. He grabbed the leash. "Now," he said loudly, "we are going home!" Wallace responded to Timothy's more demanding tone of voice. Maybe he just needed me to be in charge, he thought. Wallace pulled on the leash to go faster, but Timothy said, "No, boy!" and he slowed down.

The fence loomed in front of them. I *will* trust the Lord, thought Timothy. I *will not* be afraid. Carefully, he pulled up the fence to let the dog through. Then, holding as tightly as he could to the leash, he eased himself under the fence.

Then, covered with dirt and grass, and slowing Wallace's bounding pace to a walk by his firm commands, Timothy walked leash-in-hand down the sidewalk, all the way home.

Mr. Parker's van was in the driveway.

"Hey, Timmy, my man!" Mr. Parker's voice cracked the silence. "I'm home early. How's the old boy been treating you?"

Timothy smiled. "He's been great, Mr. Parker."

"Didn't jump all over you and scare you to death, did he?"

"Just a little."

Mr. Parker's booming laugh filled the whole neighborhood. He took the leash out of Timothy's hand and dug a ten-dollar bill out of his pocket with his other hand.

"Any idea what you're going to do with that money, Son?" he asked.

"Yes, sir," Timothy said, smiling. "I'm going to take it to the fair."

"The fair!" Mr. Parker shouted. "Good idea. Going to ride the Tingling Terror, are you?"

"Yes, sir," Timothy said. "I'm going to ride it with my mom."

Over the Top

Dawn L. Watkins
illustrated by Preston Gravely Jr.

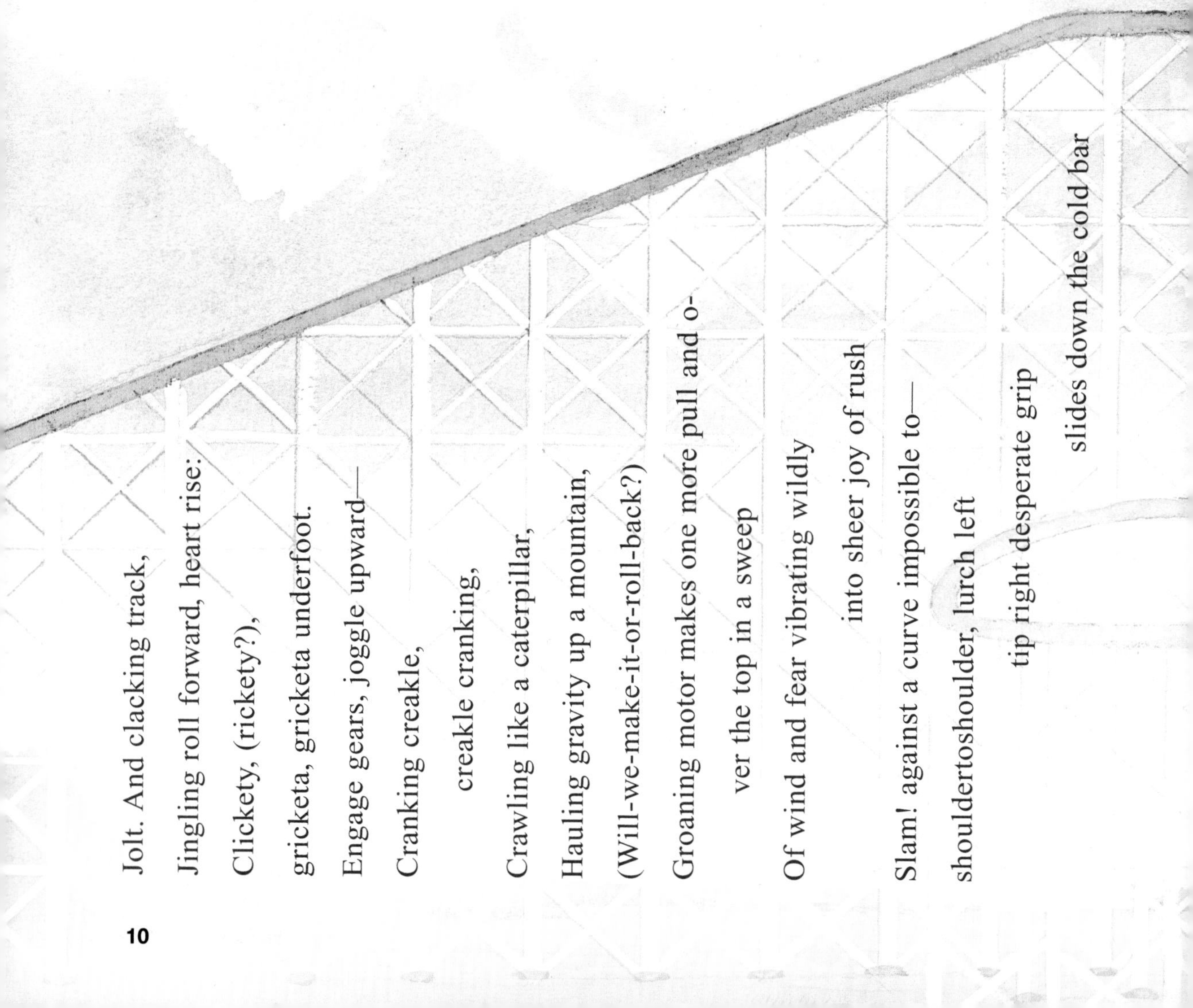

Jolt. And clacking track,

Jingling roll forward, heart rise:

Clickety, (rickety?),

gricketa, gricketa underfoot.

Engage gears, joggle upward—

Cranking creakle,

    creakle cranking,

Crawling like a caterpillar,

Hauling gravity up a mountain,

(Will-we-make-it-or-roll-back?)

Groaning motor makes one more pull and o-

ver the top in a sweep

Of wind and fear vibrating wildly

    into sheer joy of rush

Slam! against a curve impossible to—

shouldertoshoulder, lurch left

    tip right desperate grip

        slides down the cold bar

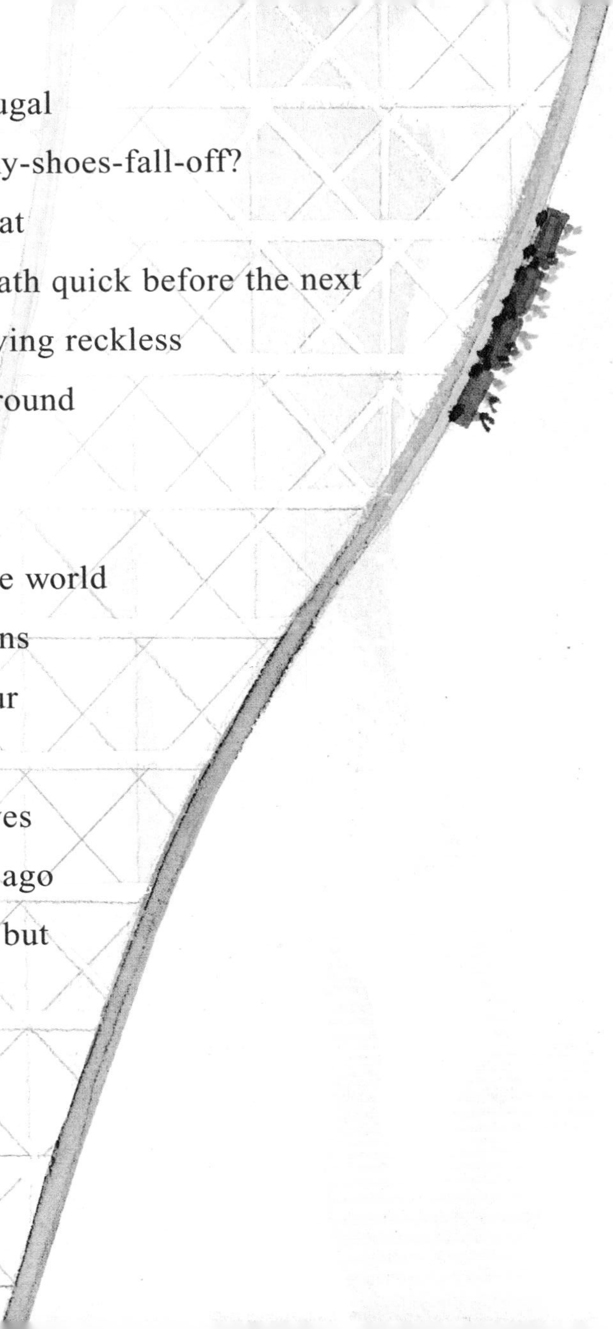

with a roar sling centrifugal

Loop up and out, will-my-shoes-fall-off?

Swoosh back into the seat

Laugh-scream, deep breath quick before the next

descent and swerving reckless

Rumbling run sky for ground

face first dazzle dive

If I live I'll never!

Swing up from under the world

through three swoop turns

Plastic people below blur

whir away, disappear,

reappear, right themselves

still smiling from years ago

when we left the planet but

Sudden slowness slurs

Creakle, crankle.

Stop.

Let's go again!

River's Rising

Milly Howard

*illustrated by Del Thompson
and Noelle Snyder*

High Water

Josh Fowler lay on the braided rag rug in front of the big potbellied stove. He marked his place in the book he was reading and looked up. Ma was rocking Buddy, gently humming "Rock of Ages." Pa was sitting at the table, reading the Bible, a mended fishnet at his feet.

Behind the curtains, April rain slashed at the windows. It drummed on the tin roof of the houseboat. Josh rolled over, listening.

Ma stopped humming to listen too. "There's nothing like rain on a tin roof," she said softly. "It's like music, first soft, then loud, then soft again."

Josh nodded, eyes half closed. The low fire in the stove had sent a cozy warmth throughout the houseboat. The rain slowed, settling into a slow drizzle, gently pinging the roof. Josh yawned and closed his eyes.

When he awoke, lamplight spread a golden circle across the room. Josh lay for a moment, watching shadows moving across the ceiling. Behind him he heard quiet clinks as Ma set the table for supper. "Stew," he thought hungrily, taking a deep breath. He could hear Pa outside on the deck, moving toward the door. Pa's footsteps stopped, and Josh knew he was hanging his slicker on the peg beside the door.

Josh was on his feet when the door opened. He watched as Pa ran his hand over his wet hair. Ma handed him a towel and gave him a questioning look. Pa nodded in answer to her unspoken question.

"River's rising," he said.

"Bad?" Ma asked anxiously.

"Can't tell yet," Pa replied as he sat down at the table, "but there was a heap of snow this winter and too much rain this spring. Wouldn't be surprised if the Reedy River really leaps the banks this time."

"Won't be any school in the morning then," Josh said, grinning. He sat down.

"You've never seen a real flood, Son," Pa said. "The Reedy's a right friendly stretch of water most times, but floodwater's deadly. We rivermen move carefully when the water's rising."

Mr. Fowler waited until Ma sat down across from him and then bowed his head. "Let's pray."

Josh listened as his father prayed for God's mercy on the land. High water had always been a part of Josh's life. Almost every spring the river and the streams that fed it would overflow their banks. When the water covered the bridges, the buses would stop running, and school would be let out until the water went back down. The grownups kept a careful eye on the water level while the children splashed happily through their holiday. No, high water had never held terror for Josh.

But when bedtime came, even Josh could tell this time was going to be different. He could feel the Reedy moving under the houseboat.

"It's rising fast," Pa said the last time he came in. "A foot since sundown. She'll be over the banks by dawn."

Josh hardly slept that night. He lay in his bunk, listening to the creaking as the river rocked the houseboat against the planks of Fowler's Landing.

When he awoke early the next morning, Josh eased out of bed quietly. Trying not to awaken Buddy and Ma, he pulled on his clothes and tiptoed to the door. Pa was already outside, walking along the dock. He had rope coiled around his shoulder and was measuring the distance from the boat to the oak tree nearest the riverbank.

Josh didn't have to use the ladder to reach the dock this morning. Water lapped at the top rung, and the houseboat rode high against the landing. Josh leaped across and ran barefoot along the planks to his father.

"What are you doing, Pa?" he asked.

"River's still rising, Son," his father answered. "It's already over the low banks downstream, and it'll soon be over the landing. Help me tie the boat to this old oak. It'll hold the boat fast."

As Josh helped Pa wind the ropes around the trunk of the tree he asked, "Are the trees on Crab Island as old as our oak?"

"Probably older," his father grunted, giving the rope one last hard pull. "That ought to do it. Run and bring me the rope from the landing."

Josh ran back down the dock and untied the rope that held the houseboat. Holding one end of the coiled rope, he walked back along the dock to the big tree. The houseboat swung away from the dock and drifted closer to the tree. Pa and Josh pulled steadily, bringing the houseboat gently to the bank. With swift movements Pa tied that rope too.

"Now she'll stay," he said in satisfaction. "And the landing will protect her from floating branches. I've never seen the river rise much higher than our landing anyway."

"How's it going?" Ma called.

"You up already?" Pa called back, teasing. "I thought you were going to sleep till noon."

Josh grinned. His folks were always teasing each other. Life on the houseboat flowed as smoothly as the Reedy River usually did. Ma cooked and took care of Buddy, singing as she did her work. Pa was a fisherman, just as Grandpa had been. When school was out Josh went with him, crabbing and fishing off Crab Island. Then they brought the day's catch home to sell in the little fish and bait house above Fowler's Landing.

Ma gave them a good-natured smile and went back inside. Josh and Pa cleared the landing and dock of anything that would float away; then they went to eat breakfast.

Shifting Current

Josh and Pa spent the rest of the morning securing everything on the houseboat. Anything that might tip over or fall was lashed down. Loose things were taken inside to be stored. Pa went over every inch of the houseboat. He was checking the roof to see if it needed any repair work when the sheriff called from the bank.

"Hello, Fowlers!" He nodded in approval when he saw the boat secured to the tree. Glancing at the water that now covered the landing, he said, "Looks like you're all set for a while."

"Reckon so," Pa replied, reaching out a hand to help the sheriff aboard. "How're things going?"

The sheriff nodded at Ma and ruffled Josh's hair. He grinned when Josh ducked. "If your family's going to be all right for a while, I could use your help," he said to Pa. "The lower part of town's already flooded, and the farms north of us are half buried under floodwater. We need every man we can get that knows the river. We've got to bring those people to high ground."

Pa nodded. "Been expecting that. My boat's secure, and my people will be all right."

After the sheriff had left, Pa kissed Ma and Buddy and motioned for Josh to follow him to the back of the houseboat. "The water's rising faster than I've ever seen it, " he said quietly. "There's going to be a lot of people stranded, and I won't be back anytime soon. You have to take care of Ma and Buddy."

Josh swallowed, "We'll be all right, Pa."

"Just remember to check those mooring lines," Pa said as he untied the rowboat. "The current is sweeping close to shore."

"Okay, Pa," Josh said. He went back to stand beside Ma and Buddy. They waved until Pa rowed out of sight.

The rest of the day dragged by. Ma went about her work quietly, and Josh could tell she was praying for Pa and the people caught in the flood. Even Buddy played quietly, running his wooden train around the braided rug.

Josh checked the water every hour. And every hour he shook his head at Ma's look. "Still rising, " he said at last. "It's over the high banks now."

Night came, and Pa was still gone. At suppertime Ma wordlessly handed the Bible to Josh. He read a chapter slowly, stumbling over some of the words. Then he tried to pray as his father did, speaking to the Lord as a friend. Suppertime was quiet. The fish and cornbread were soon removed from the table, almost untouched.

Josh checked the mooring lines again while Ma did the dishes. He held the lantern high, peering toward the bank. The water was more than a foot over the bank now, churning around the roots of the old oak. Pieces of broken branches tumbled over the landing and swept under the mooring lines. The water was too far over the landing for it to offer any protection to the houseboat.

"Oh Pa," Josh thought, "come home!" He went back inside and set the lamp down on the table.

Ma touched his arm gently. "The Lord will take care of us," she said quietly.

When Buddy was asleep, Ma sat down beside Josh. "Like me to read to you?" she asked, picking up *David Copperfield*.

Josh nodded, knowing that neither of them would sleep until Pa came home. Ma read page after page, but still there was no homecoming shout from the river. Unexpectedly, the houseboat trembled under them, rocking on the water. Ma stopped reading.

Josh reached for the lamp and stepped outside. Holding the lamp up, he looked at the mooring lines. They were only inches above the rising water that stretched out into the night. The current had shifted, pulling them away from the tree.

"A branch must have tangled for a moment," Josh called back to Ma. He had turned to go back inside when a grinding crash came from the direction of the submerged landing. He spun around, heart thudding. A large shape had lunged out of the night and smashed into the landing. Josh held his breath, listening to the creaking and grinding. Then there was a splintering noise.

b Island

"Crab Island," he said ...ghtfully.

...t his mother's questioning ..., Josh said, "We can use the ...ent itself to swing us into the ...th end of the island!"

"But that's a sandbar!"

"Not anymore," Josh said. ...ll be covered with water just ... everything else around here. ...y that sandbar is good and ...h. The water'll be shallow."

"And the island will block the ...rent," Ma whispered.

"Partly," Josh said. "Anyway, I ...nk the boat'll slow down long ...ugh for us to get some lines ...und the live oaks. You'll have ...elp, though, Ma. We'll need to ... two lines tight at once."

Ma nodded. "I'll get ready."

Josh went outside as Ma ...ked blankets around Buddy. ...e stuffed extra ones down the ...e of the crib for padding. ...aning down, she kissed him ...tly and then went to the door. ...tside, Josh was at the tiller, ...dging floating logs and planks ...enever he could. Ahead, the ...ck mass of Crab Island ...med out of the dark.

Quickly Ma tied new ropes to the ends of the houseboat, leaving them in neat coils. She tucked her skirt around her legs and tied it tightly.

The boat slid swiftly along the island. Josh edged in closer, letting underbrush and branches drag at the sides and roof. The boat slowed slightly as it neared the south end of the island.

"Ready, Ma?"

Josh saw Ma glance back at the door. If the boat got away from them, Buddy would go through the bottleneck alone. Ma's lips moved, and Josh knew she was praying.

Josh shoved the tiller hard. He heard a sharp crack as the houseboat swung to the right with a jar that almost took Josh to his knees. It slid across the sandbar into shallow water.

"Now, Ma!"

Josh and Ma grabbed the coils of rope and jumped. Water splashed into Josh's face as he plunged toward shore. Behind him he could feel the houseboat turning slowly as the current

"The landing's breaking up," he cried.

"Come inside! Now!" Ma grabbed his arm and pulled him back inside, slamming the door behind them.

The houseboat shuddered as the broken mass hit the back of the boat. Then, with a jerk, the boat began to move.

Josh stared at Ma. "The lines broke. We're loose!"

"The current'll take us to midstream," she said, her face pale. "We'll just drift downriver. "

Josh's eyes
ment before he
miles downrive
edge on both
cliffs would fo
the rushing wa
bris. There wa
river. He coul
across the fie
wrecked on sub
sheds. What co
mind searched
river for an ansv

tho

loo
cur
sou

"It
lik
On
hig

cur

thi
en
ard
to
ge

tu
Sh
sic
Le
so
O
do
w
bl
lc

from the other side of the island reached for it.

Josh ran desperately, fighting the water. He reached the first tree and flung his rope around it. Two, three times, he wound the rope before tying it. Then he scrambled across the wet underbrush to Ma. Struggling, they tied the last knot. The houseboat steadied, rocked gently, and was still. Josh and Ma fell into each other's arms, laughing and crying at once.

When they scrambled back onto the boat, Buddy was screaming. Ma took the crying baby out of the crib and held him. When his crying had settled into hiccups, she knelt beside the crib and began to thank the Lord for saving their lives. Josh knelt beside her, weak and shaky with relief.

After he had checked the lines once more, Josh lay down on the rug and slept. He did not awake again until he felt the morning sun dancing on his face through the window.

"You were so tired, I let you sleep," Ma said. Buddy padded over and tumbled on Josh. "Up," he gurgled. "Up."

"Come look," Ma said. Josh stood up and followed her to the door. Water covered the land around them as far as they could see. To the south of them the river flowed swiftly but more calmly than before. Sunlight glinted off the water and off bits and pieces carried by the current. "It's quit rising," Ma said softly. "Pa'll find us as soon as he can. He'll be proud of you, Son."

Josh turned his head. "I'd better repair the boat then. I thought it was going to rip apart when I ran it under the trees."

Josh spent the rest of the morning repairing the boat. First he hammered back the boards that had been torn by the branches. Then he patched jagged edges and loose shutters. Josh knew that the sharp crack he had heard had been the rudder. He could do nothing about that, except be thankful that it had only cracked, not broken. It was late afternoon when Josh saw a boat approaching. Quickly he called to Ma. "Pa's coming!"

Ma, Josh, and Buddy were calling across the water as soon as Pa came within hearing distance. Pa was grinning as he tied up next to the boat. "Hold on," he said. He looked over the mooring lines without speaking. Then he said, "Somebody told me this morning there was a houseboat down here. I figured out what had happened when I saw the landing."

He listened to Ma's account of the night and then put his arm around Josh. "Son, thank God you kept a clear head."

Josh hesitated. "I broke the rudder."

Pa began to laugh. "What's a rudder compared to my family? You can help me start on a new one tomorrow."

"Come in and eat," Ma said. "You look like you can hardly stand up. "

"I'm tired all right," Pa said, "but we got everybody moved. When the river settles a little more, I'll go back and help the folks salvage some of their things." He removed his cap and put it on Josh's head. "And Josh can go with me. It'll be good to have a real riverman along!"

SKILL LESSON:

Map Reading

• Maps

Maps come in different shapes and sizes and can give the reader many different types of information. Some maps include roads and highways to help the map reader find his way in unfamiliar territory. Other maps may show the boundaries of countries, states, or counties. Another type of map may emphasize the physical features of an area of the world. Many kinds of information can be shown on a map, and sometimes more than one type of information may appear.

In order for anyone to make use of the information given on a map, the mapmaker must provide a legend or a key to explain the symbols and colors used to identify the different kinds of information. In order for the map reader to understand the size of the area being shown or the distance from one place to another, the mapmaker must provide a scale which can be used to measure those distances.

• Map Scale

If Josh drew a map of the river where his adventure took place, his map might look like Map A.

To help someone reading the map to measure the correct distances, Josh would include a scale.

A map scale compares the distances on the map to the actual distances on the earth. Often the scale is shown by a straight line which may be divided into smaller parts. Each section stands for a certain number of miles. For example, one inch may represent one mile, or one inch may represent five miles, depending on the size of the map. The map reader

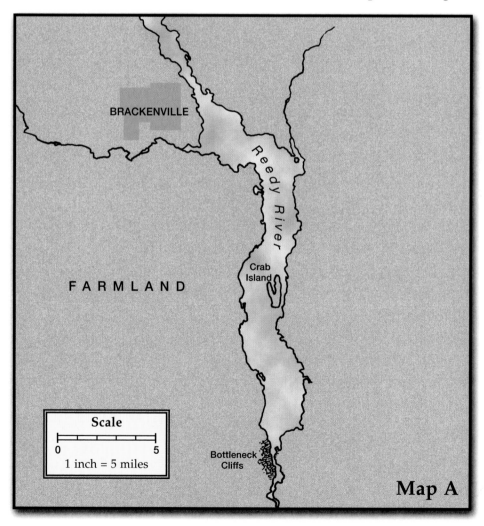

BRACKENVILLE

Reedy River

Crab Island

FARMLAND

Scale

0   5

1 inch = 5 miles

Bottleneck Cliffs

Map A

can then use this scale to measure the exact distance between two points on the map.

Next Josh might draw a map of the section of the river where his adventure actually happened. His drawing might look like Map B.

Because of the difference in the area shown, a different *scale* is needed for each map. The scale for Map A is smaller—one inch equals five miles. If the drawing of the river is five inches long on the first map, then the real river is twenty-five miles long. On Map B, one inch equals one mile. Crab Island is two inches long on this map, so the island itself is two miles long.

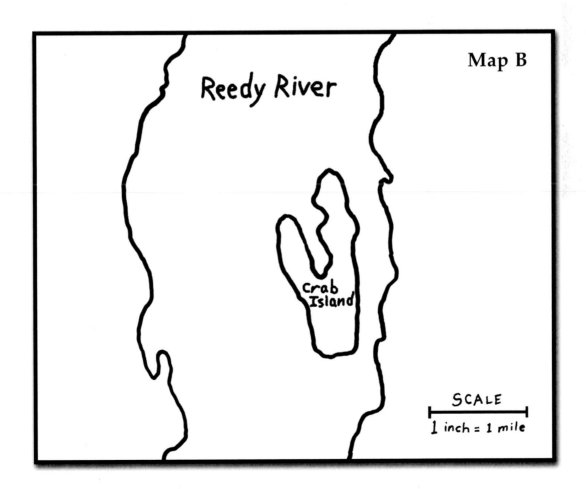

Reedy River

Crab Island

SCALE
1 inch = 1 mile

Map B

• Map Keys

Although Map B shows where the island is located on the river, it does not show the physical features of the area. Josh may wish to identify the characteristics that are important to his story.

He could do this using colors or symbols. Finally, Josh would need a key so anyone reading his map could understand at a glance the markings he used. His finished map might look like Map C.

Josh's knowledge of the river would help him draw a map of the river and the surrounding area. By identifying and labeling the features on the map, he would be able to help his teacher see more clearly exactly what had happened. And by providing a scale he could show the exact distance from place to place.

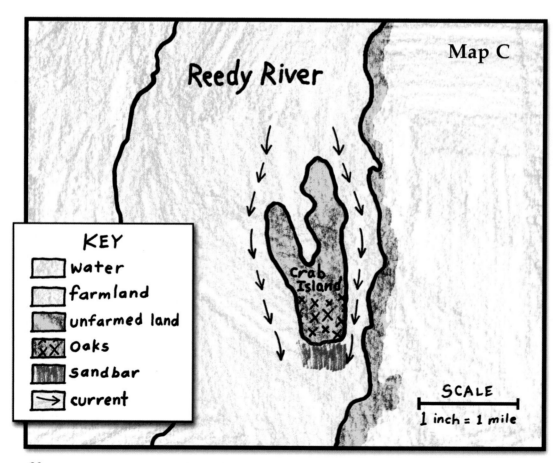

Map C

Reedy River

KEY
water
farmland
unfarmed land
Oaks
sandbar
current

Crab Island

SCALE
1 inch = 1 mile

A Wise King
and a
Wise Son

adapted by
Kristin Lehman
and Karen Wilt

illustrated by
Justin Gerard

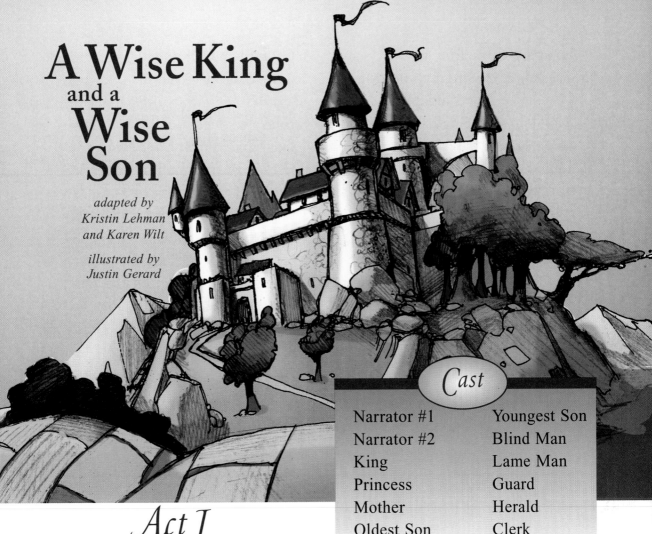

Cast

Narrator #1	Youngest Son
Narrator #2	Blind Man
King	Lame Man
Princess	Guard
Mother	Herald
Oldest Son	Clerk
Second Son	

Act I

Narrator #1: A long time ago, in a faraway land, there ruled a wise king. His great wisdom astounded the people of his kingdom, and they honored him faithfully. It put fear into the heart of every enemy, for none of them could do anything to harm him or his kingdom. During the years of his reign, wisdom came to be valued more than the brightest diamonds or the purest gold.

Narrator #2: The wise king often journeyed through his kingdom to listen to the folk who served him, and many said that each mile he rode multiplied his wisdom. His young daughter always traveled with him, winning the peasants' hearts with her charming smile and gracious heart.

Narrator #1: But as the years passed, the king grew old. Many times the good people of the kingdom wondered who would reign when the king could no longer raise his scepter. No royal son had been born to take his place.

Narrator #2: The wise king knew the thoughts of his subjects. One day in late summer the heralds of the throne rode through the kingdom, spreading news that answered the question.

Herald: *(reading from a scroll)* Hear ye, hear ye. Be it known that His Majesty, the king, desires a worthy man to marry his daughter, the princess, and to reign as king in his stead. His Majesty has planned a trial to determine the worthiness of each young man who seeks the hand of the princess.

Narrator #1: Many young men of the kingdom heard the proclamation and flocked to the palace to answer the king's challenge. One by one they failed and returned home.

Narrator #2: Meanwhile, in a far corner of the kingdom there lived a widow and her three sons. The sons plowed their stubborn corner of land, raising just enough wheat to feed themselves through the winter. The widow gave her sons all the schooling they required. Many of the villagers could not read as well as the three boys or figure half so quickly.

Narrator #1: In the middle of the harvest, the youngest boy drove the yearling calf to market to sell it. There he came upon a group of townsfolk gathered around a public notice board.

Clerk: *(whispering)* Can you read it, lad?

Youngest Son: *(standing up proudly)* Yes, sir. "Be it known that His Majesty, the king, desires a worthy man to marry his daughter, the princess, and to reign as king in his stead. His Majesty has planned a trial to determine the worthiness of each young man who seeks the hand of the princess."

Clerk: Ah me, imagine that. I'm off at once to try for such a prize! Care to join me?

Youngest Son: Oh, I'd love to try. I saw the princess once from a long distance. She's fairer than the morning sunshine on a field of honeysuckle. But alas, I have a job to do here and cannot leave my widowed mother. The best to you, sir. *(He waves farewell.)*

Narrator #2: After supper that evening, the widow's three sons discussed the notice.

Youngest Son: *(turning to his mother)* What do you think, Mother? You always give us good advice.

Mother: *(smiling)* Well, my sons, you have served me as good children and cared for me for many a long year. Soon you must go out and seek your fortunes. My blessings go with you in whatever you decide.

Oldest Son: *(jumping up from the table)* Then I'll be off at once. You'll hear news of me within the week.

Second Son: *(rising from the table)* I must try also, Mother. I believe I'll be off in the morning.

Narrator #1: So in the early morning light of the next day, the youngest son waved good-bye as his brother set out on the same road the oldest son had traveled.

Youngest Son: *(taking his mother's arm)* Mother, I cannot leave you to fend for yourself. I shall wait and see what may come to pass.

Narrator #2: The oldest brother arrived at the palace at noon. Dust rose from his shoes at each footfall, and his eyes were bleary with lack of sleep.

Oldest Son: *(boldly to the guard)* I have come to take the test for the hand of the princess.

Guard: Come this way. *(The guard leads the way to the king.)*

Narrator #1: The guard ushered him into the throne room where the king offered him meat and drink.

King: The task I require is not difficult. Yonder is a field of wheat. *(He points out a window.)* You must harvest the wheat until noon tomorrow. If you do well, the princess will be wed to you.

Oldest Son: *(smiling)* I have harvested wheat each fall since I was old enough to hold a scythe. Perhaps such a trial is too easy.

King: *(crossing his arms)* We shall see.

Narrator #1: The oldest son raced to the field. Over and over he swung the scythe, cutting the wheat. Then he bundled it in sturdy stacks and stood them on the edge of the field. The sun began to set as he worked on. Children laughed and ran home to dinner, but still he worked. All through the night the young man worked. By morning he had only a corner of the field left. Suddenly a blind man stumbled into the field.

Oldest Son: *(running to the man)* Be careful; you'll crush the grain.

Narrator #2: He lifted the man awkwardly by the arm and set him on the road.

Blind Man: Can you direct me to the palace?

Oldest Son: Yes, straight down

30

the road and to the left.

Blind Man: Thank you. *(He shuffles away.)*

Narrator #1: The oldest son increased his pace, swinging, cutting, and bundling until the field stood clean. At the last swoosh of his scythe, he saw the king drive up in his coach.

King: *(leaning out the window)* A fine job, my son, but I'm sorry you did not pass. You have done better than most, but alas, the trial requires more.

Narrator #1: And so the oldest son returned home.

Act II

Narrator #2: The second son reached the palace as the bells chimed for dinner. He was ushered into the dining room to eat with the king.

King: *(pushing his plate back)* Your trial, as all the others have been, is to harvest a field of wheat for me until dinner tomorrow. You must do well.

Second Son: *(rubbing his hands together)* Indeed, a simple task. I have wielded a scythe since I left the cradle.

King: *(wisely)* We shall see.

Narrator #1: The second son flew at once to the task of clearing a great portion of his field before dark. On through the night he worked, even more quickly than his brother. As dawn broke, a blind man stumbled across his path.

Second Son: *(taking the blind man's arm)* What do you here?

Blind Man: I seek the palace.

Second Son: I have just time to guide you there, and then I must hurry back to my task. *(He leads the blind man away.)*

Narrator #2: The second son led the blind man to the palace gates, bade him farewell, and returned to the wheat field. Just as the last wheat fell, a lame man hobbled up.

Lame Man: Can you direct me to the palace?

Second Son: *(pointing in the direction of the palace)* Yes, straight ahead and to the left.

Narrator #1: The second son pulled the last shocks into a bundle and began tying it as the lame man stumbled away. Minutes later the king drove up in his coach.

King: *(looking over the field)* A very fine job, my son. Better than anyone before you. But

alas, you too have failed. I am very sorry. *(He pats the boy on the shoulder.)*

Narrator #2: And so the second son followed the path of his brother and returned home.

Narrator #1: Both brothers told their adventures to their mother and bade the youngest brother attempt the task.

Mother: *(putting her hand on his shoulder)* Perhaps it is your turn to try your hand.

Youngest Son: Thank you, Mother. I have waited to make sure you were well cared for.

Mother: You have learned well the ways of wisdom. Now take your things and be off. Put your learning to use.

Narrator #2: Before long, the guard at the gate was leading the youngest son to the throne room. The king and his daughter sat at a game of chess. The young man stood at the door, his heart melting at the sight of the lovely princess.

Princess: *(pouting)* Father, you shall put me in check no matter where I move!

Youngest Son: *(stepping forward)* Your Highness, you do have one move that could win the game.

Princess: *(picking up a chess piece)* Why, yes, of course. I see it now. Thank you, kind sir.

Youngest Son: *(blushing and looking away)* You're welcome.

Narrator #1: The young man's heart pounded so hard in his own ears that he stepped back, fearing that she would hear it beating.

Narrator #2: When the game was over, the king set it aside and explained the trial to the boy. Bowing, the youngest son hurried to begin the task.

Narrator #1: The scythe flew as he harvested the grain, but the field stretched on and on. The king had given him the largest field of all to cut. The young man worked on through the night. The morning came and passed, and he continued working. The heat of noon beat down, and he worked on still.

Narrator #2: As evening approached, a blind man came stumbling down the road. The boy saw him from a distance and ran to help him.

Youngest Son: *(helping the man)* Where are you going, good sir?

Blind Man: To the palace.

Youngest Son: Let me guide you there.

Narrator #1: The two laughed and talked along the way.

Blind Man: My blessing on you, my son.

Youngest Son: Fare thee well. *(He runs in the direction of the field.)*

Narrator #1: He ran back down the road to the field and continued to cut the wheat. Soon a lame man approached. Again the boy ran to help, offering his shoulder and joking and talking as he led the man to the palace.

Lame Man: My blessing to you, Son. *(He sits down beside the gate.)*

Youngest Son: *(waving farewell)* Thank you and farewell.

Narrator #2: In the field the golden wheat bent and swayed with the breeze. Barely half of it lay in bundles. And far up the road, the coach of the king raised dust as it approached. The boy fell to cutting more quickly than he had ever done before, but it was too late. The coach drew to a stop.

Youngest Son: *(kneeling before the king)* I am sorry, Your Highness. I have failed to complete the task, but I thank you for the opportunity.

King: *(helping the boy to his feet)* My son, you alone have passed the test. Not only did you deal kindly with the blind man and the lame man but you also answered for your work with wisdom, showing that you alone are responsible for it. I told you only to harvest the wheat in the field. I did not say how much of the field was required.

Youngest Son: *(stammering)* Your Highness, did those men speak with you?

King: *(pointing to himself)* I was those men! Now come with me. You have yet more to learn in the ways of ruling a kingdom.

An Emergency

taken from Llamas on the Loose

Jeri Massi

illustrated by Dana Thompson, John Bjerk, and Linda Slattery

A visit from one of Dad's old friends, Doc Ericson, sends Penny and her brother Jack on an adventure. After Dad agrees to let Penny and Jack work on Doc Ericson's unusual farm, strange things begin to happen. Doc Ericson teaches Penny and Jack about the curious animals they raise and teaches them to work hard. "Beware of wild animals," Doc Ericson warns. "If the dinner gong rings and the floodlights shine, be prepared for an emergency!"

The Great Escape

Doc Ericson had to make our visit educational so he could qualify for a research grant, and during that week he taught us a lot about the history of llamas in the U.S. We also learned how to groom them and how to mix their feed.

There were forty llamas in all, thirty-four adults and six crias. There was one special male, Jock, who was boss of the herd. He took charge of all the females and every now and then had a spit-fight with the two other yearling males to remind them who was boss. Male llamas do have fangs to bite with, and if they get in a real fight, you'll see them leap up and come down on each other, biting, slashing with their hooves, trying to knock each other down, and spitting quarts at each other. But usually the lead male only has to let loose a couple of pints of spit at the other males to let them know he's still in charge.

Since female llamas don't have any upper teeth, their number one defense is to spit. And when a llama spits at you, you can consider yourself—in no uncertain terms—spit upon. They can reach right down into their stomachs to spit, unlike people, who use only their throats.

So in a sense, llamas are pretty well defended. They can sense intruders at a distance, and they will instinctively aim for an attacker's face to spit at, in order to blind him.

On the other hand, if a llama senses an approaching attacker but is trapped in a fenced pasture, he can't get away. And a llama under attack by more than one creature is pretty helpless. Two medium-sized dogs can pull down a full-grown llama. That was why Dr. Ericson had the whole place hog-wired.

Supposedly we also learned how to halter a llama, if you want to count it that way. What actually happened was that Jack got his arms 'round Ticktock's neck, and she bucked him all over the barnyard for about ten minutes. Then, when she was exhausted and wanted a drink, I got the harness around her nose and Jack fastened it before she could buck again.

"If we were taller and heavier, we could do it," Jack said. "But I can hardly reach her nose unless she keeps her head down."

"Look, two of us ought to be smarter than one of her," I told him. "Size has nothing to do with it. Even the trainer's manual says that."

"Well, I wish Ticktock would read the manual, then." But at the challenge in my words, he came up to Ticktock again and got his arms around her neck to get her

halter off. We were in the barnyard. Ticktock had been nibbling up some spilled grain. She took one look at Jack and started jumping again, taking him with her.

His legs swung up one way and then the other as she jumped and turned and bucked.

"All I want to do is get your halter off!" he yelled.

"She must think it's a game!" I called as I chased them around, trying to get a way to jump in and grab her 'round the neck on the other side.

"Sure it's a game— Kill the Kid!" Jack yelled. "Would you

do something?" But Ticktock turned away and jumped. I saw Jack's legs swing out past her. He tried to get his footing to brace himself. "Penny!" he called. I shut my eyes and jumped in.

Ticktock snorted indignantly, as though she thought I was cheating. "Quick! The buckle's on your side," I said. A second later the halter came off.

Ticktock stopped and stood stock-still.

"She does think it's a game!" Jack exclaimed. We let the tired llama go back to the pasture. "Boy," Jack said. "I'm glad Doc gets the grant just for teaching us. Because if it depended on how much we learned, I'm not sure he'd get enough to cover postage."

Of course, along with the fun stuff, we also "learned" to pick up rocks in the pasture, scrape paint on the outside of the bunkhouse, and weed the garden in the front of the house. In fact, most of what we did was just plain old work, but it was nice to have Jack there to talk to.

On our second Saturday we hurried to get the chores done early so that we could leave for home right after lunch.

"Now, you two be sure to bring Scruggs with you next Friday," Mrs. Ericson said as we sat down to eat. "We certainly can use him."

"Sure!" Jack exclaimed. I only nodded.

"And your sister Jean, too," Doc Ericson added.

Jack hesitated, looking glum, and I said, "She's not back from Alabama yet."

"Maybe next time then," Mrs. Ericson said. "Be nice to have two boys and two girls, because then nobody gets picked on and nobody gets left out."

Well, it was obvious that she didn't know Jean. Jean was just born with the tendency to get picked on and left out. I sighed heavily.

"You two eat up," Doc Ericson told us as he stood up. "I want to get the crias out to the Nursery before we leave for Peabody. The yearling males are too rough with them."

We nodded and he went out. A minute later the dinner gong that

hung on the porch started banging furiously.

Jack and I looked at each other and we both said, "Trouble!" at the same time before we rushed out. Mrs. Ericson followed.

"Look! Look!" Dr. Ericson cried as we all came bursting out the door. We looked. Everything was silent. A faint breeze kicked up dust in Pasture 1.

"Everything seems quiet," Jack said.

"Seems quiet!" Dr. Ericson exclaimed. "The llamas are gone! Gone!"

We ran down the steps.

"The gate's open," I said and pointed at the wide pasture gate. Mrs. Ericson squinted and said, "The gate to Pasture 2 is open, too."

Dr. Ericson ran back into the house and came out with his field glasses. He used them to sweep over the pastures. "All the gates are open! Quick, get in the truck!"

We scrambled for the pickup. Jack and I hopped into the truck-bed, and the Ericsons got into the front. With a mighty jerk of the gears, we took off.

Ticktock on the Loose

Pasture 1 had the gate most often used as an exit gate. By that I mean that Pasture 4's gate led into the pasture alongside it. Pasture 3's gate led into Pasture 2, and Pasture 2's gate led into Pasture 1. But Pasture 1 had a gate that opened into the barnyard, and the barnyard gate opened to the dirt road. There was an exit gate on the far side of Pasture 4, but we never used it much because it was so far from the barns, and I'm not sure the llamas even knew it was there.

We jolted down that dirt road, headed for the causeway. A welcome sight met us as we came down the bank.

The llamas stood on either side of the causeway, knee-deep in shallow lake water. Most of them ignored us. They were busy drinking or browsing at some of the plants on the banks or lifting their muzzles to catch the smells. The two yearling males were having a spit fight. Mrs. Ericson hopped out of the cab and Jack jumped out of the back. I started to follow, but Dr. Ericson yelled, "I'll get the sheriff!" and took off again before I could get out.

Jack and Mrs. Ericson nodded and waved. I don't think Doc Ericson knew I was still in the truck until we pulled into town. But he was so flustered at the llamas having been let out that he simply parked and said, "I'll get the sheriff!"

And he rushed up the sidewalk.

I felt kind of blank myself. I hopped out of the truck and looked around.

Winneca certainly wasn't a big or a busy town. Right across the street was a big warehouse-type building that said "Ernie's Everything Outlet" on it.

Instead of regular doors like any other store, it had huge garage doors that opened onto the street. The effect was that the whole front of the store seemed to be opened for the public to walk in and out. But at the moment nobody was walking out of Ernie's Everything Outlet. Instead, a huge crowd seemed to be pushing to get in.

The wholesale flowers were back there. One lady—a customer—rushed past me, but when I got there I saw the florist lady nervously holding out a bouquet to Ticktock. The llama gently sniffed along the tops of the carnations and took a nibble of baby's breath.

"She won't hurt you," I said. Ticktock glanced at me and went back to browsing. "Ticktock," I said, and put my free hand out to her.

She really wanted me to leave her alone, but as long as she had the flowers, she decided not to resist. I slipped my arm around her neck. While I talked to her I got the dog leash onto her neck and fastened it above the knot I had tied in it. That way the lead couldn't get too tight and choke her.

"Whew!" I said.

"Is she yours?" the florist lady asked me.

"No, I'm just her maid." And I laughed a little.

Just then Doc Ericson, the sheriff, and the store manager (who was mopping his face) came up the aisle. Doc Ericson was so glad that Ticktock was okay that he didn't mind how much the store manager had to say to him. He paid for the licorice and the flowers. I took the bouquet, and with that and the lead, I got the llama to come with me.

Ticktock was as mild as milk once we got her out of the store. She gladly hopped into the pickup on command. I followed her.

Lama Glama

by Wendy Harris

What has a head like a camel and ears shaped like bananas? What is white with splotches of color but can also be all black or white or brown? What has thick wool like a sheep and feet with toes? What chews its cud like a cow and hums when it's content? What can be kept as a pet but will spit on you if made angry? What is it? It's a *lama glama*.

Lama glama is the scientific name for a large plant-eating animal from South America. Its common name is *llama*. Llamas are mammals that graze on grass and browse on low bushes. At one time these woolly animals lived wild in herds. Today no more wild llama herds roam over the mountains and highlands of South America. They live with, work for, and are cared for by man. They are domesticated.

Llamas are ruminants like cattle. Ruminants have stomachs with different parts, or chambers. One chamber stores food that has already been chewed and swallowed. The stored food is called *cud*. Cud can be coughed up by the llama and chewed again.

What does the llama look like? Many people think that the llama looks like a camel. Its face is shaped like a camel's. It has large eyes, long eyelashes, and a split

upper lip. The llama's long neck looks like a camel's too. But its body is smaller and woollier, and it does not have the camel's hump.

Like the camel, llamas can go without food for several days. Do you remember the chambered stomachs? If a llama has no food, it simply coughs up some cud. It chews the food again for another meal. Llamas do not drink much water. But unlike a camel, they cannot go for days without a drink. Llamas need water every day.

How do llamas behave? Llamas are usually calm and quiet. A contented llama can make a humming noise that sounds a little like the purr of a cat. But llamas will also spit a smelly, green liquid when they are angry or when they are afraid. Usually they spit at other llamas, but if you frighten one, watch out! Llamas have great aim!

What good are llamas? Thousands of years ago, native South Americans discovered the usefulness of the gentle llamas. With little training the male llamas would carry heavy loads of goods from the mountain highlands to the lowlands for trading. Each male could carry about one hundred pounds. However, if a llama was overloaded or became too tired, it would lie down and refuse to get up. If the llama driver tried to make the llama get up, he was spit upon.

The llama's long neck is similar to a camel's, but the llama's is woolier and has no hump.

The female llamas were kept for their wool and for raising more llamas. The wool could be spun into yarn for weaving clothing and rope. The female llamas gave birth to a baby, or *cria,* every two years. The llama's hide could be used to make sandals. Its meat could be eaten or dried and stored. The native South Americans also used the llama's bones to make tools and its fat to make candles. Very little of the llama could not be put to good use.

Some llamas are kept for their wool and for raising more llamas.

Why were llamas brought to North America? Llamas proved so useful as pack animals in South America that they were imported to North America. Today there are thousands of them scattered across the United States and Canada. Some are found in zoos, but most are kept as pets and pack animals.

Do you know why someone would want a llama for a pack animal instead of a horse or donkey? The feet of the llama make it an excellent pack animal. The bottoms of the two-toed feet are covered with a soft pad. These pads do not slide on slippery, rocky paths. And the soft pads do little damage to wilderness areas our country wants to preserve. Horse and donkey hooves are hard. Hard hooves are more likely to slip on slick paths. They also wear and cut paths of dust in the land.

What is one of the most interesting animals you could ever learn about? *Lama glama,* of course!

breeches and a hooded parka, fur boots, and a fur sleeping bag. Sam was waiting for him at the sled, with eleven mighty huskies straining at their harnesses, anxious to be off.

"Better meet some of your dogs," Sam said. "This first one, your leader, is Mutt. He's been to the Yukon before, and he knows the trail."

The tawny big brute lowered its head and watched Steve with suspicion. Steve fought down his fear and leaned over to pet the dog. Its fangs bared in a snarl.

"Not too close," Sam warned. "Mutt doesn't know you yet. And you better stay clear of Kooga—this big malemute. He's a real troublemaker."

"Why is the sled tied to a tree?" Steve asked.

"Because otherwise they'd be off like a flash and we couldn't stop them," Sam explained. He pointed to an iron rod suspended above the ground at the rear of the sled. It looked like a narrow rake. "That's your brake. You step on it and the prongs dig into the snow and stop the sled."

They packed, and Steve got on top of the sled.

"Hold on!" Sam warned as he untied the rope from the tree.

The dogs were off, eleven big brutes, harnessed in pairs except for Mutt, who took the lead. They raced over the snow in full gallop. The sled bounced and flew, and it took all Steve's strength to hold on.

Standing on the runners in back, Sam gave a hearty laugh.

"Dogs are always wild to get started. They'll soon slow down."

They did. For hours they went, skirting great slopes of spruce and Norway pine, and on and on into the still white wilderness.

At midday they stopped for a few minutes' rest and a bite to eat.

"Now you drive," suggested Sam. "I'll run behind for a while to get warm. But whatever you do, don't fall off the sled. You'll not be able to stop the dogs, and you'll lose them and the sled and all your food. It's not a good way to die."

Steve leaped on the runners. "Get going!" he shouted. Mutt

turned his head back and looked at him, but nothing happened.

"Holler *mush*," Sam suggested. "When you want to go right, holler *gee*, and for left *up*. And swing the sled around corners so it doesn't tip."

Steve nodded. "Mush!" he screamed. It worked. He stood proudly on the runners. He was driving a dog team!

There was real work to it, he soon discovered. Keeping the sled upright at curves was tricky, and he had to be careful to avoid stumps and rocks that might smash the sled. On the down slopes he stood on the brake to keep from running over the dogs.

But suddenly it happened. He made the mistake of looking back too long at Sam, who was jogging half a mile behind them. He hit a slope, and his feet slipped from the runners. But he held on, dragging as the sled gathered speed down-hill until it pushed the dogs into a wild, scrambled heap. Then the sled tipped.

It started one of the wildest dogfights Steve had ever seen. Each seemed to be blaming the others for what had happened, and they snarled and slashed with white-fanged fury.

"Stop them! Stop them!" Sam yelled.

Steve stood frozen with fear. He didn't move. He didn't dare venture close.

Alone on the Tundra

Sam came up full speed, screaming at the dogs. He pried them loose one by one with a snowshoe, and straightened up their harnesses, which had become badly tangled. Then he mopped the sweat from his face.

"You'll have to learn how to do that quick," he gasped. "If you don't, you'll lose a dog or two before you know it."

For five days they went on, and then Sam began to have chills and fever. "I was in the hospital for a week before you came," he explained. "Maybe I left too soon. It's coming back."

By noon he was groaning with pain and could not leave the sled. "There's a settlement over on Carlson Creek," he whispered. "You'd better get me there fast."

Steve reached the hollow among the bluffs in three hours, but only the women and children were there to meet them. The men were out on a week-long hunt.

"This one needs the doctor," said an old woman.

Steve went cold with dread, but he knew what had to be done.

"Sam says my lead dog knows the trail well. I'll go get the doctor."

Sam mumbled in protest, "You'll stay here," he gasped. "Your uncle flies to this settlement every so often for a check."

"It might be weeks," said the old woman. "There is much sickness."

"I'll go," said Steve. He had no choice. Soon he found himself alone on the trail with a fierce pack of malemutes and Eskimo huskies, and he felt panic rising within him. He wondered if he could handle the team.

He began talking to the dogs, calling them by name as Sam had told him to do. He stopped for the night under a sheltering cliff near a staggering thicket of birches. Now the moment he dreaded had come. He had to handle the big dogs.

Steve tried not to show his fear. The big leader dog watched with yellow eyes as he approached, its ears flattened to the massive head. As Steve reached down to unfasten the harness, the wolf dog snarled.

"Easy, Mutt!" Swiftly, Steve unharnessed the dog and led it to the nearest birch tree and tied it up. He came away weak but bursting with a happiness he had never known. He could do it! The other dogs, even the big malemute Kooga, were easy after that.

One day followed another with perfect weather. The dogs were beginning to know him; some even licked his hand. But Mutt, the leader, remained sullen.

Then he saw the plane in the sky one morning. It circled above him; his uncle waved, and Steve, forming big letters in the snow, told him to go to Sam at Carlson's Settlement.

A howling Arctic blizzard started that night and kept him in his sleeping bag for two days. The third morning dawned clear, and he looked out on a white world. No dogs were in sight. They had all been buried by the snow.

As they mushed north that afternoon he became careless. He did not see the low branch until it struck him with a stunning blow in the face. He was falling. "Don't lose your sled or you die!" Sam's words came roaring back to his ears.

With all his strength he tried to hold on. But it was no use. His fingers slipped and he lunged headlong into the snow. He floundered. He tried to rise to his feet, but the earth seemed to tilt on end, and he couldn't tell which side was up.

The dogs and the sled were speeding away. He could see them vaguely. In a few moments they would be gone. There was nothing he could do to stop them. His food, his sleeping bag, even his snowshoes were on the sled. A man couldn't live very long on the lonely tundra without them.

In that reeling instant of terror he seemed doomed. His mind cleared, and instinctively he cried out at the top of his lungs. "Gee! Gee! Gee, Mutt!"

He held his breath. For a terrible instant nothing happened. But suddenly the big lead dog swung to the right. He waited until the whole team had turned. Then he screamed again "Gee! Gee, Mutt!" Once more the lead dog turned.

They were coming back now. Steve got to his feet and stumbled to meet them, waving his arms. He tripped over a snowdrift and sprawled before the onrushing team. That was all he could remember for a long time.

When he opened his eyes finally it seemed that a miracle had happened. Mutt, towering over him, was licking his face.

He threw his arms around the big dog, buried his face in the heavy fur, and let the tears come. Even a man could cry in Alaska if there was no one there to see his tears.

From that day on his uncle paid him daily visits to watch his progress and to drop sandwiches and food from Aunt Bess. In the first of these packages he found a note.

"I have seen Sam," wrote his uncle. "He's doing fine, thanks to you. If you keep up your good speed, you should reach home in three days. We'll be waiting."

Steve felt a deep inner excitement. Home! In three days! He could drive a dog team now, and he felt sure that he could be of real use to his uncle. They would not find him soft and useless. They would like him.

Near sunset, three days later, as he came down the slope into the small settlement of Unison in the Yukon, his uncle and half the village came out to meet him. They were cheering and waving and smiling. His tall uncle wore a large smile and threw an arm over his shoulder.

"Good boy, Steve," he said warmly. To the people of the village he said, raising his voice, "I'm mighty proud to introduce you to my nephew Steve. He mushed all the way from Nenana in fifteen days, and that's a record for any of us to shoot at."

When they entered the log cabin which was to be his new home, there were gifts from almost everyone in the village—snowshoes, parkas, beaded reindeer pants, a beautiful malemute pup, a carving from a walrus tusk, and bows and arrows.

Steve mumbled his thanks to the smiling villagers who stood before him. They were a strange mixture of old sourdoughs, Eskimos, Indians, and boys and girls.

One young man spoke up. "The Flying Doctor has cared for us and saved many of us from death. We love him as a father, and we are glad to welcome another of his blood."

It was not until later when Aunt Bess and Uncle Jim and Steve were alone that Uncle Jim spoke.

"I want to confess, Steve, that I've been worried about having you here. I wanted you to be happy, but I knew that a soft white boy from civilization would soon be looked upon by these people with contempt."

He smiled and took Steve firmly by the shoulders. "But I see now that I was wrong. I need not have worried. You did what had to be done. You've got the makings of a real Yukon man."

Steve turned quickly away to play with the pup—and to hide the mist of happiness that had come into his eyes.

Pecos Bill Gets a Wife

adapted by Becky Henry
illustrated by Bruce Day

Pecos Bill, that rootin' tootin' cowboy, he figured he had just about everything. Why, he had Scat the cougar. And he had Rat the python. And of course, he had Widow Maker, the biggest, brawniest horse in the West, a horse that only Pecos Bill could ride. So the cowboy was mighty content, figuring there was nothing else in the whole wide world he could ever want.

But one day Pecos Bill was moseying down the river trail on old Widow Maker's back. He was taking it kind of slow and easy, 'bout sixty miles an hour, when all of a sudden something stopped him right in his tracks.

It was a sight. A sight the likes of what Pecos Bill had never seen before in all his days. Speeding down the middle of the river on the back of a giant catfish was a cowgirl. What a cowgirl! Her hair was as red as the evening sun, all tied up in two braids, looking like two carrots sticking out of her head. Her hat flapped on the ends of its strings.

"Yippee! Yahoo!" she yelled. Her two long bony arms wrapped around the catfish's body. "Yahoo-ee! Yip-yip-yahoo!"

No doubt about it; it was love at first sight. Pecos Bill felt his heart do a double flip and the sweat stand out on his brow. He had to meet this cowgirl!

Even while he watched, the catfish took a wild leap and landed on the bank, gasping for breath. The redheaded cowgirl hopped off, and with one quick toss she flipped the catfish back into the water. Then she turned to face Pecos Bill.

"Howdy, cowboy!" She grinned wide enough to show off all six of her teeth, shining white and pearly. The freckles on her face stood out bold and orange.

Pecos Bill's heart jumped into his throat, and he couldn't speak for gazing at her beauty. So she kept right on talking.

"My name's Slewfoot Sue. I come down the river to find me new critters to ride. I done rode everything this country has to offer. I've rode grizzly bars and mountain lions and wild horses, and now I've rode a catfish too." She grinned again and poured the water out of her boot. "What have you rode, cowboy?"

All Pecos Bill could do was smile.

There was a whirlwind court-ship, and Slewfoot Sue decided she loved this cowboy as much as he loved her. But as crazy as Bill was about Sue, there was one thing he wouldn't let her do.

"Sue," he told her, "I've got to warn you. Everything I have is yours, including Widow Maker. But he's a fiery horse, and he won't let anyone ride him but me. If you try, I might never see you again."

Well, those were the very words Sue needed to hear to make her want to ride Widow Maker more than anything else in the

world. Sue didn't mention it again, but that's not to say it left her mind. She could think of hardly anything else.

Their wedding day came, and my, didn't Sue look pretty! She wore a white veil and a long white dress with a bustle the size of a bushel basket. Bustles were quite the style back then, you know, and Sue's was made from a brand new bedspring and the fanciest chicken wire around. There never was a happier man than Pecos Bill on his wedding day.

Well, no sooner had they said "I do" and the preacher pronounced his blessing than Slewfoot Sue hollered "Yahoo!" She raced outside quicker than a jackrabbit and hopped on Widow Maker's back. That was one surprised horse.

And that was one surprised bride. Widow Maker bucked hard, and Slewfoot Sue's second "Yahoo!" faded off into the distance as she disappeared from sight behind the clouds.

They all stood watching—Bill, the preacher, and all the cowboys, their mouths hanging wide open. "We might never see her again," Pecos Bill muttered. "I warned her."

Well, rumor had it that Sue had to duck her head to keep from hitting the moon. But whatever happened, she appeared again that evening, falling right out of the sky. She would have landed with only a few bruises except for the bustle she was wearing.

Instead of landing, Sue bounced.

Sue bounced up until she was out of sight in the sky again!

When she came back down, she bounced again.

This could have gone on for days or even weeks, but finally Pecos Bill decided he had had enough. He figured his new bride probably had too. So he pulled out his lariat and waited.

The next time Sue bounced, Bill lassoed her and brought her down. If it hadn't been for his strong muscles, she would have bounced again. But she stayed. She was a little dizzy and bruised, but otherwise she was fine.

From what I hear, Pecos Bill and Slewfoot Sue had a right happy life together as husband and wife. And one thing that made it happy was that never again did Slewfoot Sue ask to ride Widow Maker. She was cured of that forever.

Tall Tales

illustrated by Bruce Day

The story "Pecos Bill Gets a Wife" is called a tall tale. That's an unusual name for an unusual kind of story. A tall tale stretches the truth so much that nobody is really expected to believe it.

• The History of Tall Tales

In early America a man had to be strong just to survive. As a result, BIG stories grew up about BIG men who could do BIG, impossible things. But these impossible characters lived only in the minds of their storytellers.

The storytellers were almost always men who wished they could perform great feats. Sometimes they worked at hard, dangerous jobs. Sometimes their jobs were dull. The men wanted to have something to dream about. They wanted to know a bigger-than-life lumberjack, railroad man, seaman, or cowboy. So they invented characters like Paul Bunyan, John Henry, Stormalong, and, of course, Pecos Bill.

• Elements of Tall Tales

It could have taken a real cowboy a year to encounter the excitement that Pecos Bill met in one day. That was one reason men liked this tall tale character so much. The more impossible the feats he accomplished, the better they liked him. He was the cowboy that other cowboys dreamed of being.

However, Slewfoot Sue was hardly the kind of girl a cowboy dreamed of meeting! Adding a big dose of humor to a tall tale helped make long, lonely nights on the prairie pass more quickly.

The best tall-tale tellers also used colorful descriptions for spinning their tall tales. They wanted to draw pictures in the other fellow's mind, so they used phrases such as "her hair looked like two carrots sticking out of her head," or "her bustle was the size of a bushel basket."

Find examples of tall-tale elements in the story you just read. If you put them all together, you may be able to write a tall tale of your own!

Project Submarine

Paul and Karen Wilt

illustrated by Del Thompson and Noelle Snyder

Kyle Ellis, an average kid with an above average machine, uses current technology to unravel a security problem. Although today Kyle's computer may look strange, outdated, and useless, in the 1980s it was the most recent in computer technology. This trend of computer improvement will even make tomorrow's computers outdate today's!

Kyle Ellis punched the enter button. A bright blue "ERROR" sign flashed at him as the computer started to beep. "Oh, no!" Kyle slumped back in his chair.

"Keep trying," Mr. Javanowitz said. "Ever since your dad set up this homework-checking program, you've always got your homework done in micro-seconds." His boisterous laugh filled the office. Kyle typed "END PROGRAM" and pulled out the disk.

"Look at this, Kyle," Mr. Javanowitz said. Mr. Javanowitz was Mr. Ellis's partner and an earnest computer fan. He enjoyed Kyle's afternoon visits to the office. Mr. Javanowitz started another program, and a chessboard appeared. "The computer has had

me in check all afternoon, but I think I have a way around it."

He punched two keys, and his queen zipped across the screen and landed beside the computer's bishop. The computer hummed for a moment, then moved a knight forward. "CHECKMATE" flashed the screen.

"UGH," Mr. Javanowitz typed onto the screen.

"Well, I'll see you tomorrow," he said, closing the program.

"Good night," Kyle said. He carefully shut down the computer.

The door closed behind Mr. Javanowitz, and Kyle sighed.

Computers could do more things than he had ever imagined. They seemed able to do any-thing—or at least almost anything. But just yesterday Dad had said they couldn't think up an answer to the security problem at work. With the program Kyle had, he could check his math, but the computer wouldn't just give the an-swer straight out.

Just then the door from the laboratory opened and a man in a white lab jacket stepped out. He set his toolbox on the office floor

and held the door for a repairman. The edge of his slacks caught on the lid of the toolbox and popped it open. A disk lay on the upper shelf. Kyle could see that the other shelves were empty. He looked again. The words "PRO-JECT SUBMARINE" had been penciled on the label of the disk. Then he noticed the lower label. "High priority. Do not remove from security area."

Kyle's head spun. Dad had just mentioned the security problem at the labs. This was the leak: these men were stealing the secret infor-mation.

Quickly and silently Kyle snatched up the disk. He slid it under his chair cushion. His hands felt cold and clammy, but a drip of sweat fell off his forehead as he pretended to adjust the computer.

"Hey," the man in the lab jacket said, reaching for the tool-box. "What happened to the—Kid, did you take a disk from the box?" He leaned over Kyle, frowning and clenching his fist.

Kyle grabbed the homework disk off the desk. "Do you mean this?" he asked. He tried to keep his voice steady, but he could hear it rise in his throat.

"Yeah," the man said. He snatched it and stuffed it into his jacket.

The repairman narrowed his eyes. "I don't like the looks of this, Jake," he said.

A loud bell began clanging. "The alarm!" Jake ran for the door.

The bolt shot closed.

"Let's get out of here," the other man said. He pulled on the handle. The door didn't budge. "Come on," he said. He flung the toolbox against the window, shattering the glass. He kicked the broken pieces out of the way. "Here's our ticket out, Jake." He grabbed Kyle by the arm.

Kyle felt himself lifted out the window; then Jake tossed him into a van. He fell backward among a jumble of machines. The other man jumped into the driver's seat next to Jake.

The wheels screeched as the van jerked to life and sped into traffic.

As the van swayed from side to side, Kyle grabbed the seat in front of him and hung on with all his might.

They sped down the highway, passing cars and trucks in a swerving roller-coaster ride. A siren sounded. The driver darted in front of a car and turned into a side street, swinging the back of the van in a wide arc. The ride was a series of stops and starts, jerks and jumbles until they reached an old warehouse.

"We'll hide here," said the man who had driven the van. "I'll call Wendell. We'll have to take what we have and go."

Jake dragged Kyle into the warehouse and tied him to a pole. Then he set up a computer.

"The more you find out, the bigger problem you're gonna be, kid," Jake said. "'Cuz what are we gonna do if you find out too much?"

Kyle dropped his eyes to the floor.

Jake laughed and hit his knee. The computer beeped. Kyle peered at it without raising his head. A game flashed onto the screen.

"You're really gonna find out too much this way." Jake piloted his spaceship through asteroids, flying saucers, and enemy rockets, laughing to himself as he shot them down.

A car horn honked. Jake ran to the door. A mumble of unintelligible voices reached Kyle's ears. He pulled at the rope on his hands and felt it loosen.

Several men walked toward him, and Kyle held still.

"Well, Harvey, did he say anything else?" Jake asked.

"We'll just have to lay low for a day or two," said Harvey, the man who had driven the van. "Let's check the program we got."

He pulled out Kyle's homework program and stuck it into the machine. "RUN," he typed.

The disk drive hummed, and then the screen lit up with the program:

```
010 RANDOMIZE
020 FOR I = 1 TO 10
030 A = INT(RND(100)*100)
040 B = INT(RND(100)*100)
050 PRINT A; "+" B;
060 INPUT ANSWER
070 IF ANSWER = A+B THEN
  PRINT "GOOD WORK" :
  CORRECT = CORRECT + 1
080 IF ANSWER <> A+B THEN
  PRINT "TRY AGAIN" : WRNG
  = WRNG+1: GOTO 50
090 NEXT 1
```

"What?" Jake shrieked. He ripped the disk out of the computer. "Look; just look at this: 'Homework Program.' I bet that kid . . ." His eyes turned to Kyle.

Kyle's heart raced. "What should I do?" he thought. "I've got to think."

Jake shoved the disk at Kyle's face and broke it into a worthless mess. "We're gonna get that program," he fumed. "Like you said, Harvey, here's our ticket." He tapped Kyle's chest.

"Let's go call the boss and arrange the details," Harvey said.

Kyle heard them lock the door as they walked out. He pulled at the ropes. They seemed to loosen more, but his hand wouldn't fit between them and the pole. As Kyle twisted and turned, the rope caught on a nail. He tugged, and the rope popped loose. Kyle fell forward onto his knees. Wasting no time, he scrambled to his feet and raced to the door.

The men had locked it from the outside. Kyle searched the windows. The lowest one was at least twenty feet from the ground. He paced the floor. "If only computers could figure out a problem like this," he thought to himself.

He stopped in front of the computer. The file of disks lay in a jumble. Kyle stuck one into the slot and typed "RUN." The computer began to list names and addresses. Kyle saw his dad's company name flash by. "Hmm," he murmured.

Kyle stuck in another disk. Quickly he glanced through the files and chose the ones that looked most important. He checked a few more disks, planning to find a safe place to hide them.

Then he ran the program titled "WAREHOUSE." A set of floor plans covered the screen. Kyle reached for the return key. Then two words caught his attention— "EMERGENCY EXIT." Kyle bit his lip. If the emergency exit wasn't blocked, it would be immediately behind him. He pulled out the disk.

The front door rattled. Kyle scooped up the disks and raced for the emergency exit. A big stack of empty boxes blocked his way. Kyle shoved them aside. The emergency exit sign, covered with an inch of dust, lay shattered where it had fallen on the floor. Kyle attacked the door, praying that it would open. The hinges creaked and gave way.

"Hey, the kid's gone!"

Kyle tore blindly down the alley and then turned down another, expecting someone to grab him at any moment. His lungs felt as if they were bursting. The streetlights were just coming on. The shadows they made seemed to be filled with kidnappers. The streets were deserted. Kyle saw a gas station on the corner ahead.

The fellow pumping gas into a car brushed his long hair out of his eyes and yawned. Kyle watched from the shadows, unable to decide whether or not to trust such a character.

Just then a police car pulled into the station. Kyle broke into a run. "Help!" he yelled.

The police officer jumped out of the car. "What's the problem, Son?" he asked.

Kyle stumbled as he reached him. "I'm Kyle Ellis. I was kidnapped." He held his sides and gasped for air. "I just escaped. Please, help me."

The police officer let out a low whistle. "The radio's been screaming about you and some stolen information all afternoon. Hop in. Let's get you down to the station."

Dad was waiting in the chief's office when they got to the station. "Kyle, are you all right? They called me as soon as the officer radioed in that he had picked you up. Did they hurt you?"

"They tied me to a pole in some old warehouse and tried to scare me. They sure were mad when they found out the disk they had was that homework program you wrote for me."

"How'd they get their hands on that?" Dad looked puzzled.

Kyle grinned. "I switched the disks as soon as I realized that what they had was top security. I hid the real disk under a cushion in your office." He held up the disks. "And here's all of the rest of the stolen disks. I brought them with me!"

Dad put his arm around Kyle's shoulders. "That's quite a save you made there, Son. But how did you find your way out of that warehouse? Surely those men didn't leave you a map."

"I don't suppose they meant to." Kyle laughed. "But when you've got a computer and the right disk, you can find out just about anything."

ENCOUNTERS

Kit Carson and the Grizzly Bears

Becky Henry

illustrated by Preston Gravely Jr.

In the days when the West was wild and untamed, brave men journeyed far to explore this vast wilderness. Kit Carson was one of these brave men. He traveled across the United States, blazing trails, trapping for furs, and fighting Indians. This true story tells of one adventure Kit Carson had in the Wild West.

"Men, we need meat, and we need it soon. With no rain in so long, all the animals have gone looking for a better place to graze. I can't say that I blame them either." The leader of the camp scratched his head and looked around. "Any of you men want to try to catch us some meat?"

"I think I can." The voice belonged to Kit Carson, the twenty-four-year-old crack shot.

"That's the way, Kit!" The other men slapped his back and shook his hand. "If anyone can do it, you can."

Kit hoisted his rifle to his shoulder. "I'm heading out on foot, and I aim to come back with some supper meat."

Kit Carson was one man who usually did what he said he would do. In his soft moccasins, he padded noiselessly through the underbrush for almost a mile. Then his keen eyes spotted a clear imprint in the sand.

"Elk!" he whispered, running his fingers over the delicate grooves. "And these tracks are pretty fresh. They can't be too far away."

Sure enough, as Kit followed the tracks through the trees, he soon came upon a whole herd of elk grazing on the few plants they could find.

"Only a mile away from camp!" Kit chuckled. "And those men thought there weren't any animals anywhere near here. Well, I'll be bringing supper home pretty soon."

With a snap and a crack of his trusty rifle, Kit brought one big elk down to the ground. He headed toward it with a satisfied smile on his face.

But he never got to the downed elk. A roar sounded through the forest, and two grizzly bears lumbered clumsily through the trees. The fur on their mangy backs bristled, and their lips curled back in a snarl, showing long white fangs.

And Kit's gun was empty! There was no time to reload it.

Dropping his rifle, he scrambled hastily up a little aspen tree. Even though he climbed as high as he could, his feet were just barely out of the bears' reach. He looked down at the angry bruins trying to swipe at him with their big paws.

Kit tucked his legs under him the best he could. He watched the grizzlies rip some of the bark off the tree, pull at the roots, and tear at the branches, taking an occasional wild swipe at him.

"Well, this can't go on much longer," Kit decided. He couldn't let this situation get the best of him, so he did some thinking. Even though a grizzly was the roughest, toughest animal around, he still had one very tender spot: his nose. Kit pulled out his hunting knife and whacked off a small tree branch. This was his new weapon.

As soon as one bear nose got close enough, Kit was ready. "Well, Mr. Grizzly, I can't say that I'm too sorry to do this to you." Whap! He smacked the bear in the nose. The bear fell down and grabbed his nose with his paws, howling in pain. The other bear came toward Kit. The new weapon hit its mark again. The other bear went down. Kit couldn't help laughing.

"My life may be in danger, but you two bruins are a funny sight to see!"

Another whole hour went by before the grizzlies finally decided that this battle wasn't worth the trouble. With snorts of pain and disgust, they lumbered back into the wilderness.

After Kit was quite convinced that they were gone for good, he climbed down. Making his way with stiff legs to the spot where the elk lay waiting, he discovered that it had been eaten by wolves.

Hours after dark, Kit trudged back into camp. When he told his story, the other men laughed so hard that they cried. They didn't even mind that Kit had come back without any meat for supper.

Kit laughed too. "But I never have been so scared in all my life!"

"Kit Carson," said a friend, "you're a wonder. You're the only man I've ever known who could tussle with grizzly bears without a rifle . . . and win!"

There Was an Old Man from Pompeii

Eileen Berry and Dawn Watkins
illustrated by Jim Hargis and Sam Laterza

There was an old man from Pompeii
Who gave talks on volcanoes each day.
When the mountain erupted
He got interrupted,
And forgot what he wanted to say.

THERE WAS A YOUNG MINER IN YUMA

Unattributed
illustrated by Jim Hargis and Sam Laterza

There was a young miner in Yuma
Who once encountered a puma,
And later they found
Just a spot on the ground
And a puma in a very good huma.

Roger's Choice

Virginia Payne Dow
illustrated by Bruce Ink

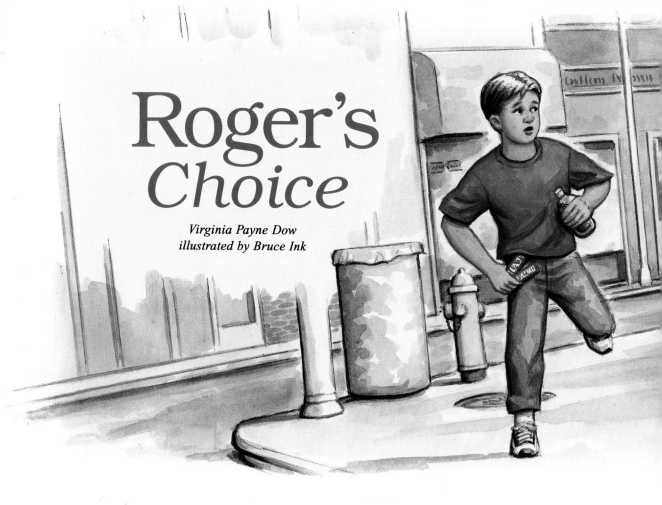

Roger felt the two candy bars under his shirt. Slowly he walked to the counter to pay for his root beer. He jingled the change in his hand and tried to whistle a little tune. His throat was dry, and the cheery notes seemed to stick.

"That all you want?" Mr. Bradley asked. He had a big jolly face. When he smiled, his dimples looked like big holes in his cheeks.

"Yes, sir; that's it."

"Can't get over how much you've grown, Roger. Two feet at least, huh?" Mr. Bradley's big hand ruffled Roger's hair before it took the change. He counted it and dropped it into the cash register. Mopping his forehead with a big white handkerchief, Mr. Bradley turned back toward Roger.

"Say hello to that little sister of yours for me, Roger."

"Yes, sir. See you around, Mr. Bradley." Roger went to the front

of the store and used the bottle opener. Tipping the bottle upside down, he let the cold, fizzy liquid run down his throat.

Roger stopped outside to bend over and tie his sneaker and then ran down the street. As soon as he rounded the corner, he took the two candy bars from under his shirt. They were beginning to melt. Then he ran the three blocks to his home.

"Wendy." Roger's whisper brought a quick scamper of little feet down the hall. Wendy was still in her long, thin nightgown. Her hair was tangled and dirty.

"Hi, Roger. Did you bring me some candy?" Wendy ran forward and clung to Roger's hand. She took her candy bar and smiled up at him.

"Yeah, kiddo. Where's Mom?"

"Sleepin' still," Wendy said, her mouth full of the melting chocolate.

"Listen, Wendy. I want you to comb your hair and get some decent clothes on. We're going for a walk," Roger said quietly. He went to the bare room that he called his own and flung himself down onto the thin mattress. He punched the flat foam pillow in frustration.

It had been two days since his mother had been out of bed. And it wasn't the first time she had stayed in bed for so long either. After Roger's dad had left, his mother had cried a lot. She stopped taking Roger and Wendy to Sunday school. Lots of times she stayed in bed for two, three—maybe even four days at a time.

Roger was sick of the makeshift meals he and Wendy were forced to eat. When everything in the apartment had been eaten, he had used the last of the money in his bank. There wasn't much there, and Wendy needed more than a few candy bars from Mr. Bradley's store.

He wanted the Lord to show him what to do. But, somehow, whenever Roger prayed these days, he felt as if his prayers didn't go very far. The Lord didn't seem to even hear.

"Ready, Roger!" Wendy came to the open doorway in a faded skirt and a bright red T-shirt. Her hair was twisted into a ponytail. She looked terrible, but Roger didn't feel like worrying about his sister's appearance.

"Okay, Wendy, out the door!" Roger jumped from the mattress.

"Where we goin'?" Wendy asked as they left the front steps. She had to skip every three steps to keep up with Roger.

"Oh, I don't know," he answered without looking at her.

"I want something to eat."

"Well, there's no money."

"So?"

"Wendy, you just can't get food without money!" Roger raised his voice and gave her arm a little jerk.

"Ouch!"

"Look, I'm sorry. Just don't talk for a few minutes. I'm thinking about how to get something to eat." Roger knew he couldn't get a job. No one hired an eleven-year-old boy.

They walked slowly down the street. It was hot. Really hot. They weren't far from Mr. Bradley's store when Roger decided to go back for some more candy. He turned into the parking lot, pulling Wendy behind him.

"Listen, Wendy, I want you to wait outside for me. You sit down

on this sidewalk—and no noise!" He showed her where to sit and walked into the store.

Roger decided that he would just wait near the candy until he could be sure that no one was looking. He couldn't stop the thumping of his heart. It seemed to be pounding right out of his chest and ears. The worst part about taking the candy was that Wendy would know. She wasn't too young to know that there was a way to get things without money. She would know that her big brother was a thief.

Roger didn't want Wendy to know, but he also didn't want her to be hungry. When he was sure that no one was paying any attention to him, he sucked in his breath and reached for a big chocolate bar. Without even looking around, he quickly slid it under his shirt.

"Roger."

Roger jumped and whirled around. Wendy was standing there, calmly eating a popcorn ball.

"Where did you get that? Why aren't you back where I told you to sit? Nobody told you to come in!" Roger angrily shoved Wendy backward. He had thought for sure he'd been caught. He could see his mother's face with tears in her eyes as she came to pick him up at the police station. Way in the back of his mind, he could hear his Sunday school teacher telling him how God hated stealing.

Tears sprang into Wendy's eyes, and Roger immediately felt sorry. He hadn't meant to yell.

"Mr. Bradley gave it to me," Wendy sniffed. "He told me to come inside out of the hot sun. He gave me some lemonade too."

Roger looked across the store. Several customers were waiting at Mr. Bradley's cash register. He looked pretty hot and tired. Twice while Roger was watching, he wiped his forehead and neck with a big, white handkerchief.

"Listen, kiddo, you go back and tell Mr. Bradley thank you, and I'll be right with you," Roger said gently. As soon as she turned around, he pulled the chocolate bar out from under his shirt and put it carefully back on the shelf.

He looked back at Mr. Bradley, punching buttons on the cash register. His big, jolly face was sweaty. Suddenly it seemed that the Lord gave Roger an idea. He walked over to the cash register and picked up a paper bag. He reached over and started putting groceries into it.

"Need a hand, Mr. Bradley?"

Mr. Bradley frowned and began to shake his head. "Roger, I can't hire you. I don't make enough to have help. I've told you that before."

"Not even for a package of hot dogs? And maybe some bread and peanut butter?" Roger asked. He continued placing groceries in the paper bag.

A slow smile spread across Mr. Bradley's face. He mopped his forehead again and nodded.

"Okay, boy. You got yourself a deal."

Roger felt like singing—almost. Just as the Lord had told him to start helping Mr. Bradley, he knew that the Lord was telling him something else now. He felt his whole face get hot, but he knew what he had to do. He watched the last customer in line pay for his groceries and walk out the door.

"Mr. Bradley." Roger felt his voice squeak a little. "Mr. Bradley, please forgive me—I've stolen some candy bars, but I want to pay for them now. I'll work for them. I'm really sorry—the Lord hasn't listened to my prayers ever since I did it. Wendy was so hungry, Mr. Bradley, but it was wrong." Embarrassed, Roger realized that tears were streaming down his cheeks.

Mr. Bradley wasn't smiling. "It's a serious thing, stealing is," he said, looking down. "It costs me a lot of money." He mopped his forehead again, slowly this time. "But I forgive you, Roger," he said. "I know you know the Lord. And He can give you the strength never to steal again."

Roger stood smiling a quivery smile while Wendy watched with big eyes. Mr. Bradley finally broke the silence. "Well, boy, if you're going to earn your keep around here, you'd better get working. Here." He handed Roger the broom. "This floor hasn't been swept in a month of Sundays. Those candy bars can be part of your pay."

"Oh, thank you, Mr. Bradley!" Roger beamed at Wendy and began to sweep the floor with all his might. "Wendy, you sit tight and watch big brother. When I'm done, I'll take you home, and we'll have the best supper ever. I bet Mom'll smell it cookin' and get up and help eat it!"

Wendy looked up at Roger. She had sticky popcorn all over her face, but her eyes were shining.

As Roger swept, he watched the pile of dust gathering in the center of the floor and smiled. That dirt was like his sins—out in the open, not swept under the rug. He felt ten feet tall. He knew he had made the right decision.

ON THE ROAD TO DAMASCUS

A choral reading from Acts 8:1-3 and 9:1-20.

arranged by Ron Shields
illustrated by Del Thompson and Roger Bruckner

Readers		**Chorus One:**	light voices
Reader One:	Saul	**Chorus Two:**	medium voices
Reader Two:	Ananias	**Chorus Three:**	dark voices

In the years after Christ's ascension, the early church suffered persecution from unbelievers. Many of Christ's followers were thrown into prison, and some of them died for their faith. One man became especially well known as a hater and persecutor of the church— Saul of Tarsus. But when Saul met the Lord on the road to Damascus, he became a new creature.

All: And at that time there was a great persecution against the church which was at Jerusalem. . . .

Reader One: As for Saul,

Chorus Two: he made havock of the church,

Choruses One and Two: entering into every house, and haling men and women

All: committed them to prison. . . .

Reader One: And Saul,

All: yet breathing out threatenings and slaughter against the disciples of the Lord,

Choruses One and Two: went unto the high priest, and desired of him letters to Damascus to the synagogues, that if he found any of this way,

Chorus Two: whether they were men or women,

All: he might bring them bound unto Jerusalem.

Reader One: And as he journeyed, he came near Damascus:

Chorus One: and suddenly

Chorus Two: there shined round about him a light from heaven:

Choruses One and Two: And he fell to the earth,

All: and heard a voice saying unto him,

Chorus Three: Saul, Saul, why persecutest thou me?

Choruses One and Two: And he said,

Reader One: Who art thou, Lord?

Choruses One and Two: And the Lord said,

Chorus Three: I am Jesus whom thou persecutest: it is hard for thee to kick against the pricks.

Saul understood immediately what the Lord meant. He had seen the pricks used to prod cattle pulling carts. If the cattle were stubborn and kicked backward, they hurt their legs on the pricks until they started forward again.

Choruses One and Two: And he trembling and astonished said,

Reader One: Lord, what wilt thou have me to do?

Choruses One and Two: And the Lord said unto him,

Chorus Three: Arise, and go into the city, and it shall be told thee what thou must do.

Choruses One and Two: And the men which journeyed with him stood speechless, hearing a voice, but seeing no man.

Reader One: And Saul arose from the earth; and when his eyes were opened, he saw no man:

Choruses One and Two: but they led him by the hand, and brought him into Damascus.

Reader One: And he was three days without sight, and neither did eat nor drink.

Choruses One and Two: And there was a certain disciple at Damascus, named Ananias; and

to him said the Lord in a vision,

Chorus Three: Ananias.

Choruses One and Two: And he said,

Reader Two: Behold, I am here, Lord.

Choruses One and Two: And the Lord said unto him,

Chorus Three: Arise, and go into the street which is called Straight, and inquire in the house of Judas for one called Saul of Tarsus: for, behold, he prayeth. And hath seen in a vision a man named Ananias coming in, and putting his hand on him, that he might receive his sight.

Choruses One and Two: Then Ananias answered,

Reader Two: Lord, I have heard by many of this man, how much evil he hath done to thy saints at Jerusalem: And here he hath authority from the chief priests to bind all that call on thy name.

Choruses One and Two: But the Lord said unto him,

Chorus Three: Go thy way: for he is a chosen vessel unto me, to bear my name before the Gentiles, and kings, and the children of Israel: For I will shew him how great things he must suffer for my name's sake.

Choruses One and Two: And Ananias went his way, and entered into the house; and putting his hands on him said,

Reader Two: Brother Saul, the Lord, even Jesus, that appeared unto thee in the way as thou camest, hath sent me, that thou mightest receive thy sight, and be filled with the Holy Ghost.

Reader One: And immediately there fell from his eyes as it had been scales: and he received sight forthwith, and arose, and was baptized. And when he had received meat, he was strengthened.

Choruses One and Two: Then was Saul certain days with the disciples which were at Damascus.

Reader One: And straightway he preached Christ in the synagogues,

All: that he is the Son of God.

The Darkest Time

Becky Henry

In the year 1861, when Abraham Lincoln was president, our country began the most terrible war of its history. Every other war that we have ever entered has been against another country. But this time, states that were part of the same country fought against each other. This terrible conflict was called the War Between the States, or the American Civil War.

Problems began because the people of the North and the people of the South lived in different ways. They believed different things, and each side thought the other was wrong. They tried to take care of their differences in peaceful ways, but the problems were too serious. To some people, war seemed to be the only solution.

No other war in United States history has created such bitterness. Sometimes even brothers sincerely believed differently from each other and fought on opposite sides of the same battle. The War

Between the States tore apart families and friends. It was one of the darkest times in our nation's history.

Abraham Lincoln was the man the Lord gave us to lead our country through that bleak time. He had patience, compassion, a gentle sense of humor, and a real love for his country. After years of toil and heartache, he led the nation to the end of the war. How thankful Mr. Lincoln was then! But only five days later the president was shot and killed. He did not live to see his beloved states become one strong nation again.

When President Lincoln died, many people in the North and some people in the South grieved over his death. Today people in both the North and the South remember him as one of the greatest presidents this country has ever had. He guided our nation through its darkest time, and in the end he brought it to a better light.

Abraham Lincoln
Was My Friend

by Keith W. Jennison
illustrated by Mary Ann Lumm

Billy Brown and Abraham Lincoln were neighbors in Springfield, Illinois. When Mr. Lincoln became the president of the United States and went to Washington, Billy stayed behind. Each day he eagerly read the newspaper for news of his good friend Abe. He read about the war and learned that some people blamed Mr. Lincoln because it lasted so long. He read that each day the president saw dozens of people and that he helped them whenever he could. Billy often wished he could do something for his old friend.

In 1864 Billy Brown made a trip to Washington to see the president. Billy tells of his visit with the president when Mr. Lincoln was staying at a home very near a battlefield.

I footed it up to the Soldiers' Home where Mr. Lincoln was living then, right among the sick soldiers in their tents. There was lots of people settin' around in a little room waiting for him. A door opened, and out came little John Nicolay. I went up to him and said, "How'd you do, John? Where's Mr. Lincoln?"

"Have you an appointment with Mr. Lincoln?" he says.

"No sir, I ain't, and it ain't necessary. You just trot along,

Johnnie, and tell him Billy Brown's here, and see what he says."

In about two minutes, the door popped open and out came Abe Lincoln, his face all lit up. He saw me first thing and shook my hand fit to kill. "Billy," he says, "come right in. You're going to stay to supper with Mary and me."

He had a right smart lot of people to see, but as soon as he was through, we went out on the back stoop and talked and talked and talked. I told him about everybody in Springfield—the weddings, the births, the funerals, and the buildings. I guess there wasn't a yarn I'd heard in the last three-and-a-half years that I didn't spin for him. Laugh— you'd ought to have heard him laugh! It just did my heart good, for I could see what they'd been doing to him. He always was a thin man, but he was thinner than ever now, and his face was drawn and gray. It was enough to make you cry.

Well, we had supper, and then we talked some more. About ten o'clock, I started to leave.

"Billy," he says, "what did you come for?"

"I came to see you, Abe."

"But you haven't asked me for anything, Billy. What do you want me to do for you?"

"Nothing, Abe. I just wanted to see you. I felt kind of lonesome 'cause it had been so long since I'd seen you. And I was afraid I'd forget some of those yarns if I didn't see you soon."

Well, sir, you should have seen his face when he looked at me.

"Billy Brown," he says slow-like, "do you mean to tell me that you came all the way from Springfield, Illinois, just to visit with me? You don't have any com- plaints in your pocket or advice up your sleeve?"

"Yes, sir," I says. "That's about it. Why, I'd go to Europe to see you if I couldn't do it no other way, Abe."

Well, sir, I was never so aston- ished in all my life. He just grabbed my hand and shook it nearly off, and the tears just poured down his face.

"Billy," he says, "you'll never know just what good you've done me. I'm homesick, Billy, just plumb homesick, and it seems as if this war will never be over. Many a night I can see the boys dying on the fields, and I can hear their mothers crying for them at home. And I can't help it, Billy; I have to send them down there. We've got to save the Union, Billy. We've got to."

His Mule

was ringing; they might catch the end of the line as it was marching into the building; they might even tiptoe fearfully into the room after classes had started—but never Johnny! He was always in his place as the line marched in and always in his proper seat when classes began. In the fall, in the winter, and in the spring, it was always the same. Johnny was always on time.

But one day, toward the end of the school year, Johnny was late! The last bell rang—Johnny was not there! Nine o'clock came—and still no Johnny. Ten o'clock rolled around, half past ten, and not a sign of Johnny.

It was so very late now, the teacher and the children began to wonder what had happened. Perhaps Johnny was sick, or perhaps he had fallen over the steep mountainside on the way to school. But a half hour later, at eleven o'clock, there was a shuffle-shuffle outside the door. It opened slowly, and Johnny creaked guiltily into the room.

"Why, Johnny!" cried the teacher. "It's eleven o'clock! Why are you so late?"

"I just couldn't help it, Miss Mary!" stammered Johnny, and he looked as though he might cry at any moment.

"But tell me, what happened?" urged Miss Mary.

"I got into town early this morning, Miss Mary," began Johnny, "in plenty of time for school, but I stopped for a minute in the town square to watch the auction."

Everybody knew about the auction. It was held every Friday, and the mountaineers called it "Trade Day." They came in from all the surrounding hills and ranges bringing anything they had on hand that they wanted to swap or sell. Handmade chairs, baskets,

turkeys, jackknives, horses, preserves, feather pillows, anything and everything went on sale in the town square on Friday.

"And so," continued Johnny, "while I was standing there, an old mule was put up to be sold. The auctioneer began shouting, 'What am I offered for this mule? What am I bid? What am I bid?'

"Nobody would begin the bidding, and so, just to get the sale started, I hollered out, 'I bid five cents!' I thought sure somebody would bid higher because mules cost a lot of money. But nobody did, and so they gave me the mule.

"And there I stood, Miss Mary, holding the mule by the halter. I didn't know what to do with him. About the only thing I could think of was to take him along to school with me. So I started toward the schoolhouse leading the mule.

"I soon found out why nobody wanted that mule. After we had gone about a block, he stopped stock still. I tried every way to get him to go along, but he wouldn't budge an inch. He was a balker! Lots of other people tried to make him go, but no sir! That mule wouldn't go until he felt like it. After a while, all by himself, he took a notion to start. He walked another block and then he balked again. Miss Mary, I tell you the truth, it took me two hours to get that critter four blocks to the schoolhouse! That's why I'm late, it really is!"

"Why Johnny!" exclaimed Miss Mary. "I never heard such a tale!"

"If you don't believe it, Miss Mary, just look out the window," replied Johnny.

The teacher gazed through the window and so did all the pupils. There, tied to a tree, was a mule. His head hung down and his large ears flopped sadly. There was no doubt about it, Johnny's tale was true.

Lessons began again and the day wore on. Johnny did not pay much attention to his lessons. The thought of his mule lay heavy on his mind. What could he do with him?

Budging the Balker

When the bell rang for closing time, all the children rushed into the schoolyard and gathered 'round the mule. They were in a jolly mood, laughing and joking and poking fun at Johnny and his animal.

"Such a sad looking critter! What are you going to do with him, Johnny?" asked his little friend Matthey.

Johnny did not feel very happy. "I don't know what to do with him," he said wretchedly. "It took me two hours to get him a few blocks to school; how long will it take me to get him home? I live five miles over the mountain. It will be black night and the owls a-hooting before I get him halfway there!"

Johnny leaned against the tree beside his mule and began to cry.

The children stopped laughing and looked solemnly at each other.

"Hold on there, Johnny, you never can tell about a balking mule," comforted Matthey. "He may be ready to go by now. Maybe he'll start right off!"

Johnny brightened. He untied the mule's rope and tried to lead him forward. But the mule was not ready to go, and he did not start right off. Johnny braced himself and pulled. But the mule was not in the notion.

"Give me a handhold, and I'll help you pull," said Matthey.

"I'll help too," said Nancy Belle. Both children threw their weight against the mule. But he did not budge.

"Make room for us. We'll all pull!" said Hetty and Hank. They grasped the mule's halter and hauled with all their might. But the mule only braced himself and stood in his tracks.

While the children were pulling and straining and puffing and blowing, the teacher came out of the schoolhouse. "Let me get a hold. I'll pull too!" she said. But one more made no difference to the mule. His mind was made up.

"My father once had a balking mule," piped up Nancy Belle, "and he used to get him to go by twisting his ear."

"Twisting his ear?" echoed Hezekiah. "Whoever heard of making a mule go by twisting his ear?"

"Well it's true," insisted the little girl. "That made him go."

"It wouldn't hurt to try it," said the teacher. "Go ahead. Nancy Belle, you are the one who knows how. You twist his ear."

Nancy Belle grasped the long droopy ear and twisted.

The mule stood pat.

"Twist again! Twist harder!" said the children, and Nancy twisted, but it was no good. The mule did not care to move, and twisting his ear did not make him change his mind. He only rolled his eyes and wiggled his ear to make sure it was all in a piece.

"My uncle once had a balking mule," offered Hetty, "and he used to get behind him with a plank and push him."

"That's right," added Hank. "They used to push the mule a

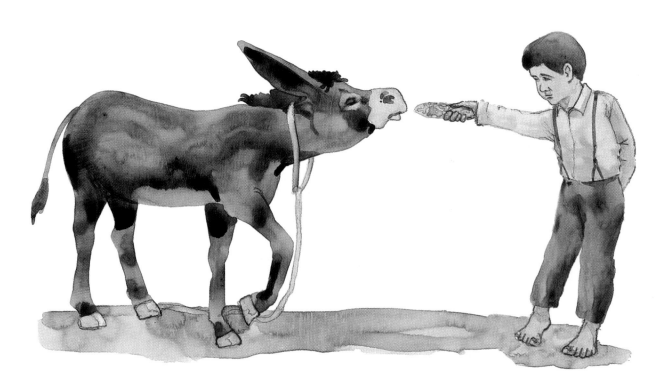

few steps forward, and after that he would go all by himself."

"Maybe that's just what this mule needs," said Miss Mary. "Where can we find a plank?"

The children hustled around, and underneath the edge of the schoolhouse they found a long plank. They put it behind the mule's haunches and pushed. They huffed and puffed, but the mule stood pat! They stopped for breath.

"Maybe the mule's hungry," spoke up Nancy Belle. "If we got a piece of corn and held it out to him, maybe he'd follow after it."

Johnny ran to the nearest house and brought back an ear of corn. He held it out to the mule. Yes, the mule was hungry. He stretched his neck toward the corn.

The children held their breath. The mule took one step forward. Johnny backed away, holding the corn just out of reach. The mule took another step forward, then another, and another. A loud shout rose from the children.

"Hurrah! Hurrah! He's going!" they yelled.

The teacher held the mule's halter while Johnny danced ahead with the corn. Through the town they went, clip-clop, clip-clop. Over the mountain trail they started as fast as they could go. But still Johnny did not seem very happy.

"A balking mule is no good to anybody," he grieved. "I'm afraid my Pappy will be cross when he sees this critter. Like as not he'll give me a good licking."

"No use borrowing trouble," said the teacher. "Let's sing a song and forget all about the mule."

Johnny struck up an old mountain song, and along they went singing.

Moon's a-rising on Thunder-head Mountain,
Heigh! Heigh! Step and go lightly!
Hound dog's a-baying and we're a-going hunting,
Heigh! Heigh! Step and go lightly!

Chased a coon into a gum tree,
Heigh! Heigh! Step and go lightly!
Shoot at the coon and hit a froggie,
Heigh! Heigh! Step and go lightly!

Thought I had a possum in a tree there,
Heigh! Heigh! Step and go lightly!
Shook that tree and down came a he-bear!
Heigh! Heigh! Step and go lightly!

Mr. Bear, please don't ketch me, sir!
Heigh! Heigh! Step and go lightly!
Ketch that fellow behind the tree, sir!
Heigh! Heigh! Step and go lightly!

Moon's going down, my song is ended,
Heigh! Heigh! Step and go lightly!
Mighty good thing, for I'm pretty nigh winded!
Heigh! Heigh! Step and go lightly!

Cause for Concern

After that Johnny felt better. "You never can tell," he said cheerfully, "maybe Pappy'll be pleased to have a mule. He needs some kind of critter to help him plow his potatoes. He has to do it now all by himself with an old hand plow."

"Why yes, of course," agreed the teacher. "It's likely he'll be glad to get him."

"If only he wasn't a balker," said Johnny, wrinkling his forehead again. "Hardly anybody would want a balker."

"Oh don't think about it," the teacher tried to cheer him up. "It's too beautiful on the mountains to get a head full of worry."

"Yes, it is pretty on the mountains." Johnny looked all around and forgot to worry about the mule. The air was full of the nice smell of pine and balsam and the pink rhododendron was blooming everywhere.

But the mule did not care for anything except the ear of corn that was always just out of reach. He kept his eyes upon it and went clop-clopping along.

Johnny and the teacher felt cheerful until they came opposite Aunt Betsy's house.

Aunt Betsy was sitting on the porch busily spinning some yarn to weave into a bedspread.

"My me! What have you got there?" she cried when she saw Johnny and the teacher and the mule.

"It's a mule," Johnny replied. "I bought him at the auction for five cents."

"Five cents!" Aunt Betsy threw back her hands and laughed. Then she grew sober. "But he's not a balker, is he? I never heard of a mule's going that cheap unless he was a balker. "

"Yes'm," Johnny admitted uneasily. "He's a balker, all right."

"Oh, my." Aunt Betsy shook her head dolefully. "I don't know what you'll do with a balker."

After that there was hardly anything the teacher could say to comfort Johnny.

On up the trail trudged Johnny, feeling more dismay every minute. "The worst of it is: a mule has got a terrible appetite," he worried. "Why, that old mule could probably eat us out of house and home in no time. Miss Mary, I'm going to get that licking sure as anything. I wish I didn't have to go home at all."

But the mule took them there in a hurry.

Mammy and Pappy were waiting in front of the cabin, looking down the road, wondering what kept Johnny so long. When they saw him tolling the mule along, and the teacher holding the rope, their eyes popped open.

"What have you got there?" cried Mammy, laughing.

"It's a mule," replied Johnny nervously. "I bought him at the auction for five cents."

"For five cents! Then there must be something wrong with him," said Mammy.

"Yes'm there is—a little something wrong. He's a balker, I reckon."

"A balking mule!" exclaimed Mammy. "Whatever could we do with a balking mule?"

"I-I don't know ma'am," exclaimed Johnny, glancing uneasily at Pappy.

Pappy did not say anything at all. He just rubbed his chin and looked thoughtfully at the mule.

The sun was setting by this time. It was much too late for the teacher to return to town. She de-cided to spend the night with Johnny and his parents.

Mammy set a chicken on to stew in a big iron pot and later on they had supper, chicken and dumplings, hot biscuits, and nice cold buttermilk. For dessert, there was honey from their own beehive and a pot full of sassafras tea.

It was a fine supper, but Johnny could not enjoy it. What was his Pappy thinking about that old balking mule? What was he going to do with him?

After the meal, everyone sat around the fire, which leaped brightly in the old stone fireplace. Pappy got out his fiddle and played some merry jigs. Mammy sang some old mountain ballads for the teacher.

Johnny sat in the chimney corner. He did not feel very happy because he kept wondering if his Pappy felt angry about the mule. At last he screwed up his courage and asked him.

"Pappy," he said timidly. "That balking mule is going to be sort of a nuisance, I reckon."

"Nuisance!" cried Pappy. "Why, I know how to make that

Rhody." This song tells a story, but it leaves out most of the details. It also includes a catchy, rhythmic tune and lines that are repeated often.

When slaves came to America, folksongs changed a little more. Slavery songs added much sadness and tenderness to American folk music. The slaves sang about everything in their lives: the land, the weather, their hard work, even the tools that they used. They sang "Jump Down, Turn Around, Pick a Bale of Cotton" to keep in time with the backbreaking work they had to do.

The slaves, of course, were the ones who developed the Negro spiritual. This type of song became a part of American folk music too. Some Negro spirituals are not accurate about the Bible or about God. Because most slaves could not read, they made some mistakes. The song "Michael, Row the Boat Ashore" does not have a spiritual message, but many slaves thought it did.

Many spirituals, however, are a testimony of the faith and cheerfulness of black Christians in early America. They were locked into slavery on earth, but they were spiritually free by the blood of Christ.

• Differences in Folksongs

American folk music differs throughout the country. The lumberjacks in Oregon sang songs different from those sung by the farmers in Georgia and South Carolina. This difference occurred because folksongs were passed down only orally. Nobody wrote down the tunes or the words. The songs were not sold to be recorded or to be printed in music books. Only the common people sang them.

Because the common people did not travel far, their music did not change a great deal. Southern folksongs tend to tell about life on the farms, the crops, and perhaps hunting. Folksongs from the West often tell about cowboys, cattle-drives, Indian attacks, and buffalo herds. But the source of folk music has not changed. It is still the music of everyday people doing everyday things.

Were You There?

Spiritual

1. Were you there when they cru - ci - fied my Lord? Were you
there when they cru - ci - fied my Lord? Oh!_____

Some - times it caus - es me to trem - ble, trem - ble, trem - ble.

Were you there when they cru - ci - fied my Lord?

2. Were you there when they laid Him in the tomb?
Were you there when they laid Him in the tomb?
Oh! Sometimes it causes me to tremble.
Were you there when they laid Him in the tomb?

3. Were you there when He rose up from the grave?
Were you there when He rose up from the grave?
Oh! Sometimes I feel like shouting glory!
Were you there when He rose up from the grave?

Word of Honor

Eileen Berry
illustrated by Del Thompson

The Signature

When I grow up, I'm going to be just like Mr. Hines, David thought. He watched his Sunday school teacher handing out the permission slips. Mr. Hines attended a faraway college where he was training to be a pastor, so he was never home during the school year. But this summer, he had taught David's fourth-grade boys' Sunday school class. And now, just before the new school year started, he was taking them all on an overnight hike. No parents, no brothers or sisters—just Mr. Hines and the guys.

"Now remember, guys." Mr. Hines leaned against the edge of the desk and folded his arms. "It's not just your parents' signature that I need. For you to be eligible for this hike, you have to sign the top line on the form—the line that says you've read the book of John all the way through. Be honest now. Your signature on that line is your word of honor. You've had all summer to read, so I hope you'll be able to sign. I'll need these forms back next week."

The bell rang and Mr. Hines lifted his hand in a wave. "See you next time."

David stuffed the permission form into his Bible and raced for the door. Mr. Hines caught up with him in three long strides and clapped a friendly hand on his shoulder. "Hey, David," he said. "How's your reading in John coming?"

David gave a slight shrug. He tried to match his steps to Mr. Hines's. "I've still got a ways to go," he said, glancing up.

Mr. Hines's eyes were kind. "Keep plugging," he said. "You'll make it."

David thought about the book of John after supper the next day. He even picked up his Bible and opened it to where his bookmark was in the fifth chapter. But then Aaron called and asked him to come over and play catch. *I'll read tomorrow,* he thought.

Tuesday night his mother asked him to help her in the garden. Wednesday night was church. He spent all day Thursday playing with his brother Ben in their tree fort. And on Friday evening he forgot all about the book of John and read a library book.

On Saturday evening, he took his permission slip to his mother. "Mom, will you sign this? It's for the hike," he said.

Mom set her knife down by the heap of potato peelings and wiped her hands. She studied the form for a moment. "Have you read the book of John yet?" she asked. "You haven't signed on the top line."

David shoved his hands deeper into his pockets. "Almost," he said. "I'll sign it as soon as I'm done."

Mom signed her name in tall, even lettering on the bottom line. "Better finish up that reading tonight," she said. "Mr. Hines wants these forms back tomorrow, doesn't he?"

"Yes."

David brushed his teeth and got ready for bed. Then he switched on his bedside lamp and sat up against his pillows with his Bible. *Seventeen chapters to read,* he thought. *Maybe they won't take long.*

David had gotten only to chapter seven when his head sank low onto his chest. His eyelids felt like lead weights pressing down. *Maybe tomorrow,* he thought, halfway between daydreams and sleep.

When David awoke the next morning, his lamp had been turned off and his Bible lay open on the bedside table. "John chapter seven," he mumbled sleepily. "There's no way I can make it to the end of the book before Sunday school."

David pulled the permission slip out of his Bible and stared at it for a few moments. He picked up a pen and hesitated. Mr. Hines's voice echoed inside his head. "Your signature on that line is your word of honor."

David glanced out the window. He thought about the new backpack his father had bought him earlier in the summer. If he didn't go on the hike, when would he ever use it? He took a deep breath, trying to ignore the ham-mering of his heart. Then he signed his name on the line.

David ate very little of his pancakes for breakfast. Dad looked at his plate with a raised eyebrow when David stood to leave the table. "You ate hardly enough to keep a bird alive," he said. "Feeling all right?"

David nodded, studying the pattern in the rug.

Mom smiled. "He was up late last night finishing his Bible reading," she said. "Did you get it all done, David?"

David waited only a second before answering. "Yes," he said without looking up.

"Good job," said Dad. David could feel Mom's eyes still watching him as he trudged off to his room.

The Acknowledgment

Mr. Hines was wearing a tie with golf clubs on it. As David handed the permission slip to him, he stared at the golf clubs rather than looking at Mr. Hines's face.

"I'm glad to see most of you got those permission slips turned in," Mr. Hines told the class. "We'll meet here at the church Friday afternoon at two o'clock." He held up a stack of papers. "This paper I'm handing out now is a list of stuff to bring. Keep it handy while you're packing so you don't forget anything important."

David noticed that the first item on the list was a Bible. All at once, his stomach felt like someone had used it for a punching bag.

David tried to forget about the permission slip for the rest of the week. He concentrated on getting together all the items he would need for the hike. Mom took him shopping for things like insect repellent and flashlight batteries. The stack on the floor beside his backpack grew larger and larger as the week went on.

"Jacket, hat, pocketknife, sleeping bag . . ." He checked off each object on the list as he stashed it in the pack Friday morning. "Bible." He went to his shelf, picked up his Bible, and stood staring down at it. He still hadn't finished the book of John. In fact, he couldn't remember reading the Bible at all this week. Every time Dad had read it after supper, David had gotten that sick feeling in his stomach again. David buried the Bible at the bottom of the pack.

That afternoon the boys gathered in the church parking lot. Mr. Hines looked like a gym teacher with a baseball cap on his head and a whistle around his neck. "The first thing I'm going to do is assign each of you a buddy," he said. "From the minute we get on the bus, you should know where your buddy is at all times."

David and Aaron were assigned to be buddies. "Mr. Hines is the greatest," Aaron said as they boarded the bus to drive into the mountains. "Aren't you glad you got your reading done so you could come?"

Why do people have to keep asking me about my reading? David wondered. He just nodded and said nothing. A moment later, the boys started singing a camp song at the tops of their voices, and Aaron joined in. David turned his face to the window.

When they all got off the bus, Mr. Hines gave each set of buddies a map of the trail they would be hiking. "The trail forks into two different trails at one point," he said, "but we'll go to the right. I've marked the fork we'll take in blue on all the maps. We'll all stay together—the maps are just a safeguard in case someone gets lost."

They set off with Mr. Hines leading the way. "Where He leads I'll follow," Mr. Hines started singing. The boys joined in.

"Follow all the way; where He leads I'll follow, follow Jesus every day."

Sunlight slanted through the branches of the pines and dappled the trail with shadows. The air felt cleaner and cooler as they climbed, and at one point they all stopped to pull jackets or sweatshirts out of their packs.

Near suppertime, they reached the spot Mr. Hines had marked with a star and the word "campsite" on the map. In a few moments, the boys all had assignments. Some were helping Mr. Hines set up tents, some were unpacking food supplies, and some were gathering pieces of wood for a fire.

Mr. Hines set lighted matches among the pile of sticks until a steady fire was blazing. David stood with his arms folded across his chest, watching the flames.

Mr. Hines stepped up beside him. "How's it going, David? You've been pretty quiet on this trip. Everything all right?"

David felt like shrinking away from Mr. Hines. What would he say if he knew? David tried to imagine the look on Mr. Hines's face if he found out about the lie on the permission slip. David worked on a design in the dirt with the toe of his shoe, wondering what to say.

Mr. Hines waited a moment, watching him. Then he laid a hand on his shoulder and said, "If you need to talk, you know where to find me." He walked away.

After the hot dogs and marshmallows had all been roasted and eaten, Mr. Hines led them in a few songs. When the stillness closed in after the last notes died, he held up his Bible. David stared at the words "Holy Bible" that glowed on the cover in the firelight.

"This book," Mr. Hines said, "is your trail map for life. Just like the maps I gave you, this book will tell you the right forks to take—the right decisions to make—every day."

David shifted his feet and looked away from Mr. Hines to watch the fire.

"Before you came on this hike, you read the book of John," Mr. Hines went on. "You signed your name on a line, telling me you had finished. You gave your word of honor."

Mr. Hines was quiet for a moment. A stick on the fire cracked with a loud pop and sparks shot up.

"Everything God says in this book is His Word of honor to us," said Mr. Hines. "Every promise He makes, He will keep. The Bible says in Psalm 138 that He has magnified His Word above His name. The honor of His name rests on His ability to keep His word. So you'd better believe if He says something, He'll do it. Let's name some of the promises God gives us in His Word."

David was quiet, listening to the other boys naming promises.

God never leaves or forsakes. God saves. God hears and answers prayer. When all was quiet again, Mr. Hines said, "I'd like to read one more of God's promises. It's in I John 1:9. 'If we confess our sins, He is faithful and just to forgive us our sins, and to cleanse us from all unrighteousness.' Let's pray."

David hardly heard the prayer over the beating of his heart. *How had Mr. Hines known to read that verse? Does he know I lied?* David wondered. *Did he read that verse just for me?*

"Hey, David, want to get our flashlights and play hide and seek?" asked Aaron as soon as the prayer was finished.

"I'll be there in a minute," David said. The other boys were wandering off toward the tents. Mr. Hines stood by himself, throwing a few more sticks on the fire. David hurried to him before he could lose his nerve.

"Mr. Hines? I'm ready to talk now." With his eyes on the ground, David blurted out the whole story—the lie on the permission slip, the lie to his parents, and the lie he had let all the other boys on the hike believe. "My word of honor isn't good for much," he finished.

He couldn't bring himself to look up at Mr. Hines's face. *What must he think now? He'll probably never be as friendly to me anymore now that he knows he can't trust me,* David thought.

He heard the rustle of paper and looked up to see Mr. Hines turning the pages of his Bible. "I'm glad you told me this, David," Mr. Hines said. "You did the right thing in coming to me. I'll talk to you about this further. I think you'll want to say something to your parents and to the other guys as well. But first, there's Someone else you need to talk to." He handed David the open Bible.

"Psalm 51," he said, "was written by another David long, long ago. Why don't you sit here and read it and then pray it back to God? Remember—He keeps His Word."

As Mr. Hines walked back toward the tents, David sat by the dying fire and read. " 'For I acknowledge my transgressions: and my sin is ever before me. Against thee, thee only, have I sinned, and done this evil in Thy sight. . . . Create in me a clean heart, O God . . . a broken and a contrite heart, O God, Thou wilt not despise.' "

A leaf blew into the fire, and David watched it shrivel and break apart in the flame. Then he bowed his head.

Hamlet, Augusta Jones, and Me

James Townsend

illustrated by Tim Davis and Noelle Snyder

Mimosa Street Drama Club

Since Augusta Jones moved into the house next door to mine, Mimosa Street has changed. I had never met anyone like her, and I don't think Mimosa Street will ever be the same again.

Right off the bat I thought that girl was really strange. It's not that I don't know about girls. I have two sisters. It's just that Augusta is different. When she gets out a box of paper dolls, it's not to play with them but to try out costumes for those plays of hers. She hadn't been here for very long before she had every girl on Mimosa Street acting the part of this princess or that one or, worse yet, some animal or other.

When she first started this play business, she tried to get us boys interested too. But we were too smart to get caught. After all, who wants to be a giant rabbit when we could be playing kick ball in my back yard instead?

At least, that's what we were doing before one of my sisters volunteered our garage for a play-house. Then the Mimosa Street

Drama Club started meeting at our place every day. "Nothing but trouble," I predicted. And sure enough, one day when Barry Horton tried for a home run, a princess and something that looked like a frog dashed across the yard from our house to the garage. We lost the game five to nothing!

Then Augusta came out, apologizing all over the place. The boys were pretty sore until she started talking about swords and fighting battles. It wasn't long before the whole kick ball team was over in the garage signing up for parts.

Fighting! I thought she probably meant setting out to kill a giant rabbit or something. But who would she get to be the rabbit?

Well, I couldn't play kick ball alone. I thought that maybe if I signed up too I could talk some sense into those guys. But I knew one thing: If Augusta thought she was going to get me into a rabbit

suit, she would have to think again!

When I reached the door of the garage, Augusta gave me a sticky smile. For a moment I thought she had been waiting for me. Not likely, since Augusta and I didn't get along too well . . . and ruining my kick ball game didn't help any either.

"Hello, Thomas," Augusta said.

Now that's not any way to smooth things over. Thomas! Everybody knows my name's Tom. "Ahem," I said, clearing my throat. "Er, how're things going?"

"Just fine," she replied, pulling me inside. "Look."

I whistled in spite of myself. So this was what they had been doing all week! The garage hadn't been really dirty. Dad didn't use it for storage. But still it was cleaner than I had ever seen it. Just inside the doors was the open space where the car usually parked. Beyond that was the platform that had been brushed clean and made into a stage. Sheets hung from the rafters. They were pulled back at either side and tied to make curtains for the stage.

"Neat, isn't it?" Augusta beamed. "And take a look at the layout. The paying customers come in the front doors and sit in the open area. The actors are on the stage. They won't even have to enter from the audience. That side door opens onto the stage. We can do our entrances and exits there."

"Paying customers?" I said, a little dazed.

"Sure, why not?" Augusta replied cheerfully, but I wasn't listening. My attention had been caught by a flash of steel. Jonathan Lee was chasing a girl across the stage, waving a sword over his head.

"That's real!" I croaked. "Are you crazy?"

Augusta gave Jonathan a cold look. "That's enough," she called, "or you're out!"

I watched in amazement as Jonathan meekly returned the sword to a big trunk near the side door. The prospects of getting the boys back to the game seemed smaller and smaller.

Auditions

"Have you got permission for all this?" I demanded triumphantly, seeing a loophole.

"Why of course, Thomas," Augusta replied haughtily. "I am a responsible person."

I winced.

"The swords and costumes are from my attic. No, they aren't real. My mother used to run a small theater, and she's delighted that I want to follow in her footsteps. Good stuff, you know. *Hamlet, Macbeth,* all those," she said with an airy wave of her hand. "Oh, and of course both your parents and mine gave permission to charge a slight fee. Twenty-five cents. We'll make a fortune!"

"Oh," I said weakly.

"Come on," she said. "We're auditioning for parts already."

She pushed me up to the stage where my sister Eva was listening to Benny reading—or rather, trying to read. What was coming out didn't resemble anything I had ever heard before.

"Try again," Eva said encouragingly. "You can do it."

" 'But look, the morn, in . . . russet mantle clad, walks o'er the dew of yoon . . . yon high eastward hill. Break we our watch up.' . . . What watch?" Benny stopped, puzzled. "Why would anyone want to break a watch?"

"Never mind," Augusta said. "Isn't it beautiful? The morning walks over the dew of the hills— just beautiful!"

"But Augusta," Eva protested, "it may be pretty, but nobody knows what anybody else is talking about. How can we put on a play when we don't understand each other?"

"It's just the language," Augusta said thoughtfully. "Why don't I rewrite it so we can understand it?"

"Whew," Benny said. "Anything would be better than this!"

"Okay, okay." Augusta stepped onto the stage. "Listen up, everybody. Come back tomorrow at four o'clock, and we'll audition for parts then."

There was a lot of bike traffic on Mimosa Street after school the next day. By four o'clock there must have been twenty kids in our back yard. How the word got passed around, I'll never know. Every kid there wanted either a crown or a sword. I knew even Augusta didn't have that many, so I wandered out to watch the fun. Augusta was moving about quickly, giving out copies of the play and organizing the kids into groups. I picked up a copy and sat down on the edge of the stage.

"Hmmm," I thought as I flipped through the pages. "Typewritten and photocopied! Wonder who Augusta got to do that?" I settled down to read.

"Thomas! Thomas, hurry up!" Augusta thumped me on the head. "I've called you three times already. Come on!"

I glanced around. Most of the kids had been given scripts and sent home. Only a few were still reading. I stretched and got up, holding the script.

"Hey, Augusta," I said. "This is a great story. Who wrote it anyway?"

"Some man named William Shakespeare," she replied. "I think I'll test you for the part of Hamlet."

"Did he write any others?" I asked, following her to the center of the stage.

"Sure, lots of them. Now turn to page two and read where it says 'Hamlet.' "

"I'd rather be the ghost."

"No, silly, that part is perfect for Benny."

"Why?"

"Because Benny can make more noises than any boy I have ever heard," Augusta said patiently. "Now read!"

I read.

Two weeks later we were still practicing. We had shouted and whispered and murmured. We had lunged and dodged and thrust. Finally the mutters that arose from the cast had nothing to do with the parts.

"Are we ready yet?"

"When do we get our swords?"

"I'm tired!"

"Well," Augusta said, "you know, practice makes perfect, but I guess we can get out the costumes."

With a shriek of joy the cast raced for the trunk. Augusta was the first there, but she really had to move fast.

Silks and velvet, iron and steel! What a rainbow of colors came from that old trunk! Squeals of delight came from the girls as yards of material slid over their heads and trailed on the floor.

"Here. I knew they'd be too big," Augusta said, opening a box full of twine and pins. "This should help."

When everyone had been pinned and tied as much as possible, Augusta lined us up along the platform and looked us over. I think that's the first time I had ever seen Augusta without a cheerful face. I looked slowly down the line of kids. Eva's dress was all bunched around her waist, and her coronet had slipped over one ear. Benny's hose had settled around his ankles in deep folds, and Jonathan Lee's doublet reached to his knees. The rest of them didn't look much better. Personally, I thought my costume looked fine.

"I guess we could make our own costumes," Augusta said hesitantly.

"Oh, no!"

"I like mine!"

"Mine is perfect," Eva called, spinning around and making her

veil fan out behind her. "Let's put the play on tonight."

"Not tonight," Augusta said. "We need a dress rehearsal."

"Aw, Augusta, we've practiced enough," Benny pleaded.

"Yes, let's do it," the others said as they gathered around her. "We know our parts. And we can go around the neighborhood, telling everyone to come tonight."

"Well," Augusta said doubtfully. "I guess we can use tonight as a trial performance."

How much of a trial it was going to be we didn't know. Otherwise, I'd have been in the audience, not on the stage.

The Performance

The first thing that went wrong happened in the first act. Benny was playing the ghost of the dead king, Hamlet's father. He was doing a fine job, too, until he reached the front of the stage. He wouldn't have had any problem if his sagging hose hadn't unrolled over his shoe. Benny grabbed for my arm and missed. He pitched headlong into the first row, right where we had put the little kids so they could see. Well, they could see all right. They scattered everywhere, screaming and yelling.

Augusta called a brief intermission to calm things down. Then with a "the-show-must-go-on" expression, she motioned us back on stage.

From then on things went from bad to worse. The problem was the costumes. Terrific as they were, they definitely were too big. Since we didn't know what to expect from the cumbersome outfits, we had a hard time moving around. I wasn't doing too badly because I had double-pinned everything and

even put square knots in the twine. But being Hamlet, I was on the receiving end of some clumsy sword thrusts that kept me dodging. It's hard to look brave when you duck instead of facing the other person. By the end of the second act (Augusta had shortened the play a lot), the audience was roaring with laughter.

"This is a tragedy," Augusta moaned as the curtain closed. "Why are they laughing?"

"They won't laugh in the next act," Eva promised. "Nobody laughs at a drowning person."

"I certainly hope not," Augusta murmured.

But she was wrong. The girl who played Ophelia had been having trouble all night. She was a thin girl anyway, and that dress had been made for a very healthy woman. When "Ophelia" had been on stage with me, the dress had kept slipping. Pins or not, I didn't think it could last much longer, and I was right.

"Ophelia" must have been expecting the same thing, because when she felt the dress slip, she caught it at her waist. Quickly looping one end of the twine around it, she continued her speech. She didn't miss a word, but the sight of all that rich material wadded at the waist of a T-shirt was too much for Augusta. She walked out the back door. I started to go after her, but Benny hissed, "Hamlet! You're on!"

The last scene was where the wicked King, the Queen, Laertes, and finally Hamlet all die. It was the best part of the play, if I do say so myself. The audience loved it. We were used to the clothes by then, and I didn't have to dodge so much . . . although Laertes got tangled up in the Queen's trailing skirts and almost didn't manage to kill me. For a moment I was tempted to rewrite Augusta's play and finish him off so I could live and become the new king. But Augusta was feeling so bad already that I couldn't. I just leaned on my sword and waited until he got to his feet again.

Well, surprisingly enough, the play was a success. Everyone clapped and clapped. While the others were taking their bows, I slipped outside. Augusta was sitting on the porch steps. She was looking surprised to hear all the clapping and whistling going on.

"Come on," I said, pulling her to her feet. "They loved us. You have to take a bow too."

"They liked it?" she said in an unbelieving voice.

"Not liked—loved."

After a few bows, that happy light was back in Augusta's eyes. When the curtain went down for the last time, she turned to the cast. "Thank you all for doing such a good job. And forgive me for not believing in you."

Well, I've still never met anyone like that Augusta Jones. But you know, I guess she isn't so strange after all. You just have to get to know her. When we left, she was sitting on the trunk, murmuring something about *Romeo and Juliet*. I wouldn't mind doing another play, but *Romeo and Juliet?* Not me. Augusta will just have to find herself another boy. Absolutely no. Never. Not me.

William Shakespeare, Playwright

Beki Gorham   illustrated by Bob Martin

Have you ever sat down at a crowded table and had to ask for more "elbow room"? Have you ever told anyone that you had "caught a cold"? Or have you ever heard that someone was "full of the milk of human kindness"?

If you have, you were using or hearing language written down over four hundred years ago by a man named William Shakespeare. William was born in Stratford-on-Avon, England, a little over a hundred miles from the big city of London. It was a small town on the Avon River, full of houses and shops and bordered by meadows, orchards, and rolling fields. Merchants and sailors visited this town, so William could sit and listen to the stories they told about shipwrecks and people in faraway places. It was a fine place to grow up.

William attended the Stratford grammar school with the other boys. Every morning at six o'clock he was in his seat, ready to study Latin and literature. All day long, till five or six at night, the boys sat up straight on wooden benches. Perhaps it was here that William read the plays that inspired him to write. At any rate, he was a good student.

William's father, John Shakespeare, was mayor of Stratford and owner of one of its small businesses. William had a sharp sense of humor, which may have come from his father, who was said to have been a cheerful and clever man. Perhaps William also helped in his father's glove-making shop, along with some of his brothers and sisters.

Little is written of William's early childhood, so we can only imagine what it would have been like to live in Stratford-on-Avon in the 1500s. In the spring and fall a boy could visit the fair in town, or he could go to see a play in the guild chapel. When he grew tired of the town, he could run off to play with friends in the

woods and fields outside the city. Perhaps he could fish in the Avon River or sail toy boats made of leaf and bark in a shallow stream. He could make forts in the Forest of Arden, which edged the sunny fields. Surely William must have been fun to be with. His rich imagination could have provided hours of games and adventures for his companions.

When William was about thirteen, John Shakespeare had business misfortunes and went into debt. So William left school to earn a living. Later he married

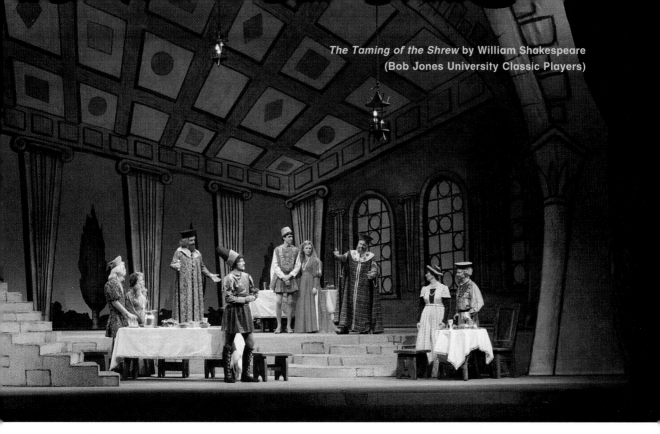

The Taming of the Shrew by William Shakespeare
(Bob Jones University Classic Players)

and then went to London. There he began to act and to write plays.

His plays became popular, and William Shakespeare prospered. He wrote comedies and tragedies, poetry, and tales of kings. *The Comedy of Errors* might have been his first play, written around 1591. Others of his comedies, or funny plays, are *The Taming of the Shrew, All's Well That Ends Well, Twelfth Night,* and *The Tempest.* The tragedies, or plays that end sadly, include *Romeo and Juliet, Julius Caesar, Hamlet,* and *Macbeth.*

Today, William Shakespeare's plays are produced all over the world, and millions of students study his work in high school and college. Hundreds of magazine articles and books have been written about him. He is probably the most famous writer in the world.

So the next time you hear the name William Shakespeare, or you find yourself "catching a cold," don't forget the little boy who lived in Stratford-on-Avon, who went to school and played with his friends just as you do today.

Diagrams

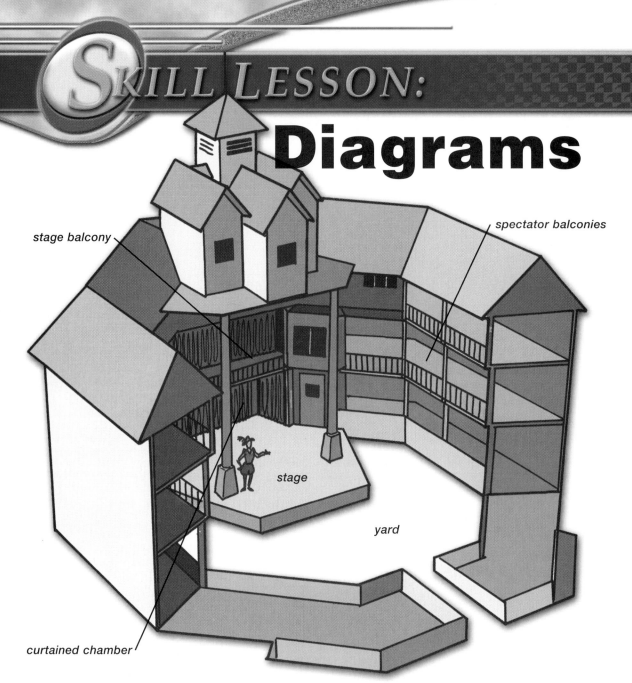

stage balcony

spectator balconies

stage

yard

curtained chamber

Cutaway diagram of the Globe Theater

Some things are hard to explain with just words. How would someone explain the parts of a car to a friend who had never seen one?

A diagram comes in handy then. A diagram is a drawing of the object you want to explain. It labels the important parts of the drawing.

• Reading a Diagram

The stage where William Shakespeare's plays were performed wasn't like the one Augusta Jones used in the story "Hamlet, Augusta Jones, and Me." Many of Shakespeare's plays were performed in a theater in London called the Globe Theater. Notice the labeled parts of the Globe Theater in the diagram as you read the following paragraph.

In the Globe Theater there was no curtain for the stage. Performers would show that a scene was changing by simply leaving the stage and going behind the curtained chamber. The stage balcony could represent the deck of a ship, a prison window, or the balcony where Juliet waited for Romeo. The stage itself reached right into the first rows of the outside audience, the poorer people who sat in the yard. The yard was the area in front of the stage that was always exposed to weather. The rich people could sit in three tiers of covered spectator balconies where they would be protected from the rain.

• Uses for Diagrams

If you had read the above description without a diagram, it might have been hard to picture the Globe Theater. But the diagram helped you to understand much better.

Suppose you were reading instructions about how to make a costume for a play or build a piece of scenery. One diagram or a series of diagrams could help you then.

Remember how useful a diagram can be the next time you have to explain something to a friend. It may make all the difference between confusion and understanding!

JANWAHR'S BRIDGE

Dawn L. Watkins
illustrated by Del Thompson and John Bjerk

Silver Horn

Janwahr, the youngest son of King Rolday, was blind. He sat in his tower room and pulled at the leather strap of his boot as if the boot could be on any more securely than it already was. He always did everything twice, just to be sure.

In the courtyard below, his brothers, Taytan and Nadar, called for their horses to be saddled. Servants ran across the cobblestones to the stables.

"I wonder if Gemla is going riding this morning," he thought. Gemla, his sister, whom everyone called beautiful, would let him ride behind her sometimes, but only when Taytan and Nadar were not there to scold about his getting hurt.

He tugged the strap of his other boot a second time.

"Bandeen," he called.

"I am here, Prince Janwahr," a servant about the prince's age answered.

It was true that the palace servants addressed him as Prince Janwahr; the stablemen and yeomen always said "Your Highness" when they spoke to him. But in all his nine years he had never felt like a prince.

" 'Janwahr' would do," he told his servant.

"I know you do not want me to use your title, sir, but I should not call my master by his name only—it is disrespectful."

Janwahr nodded. "Shall we go?"

The prince put out his arm for Bandeen. The servant took it.

"To the river as always, Your Highness?"

"Yes, to the river."

As Bandeen stepped forward, Janwahr felt confirmed in his belief—a blind boy could never truly be a prince.

Janwahr and Bandeen walked out onto a gray marble portico. The prince felt the smooth sun on his cheeks and neck.

"Is the sky clear?" he asked.

"As blue as . . ." the servant began.

There was silence.

"The sky is cloudless, Prince Janwahr."

"It is all right to say blue, Bandeen. I think of blue as the way the air feels on a calm summer evening."

"How is red to you, sir?" the servant asked.

"Like my brother Nadar when our sister outshoots him on the archery fields."

Bandeen and the prince laughed together and then went down the jade steps.

At the river, Janwahr sat under his favorite wildalia tree. He had sat there so often that he had worn a comfortable hollow between two big roots. The roots now stuck up so far that they made armrests for the prince. The upper branches of the huge old wildalia reached far out over the river and kept it as cool as early morning around the roots all day.

"Come back for me at noon," said Janwahr, and the servant left him, as always, without a word.

Where Janwahr sat was at the narrowest point in the river. Bandeen had told him once that it was two palace lengths to the other bank. Janwahr could not imagine how high and rough the ridges were behind him, but Bandeen had said they were treacherous. He leaned back against the tree, smelling the river flowers and the damp earth. The julas sang above him, and the water sloshed against the bank just below him. When he was sure Bandeen had gone, Janwahr whistled—a high, swift whistle—and listened. Some way off he heard a rush and swirl of water. He smiled widely. Then there was a sound like milk being poured into a tall glass, and Janwahr knew that his companion was coming.

"Good morning, Danzee," he called out.

A rolling roar answered him.

"You are such a noisy fellow in the morning. We could never have you about the palace."

Janwahr heard splashing right at his feet, and he knew Danzee had reached the bank and was tossing the water off his great head.

The prince reached forward, and Danzee laid his head on the bank. Janwahr patted the broad expanse familiarly. He ran his hand over the rough scales, each of which was bigger than his hand.

"I never get used to how big your nose is. Just the tip of it is bigger than I am!"

Danzee gurgled deep in his throat in response.

Janwahr came forward on his hands and knees, climbing right up Danzee's massive nose until he came to the giant curved horn.

The horn was always cold and smooth like the silver cups in the palace. Janwahr was sure the great horn was solid silver. He looped one arm halfway around the horn, pulling himself onto it, straddling the base as he would a horse. He adjusted his position on the inside of the sweeping curve.

"Let's go, Danzee!"

The huge beast lifted his head. Up and up went Janwahr through the air, through the leaves of the wildalia, into the strong sunlight. Then Danzee swayed his head from side to side, gently swinging the prince about like a blade of grass.

Janwahr thought, "Someday I will bring Nadar and Taytan here to see me ride. Then they will let me on the horses."

The prince laughed aloud with delight.

"Now roundabout!"

Danzee swung his head in a wild circle, first clockwise, then counterclockwise, then clockwise again, and again, and again.

"Well done, Danzee," said the prince, patting the vast cheek as soundly as he could. "Good boy."

Danzee glided to the shore and lowered his head as softly as the snow comes down. He blew gusts of wind from his nostrils as he waited for the boy to get off.

"All tired out, are you? Then you rest, and I will sing a song I made up for you." In clear tenor, Janwahr picked up a merry tune:

The banks are steep,
The water's deep,
But I shall never have a fear-O.
For I can fly
Like the julas shy
When Danzee Boy is near-O.

Danzee gurgled and blew out one big gust.

"Well, let's see you do better, then," said the prince, and gave the beast a tap on his nose.

Danzee dozed awhile, and Janwahr tried to make up another verse for his song. He could not come up with a rhyme for *silver;* so by and by he gave up the effort.

"Wake up, Danzee, you old snoozer. Do you want your back scratched?"

Danzee stirred himself lazily.

"Hurry along. It takes some time, you know," Janwahr said.

Danzee snorted and nudged the prince.

The boy pulled a sturdy, forked branch from beside the tree and held it firmly out over the bank.

Danzee ducked his head under the branch and began to swim forward, close to the bank. Janwahr pointed the branch downward until he felt it touch the back of the beast. Danzee swam on, arching his great length to come under the prongs of the branch.

For ten minutes he passed by, until at last he slapped the tip of his tail in the water to let Janwahr know he could stop holding the branch.

"You get longer every day, Danzee!"

Invasion

The beast had made a mighty circle; his head was nearly to the bank again. He roared his gratitude.

"Someday I'll bring my sister here to see you. You'll like her. She is beautiful, they say. And she will know how to appreciate so fine a creature as you. The gift I bring you today," said the prince, "is the North Star. My father's sailors say they use it to steer their ships. You may have it."

Danzee slapped the water with the end of his tail and roared.

"You like that gift, do you?" said Janwahr. "Do you like it better than the summer breeze I gave you yesterday?"

Janwahr could feel Danzee's head very near.

"You had better go now, before Bandeen comes. I'll see you to-morrow, my friend."

Danzee put his nose against Janwahr and then swam slowly backwards, submerging himself as he went. He left so quietly that the prince was often not sure he was gone.

On this day, Danzee had hardly disappeared before the prince heard Bandeen calling.

"Prince Janwahr!"

Janwahr stood up and turned toward the sound.

"Your Highness!" Bandeen called.

"What is it? Why are you early?"

Bandeen came thrashing through the tanglebriars, forsaking the safer but longer path. He arrived before the prince, breathless and scratched.

"What is it, Bandeen?" Janwahr reached out to take his servant by the shoulders.

"An invasion," he said between pants. "The kingdom to the south!"

"Are we under siege right now?" Janwahr felt his heart leaping.

"No," the servant puffed.

"What then?"

"A messenger delivered a declaration of war this morning. The southern king begins his march tomorrow!"

"Why?"

"For your sister, Your Highness."

"Gemla! Come, take me home. Quickly!"

At the palace, an argument was going on in the court. "Give me five hundred horsemen, Father," Nadar said. "I can meet the invaders in the third valley."

"No, no," said Taytan, the eldest. "We must send a delegation to discuss the matter."

"Stop it, all of you," said Gemla in her quiet voice. "I will marry the southern king to spare our father all this trouble." She turned away to the window.

"Five hundred men, and I will hold them in the valley," Nadar began again.

"You only know how to settle things by taking sword in hand!" Taytan glared at Nadar.

"And you would send old philosophers and the aged of our court into the very teeth of war!"

"Silence!" King Rolday stood up, and the hall went silent.

Janwahr still stood at the west door with Bandeen.

"Hear what I say," said the king. "Your solutions are not real solutions at all. First, I ask you, Gemla, do you love this king?"

"I love the rats in the grain more," said she without raising her voice.

"As I thought. The king of Wehdona is more to your liking, is he not?"

She blushed in answer.

"So no more foolish talk from you then. You will not marry so wicked a man as the southern king for any reason. Now, Nadar, do you know the size of the invading army?"

"No, sir," he replied.

"Then how can you say five hundred of my horsemen will hold them? In years past I have known this king to go to war with two thousand soldiers. He may have as many now."

Nadar studied the toe of his boot.

"And you, Taytan, what is there to negotiate? War has been declared already. It is too late for talking."

No one there, not the princes, nor the counselors, nor the captains, made any answer to the king.

Janwahr listened, every nerve tight. He would die to save Gemla, but what could he do? He could not ride; he could not hold a bow. He strained forward, hoping to hear comfort from his father.

But before the king could speak, one of his outriders appeared at the north door, winded and pale. He bowed low and waited.

"Speak, man," said the king.

"Your Majesty," he said, "the southern army is in the second valley!"

Astonishment gripped the hearers.

"Say on," said the king.

"If they march on at the rate they are coming, they will be here at dusk."

"How many men?" said the king.

"About a thousand, sir."

The king's mouth was set and grim. He scanned the room as if searching for an answer.

Janwahr felt his heart throbbing against his ribs. He wanted someone to think of a way to save Gemla. But no one spoke.

"Call up a thousand horsemen," said the king.

Nadar paced toward the door.

"Wait!" cried Janwahr.

All eyes turned to him. The king was amazed.

"Janwahr. What is it?" he asked.

"I have a plan, sir."

The king saw the desire in the boy.

"Quickly, Son."

"Let Nadar take the horsemen to the ridges above the river at the narrow place and stay out of sight. I will get Gemla to the other side. When the southern army comes to the river, let Nadar and the men sweep down and trap them against the river. The ridges will be too steep and the pass too narrow for them to escape. Then let Taytan and the counselors talk."

Everyone waited for the king to dismiss the plan.

"How will you get Gemla across quickly enough? Our best rowers cannot steer across that current in one whole day."

"I know a bridge, my father."

"What bridge? There are no bridges."

"A bridge that comes out of the water."

"And what is to stop the southern king from sending his men across that bridge?"

"It is a secret bridge, sir."

King Rolday weighed the risks. He wanted to believe his son for many reasons.

Then to the surprise of all he said, "We will do as Janwahr suggests. Obey him."

Janwahr could hardly breathe in the silence that followed.

"Please bring up the horsemen, Nadar," he said.

Nadar glanced at the king, who nodded once. Nadar left immediately.

"Sir," said the youngest prince, "Bandeen and I will take Gemla to safety. Taytan and what counselors you choose should come behind the horsemen. Yes?"

"As you say, Son," the king replied. "But I will come with you. I want to see this miraculous bridge that even I did not know existed in my kingdom."

Before long, the king, Princess Gemla, the king's guards, Bandeen, and Janwahr stood at the bank by the wildalia tree.

"Where is the bridge?" Gemla asked, a quiver in her voice.

Janwahr gave a high whistle and then another.

Near the other shore a huge blue sea dragon's head broke the surface, roaring. The king and the princess gasped in wonder. Bandeen and the guards fell back.

The dragon lifted its head high out of the river and shook the shining water off in all directions. Its horn glistened in the sun.

"That horn must be solid silver," said Gemla under her breath, holding Janwahr's arm.

"Is it silver?" Janwahr said. "I thought it was."

Danzee swam forward.

"It's coming here," said Bandeen, running behind the wildalia.

Janwahr smiled. "Danzee won't hurt you."

When the shining monster neared the shore, even the king stepped back. Two of his guards advanced and crossed their swords in front of him. The great beast put his head beside the roots of the tree and waited.

Trapped

"Danzee, this is my father, the king, and my sister, Princess Gemla. We need your help." Janwahr heard Danzee gurgle. "Can you stretch from one bank to the other?"

Danzee swirled himself around. He arched himself in several dozen places and made the water toss out beside him for yards and yards.

Then, from far across the river, a slap of his tail sounded.

"He's ready," said Janwahr.

Gemla, still holding her brother's arm, hesitated.

"It's all right," the prince said. "Danzee will help us. I would go with you, but I must wait here for the invaders."

At last Gemla stepped forward, and at the king's command four guards took her across the dragon bridge to the other side.

"Is he beautiful?" Janwahr asked his father as Gemla was crossing.

"Worthy of a prince," said the king.

Janwahr said nothing.

"Thank you, Danzee," said the king. And Danzee dropped beneath the surface, flashed the tip of his tail once, and was gone.

After some hours Janwahr could hear hoofbeats and trumpets and shouts.

"Can you see them yet?"

"Not yet," said King Rolday.

"If my plan fails—" the prince began.

"Never doubt your plan once it's under way. Choose the best plan and stay with it. A king must believe in himself if he would have his men's trust."

Janwahr remained silent. It was good to stand here by the river with his father. He straightened and clasped his hands loosely behind his back.

At length the king said, "They are here."

The whole pass between the ridges was suddenly filled with riders on huge battle horses. The armor and swords shone out in the setting sun. On and on they came, leather creaking and metal clinking. The horses tossed their heads, rattling their martingales and chest plates. They drew up before King Rolday and Prince Janwahr.

The southern king leaned forward in his saddle, throwing back his black hood. "Where's your feeble army, Rolday?"

All along the ridges above and in the pass, Rolday's soldiers appeared silently, gray and solemn against the dusk. King Rolday pointed.

The southern king looked back and started. His men tensed in their saddles and put their hands to their scabbards.

The southern king swung back around. "A stupid trap! You do not have me—I have you!"

And with that he sprang from his horse and drew a dagger against Rolday's throat. He leaned toward Rolday's ear. "Call them down, or I kill you!"

Janwahr whistled high and long and loud. Just behind them the river burst open with a great rush and a horrible roar. The silver horn gleamed as the water streamed off the giant creature.

Danzee saw the armies and raised himself a hundred feet out of the water, shaking his head and screaming.

The southern king staggered back.

"Help us, Danzee!" Janwahr called.

The great head swooped down. Danzee caught up the evil king by his tunic and held him there.

"Your men surrender, or I give you to my friend here—for his supper!"

The two armies stood frozen in horror and awe. But the southern king refused to speak.

"Roundabout," called out Janwahr.

Danzee took the southern king in four giant circles, skimming the water with him on the downward moves, raking him through the wildalia on the upward.

"Enough," the king called. "We surrender!"

"Well done, Danzee! Drop him," called the prince.

In mid-arch, Danzee opened his jaws and the king flew out and down into the water.

As he clambered about in the water, Taytan and the counselors came forward through the invading armies. The southern king dragged himself onto the bank.

"Shall we discuss the terms of surrender?" said Rolday to the dripping king.

Bandeen, overcome with the wonder of it all, ran forward to his master. "Well done, Janwahr!"

"Prince Janwahr," said King Rolday.

Janwahr smiled broadly and straightened his tunic—once.

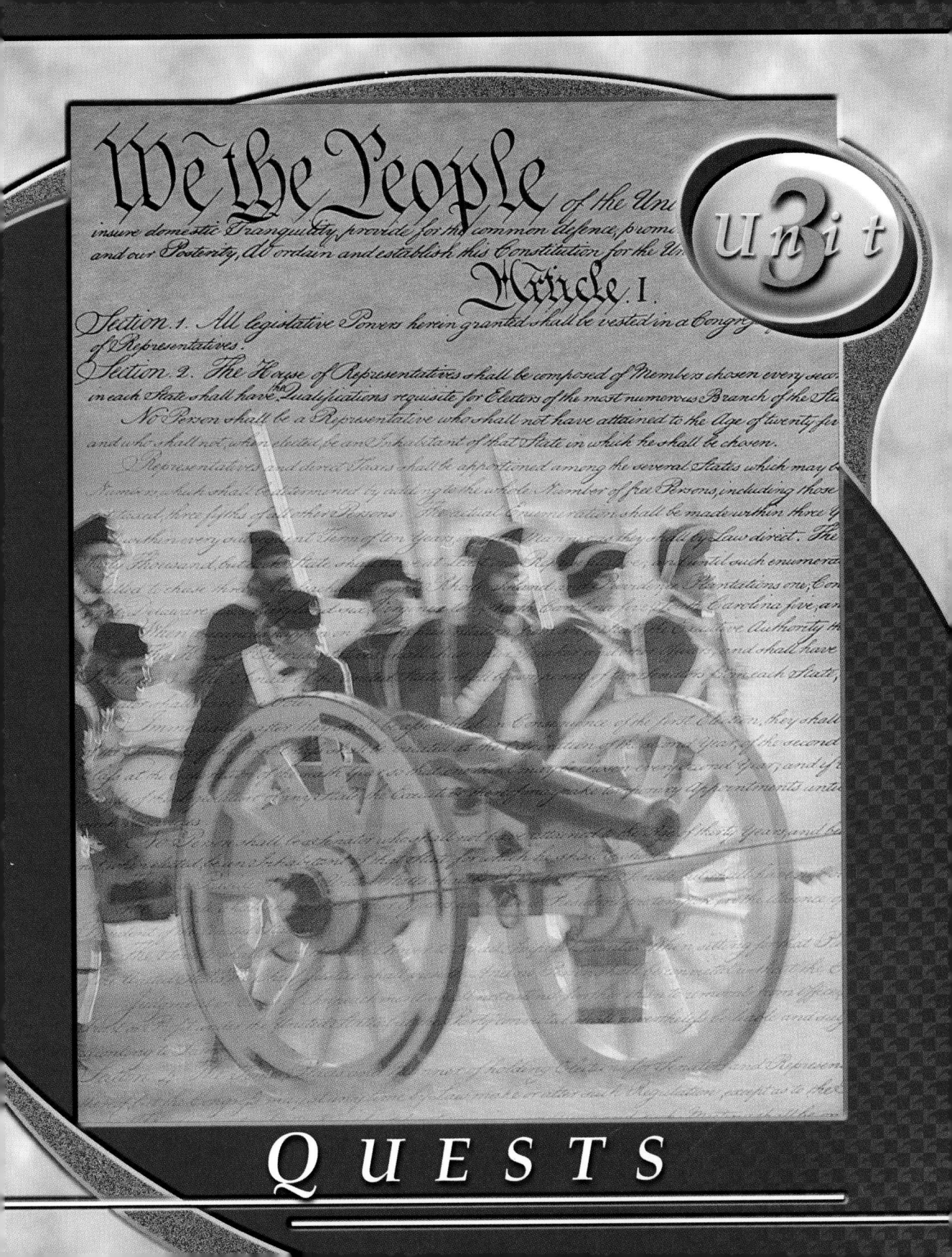
We the People
of the Unu
insure domestic Tranquility, provide for the common defence, promo
and our Posterity, do ordain and establish this Constitution for the Un
Article. I.
Section. 1. All legislative Powers herein granted shall be vested in a Congre
of Representatives.
Section. 2. The House of Representatives shall be composed of Member
in each State shall have the Qualifications requisite for Electors of the most numerous Branch of the Sta
No Person shall be a Representative who shall not have attained to the Age of twenty fi
and who shall not, when elected, be an Inhabitant of that State in which he shall be chosen.
Unit
3

QUESTS

Pony Penning Day

taken from Misty of Chincoteague
Marguerite Henry

illustrated by Preston Gravely Jr.

In the book Misty of Chincoteague, *two children named Paul and Maureen want very much to have a horse of their own. The following story, taken from that book, tells how Paul and Maureen try to make that dream come true.*

The Straggler

Pony Penning Day always comes on the last Thursday in July. For weeks before, every member of the Volunteer Fire Department is busy getting the grounds in readiness, and the boys are allowed to help.

"I'll do your chores at home, Paul," offered Maureen, "so's you can see that the pony pens are good and stout."

Paul spent long days at the pony penning grounds. The pens for the wild ponies must be made safe. Once the Phantom was captured, she must not escape. Nothing else mattered.

Paul and Maureen Beebe lived on their grandfather's pony ranch on the island of Chincoteague, just off the Virginia shore. Across a narrow channel lay another island, Assateague, which was the home of the wild herds. They were said to be the descendants of a bunch of Spanish horses off a Spanish galleon which had been shipwrecked there several hundred years ago. Once every July the men of Chincoteague crossed the channel to Assateague and rounded up wild ponies. They swam them across the channel to Chincoteague to be sold on Pony Penning Day.

Paul and Maureen had gentled many a wild colt. But just as the colt was learning that they were his friends, Grandpa Beebe would sell it and the children would never see him again. They had earned a hundred dollars to buy a horse of their own—and the horse they wanted was the Phantom. This was the mysterious wild mare about whom so many stories were told. None of the roundup men had ever been able to capture her. But this year Paul was old enough to go with the men and he was determined to get her.

"When I do," he said, "I'll tie a rope around her neck to show she's already sold. To us."

The night before the roundup, Paul and Maureen made last-minute plans in Phantom's stall. "First thing in the morning," Paul told Maureen, "you lay a clean bed of dried sea grass. Then fill the manger with plenty of marsh grass to make Phantom feel at home."

"Oh, I will, Paul. And I've got some ear corn and some 'lasses to coax her appetite, and Grandma gave me a bunch of tiny new carrots and some rutabagas, and I've been saving up sugar until I have a little sackful."

It was dark and still when Paul awoke the next morning. He lay quiet a moment, trying to gather his wits. Suddenly he shot out of bed.

Today was Pony Penning Day! He dressed quickly and thudded

barefoot down to the kitchen where Grandma stood over the stove, frying ham and making coffee for him as if he were man-grown!

After a hurried breakfast, he ran out the door. He mounted Watch Eyes, a dependable pony that Grandpa had never been able to sell because of his white eyes. Locking his bare feet around the pony's sides, he jogged out of the yard.

Maureen came running to see him off.

"Whatever happens," Paul called back over his shoulder, "you be at Old Dominion Point at ten o'clock on a fresh pony."

"I'll be there, Paul!"

"And you, Paul!" yelled Grandpa. "Obey yer leader. No matter what!"

Day was breaking. A light golden mist came up out of the sea. It touched the prim white houses and the white picket fences with an unearthly light. Paul loped along slowly to save his mount's strength. All along the road, men were turning out of their gates.

"Where do you reckon you'll do most good, Bub?" taunted a lean sapling of a man. He guffawed loudly, then winked at the rest of the group.

Paul's hand tightened on the reins. "Reckon I'll do most good where the leader tells me to go," he said, blushing hotly.

The day promised to be sultry. The marsh grass that usually billowed and waved stood motionless. The water of Assateague Channel glared like quicksilver.

Now the cavalcade was thundering over a small bridge that linked Chincoteague Island to little Piney Island. At the far end of the bridge a scow with a rail fence around it stood at anchor.

In spite of light talk, the faces of the men were drawn tight with excitement as they led their mounts onto the scow. The horses felt the excitement, too. Their nostrils quivered, and their ears swiveled this way and that, listening to the throb of the motor. Now the scow began to nose its way across the narrow channel. Paul watched the White Hills of Assateague loom near. He watched the old lighthouse grow sharp and sharper against the sky. In a few minutes the ride was over. The gangway was being lowered. The horses were clattering down, each man taking his own.

All eyes were on Wyle Maddox, the leader.

"Split in three bunches," Wyle clipped out the directions loud and sharp. "North, south, and east. Me and Kim and the Beebe boy will head east, Wimbrow and Quillen goes north, and Harvey and Rodgers south. We'll all meet at Tom's Point."

Paul touched his bare heels into Watch Eye's side. They were off! The boy's eyes were fastened on Wyle Maddox. He and Kim Horsepepper were following their leader like the wake of a ship.

Misty

Watch Eyes plunged on. There was a kind of glory in pursuit that made Paul and the horse one. They were trailing nothing but swaying bushes. They were giving chase to a mirage. Always it moved on and on, showing itself only in quivering leaves or moving shadows.

What was that? In the clump of myrtle bushes just ahead? Paul reined in. He could scarcely breathe for the wild beating of his heart. Here it was again! A silver flash. It looked like mist with the sun on it. And just beyond the mist, he caught sight of a long tail of copper and silver.

He gazed awestruck. "It could be the Phantom's tail," he breathed. "It is! It is! It is! And the silver flash—it's not mist at all, but a brand-new colt!" he murmured.

He glanced about him helplessly. If only he could think! How could he drive the Phantom and her colt to Tom's Point?

Warily he approached the myrtle thicket. Just then the colt

let out a high, frightened whinny. In that little second Paul knew that he wanted more than anything in the world to keep the mother and the colt together. Shivers of joy raced up and down

his spine. His breath came faster. He made a firm resolution. "I'll buy you both!" he promised.

But how far had he come? Was it ten miles to Tom's Point or two? Would it be best to drive them down the beach? Or through the woods? As if in answer a loud bugle rang through the woods. It was the Pied Piper, the pinto stallion in command of the herd. And unmistakably his voice came from the direction of Tom's Point.

The Phantom pricked her ears. She wheeled around and almost collided with Watch Eyes in her haste to find the band. She wanted the Pied Piper for protection. Behind her trotted the foal, all shining and clean with its newness.

Paul laughed weakly. He was not driving the Phantom after all! She and her colt were leading him. They were leading him to Tom's Point!

Tom's Point was a protected piece of land where the marsh was hard and the grass especially sweet. About seventy wild ponies, exhausted by their morning's run, stood browsing quietly, as if they were in a corral. Only occasionally they looked up at their captors. The good meadow and their own weariness kept them peaceful prisoners.

At a watchful distance the roundup men rested their mounts and relaxed. It was like the lull in the midst of a storm. All was quiet on the surface. Yet there was an undercurrent of tension. You could tell it in the narrowed eyes of the men, their subdued voices and their too easy laughter.

Suddenly the laughter stilled. Mouths gaped in disbelief. Eyes rounded. For a few seconds no one spoke at all. Then a shout that was half wonder and half admiration went up from the men. Paul Beebe was bringing in *the Phantom and a colt!*

The roundup men were swarming around Paul, buzzing with questions. "Beats all!" he heard someone say. "For two years we been trying to round up the Phantom and along comes a spindling youngster to show us up."

" 'Twas the little colt that hindered her."

" 'Course it was."

"It's the newest colt in the bunch; may not stand the swim."

"If we lose only one colt, it'll still be a good day's work."

The men accepted Paul as one of them now—a real roundup man. They were clapping him on the shoulder and trying to get him to talk. "Ain't they a shaggy-lookin' bunch?" Kim Horsepepper asked.

"Except for Misty," Paul said, pointing toward the Phantom's colt. "Her coat is silky." The mere thought of touching it sent shivers through him. "Misty," he thought to himself wonderingly. "Why, I've named her!"

He looked out across the water. Two lines of boats were forming a pony-way across the channel. He saw the cluster of people and the mounts waiting on the shores of Chincoteague and he knew that somewhere among them was Maureen. It was like a relay race. Soon she would carry on.

"Could I swim my mount across the channel alongside the Phantom?" Paul asked Wyle Maddox anxiously.

Wyle shook his head. "Watch Eyes is all tuckered out," he said. "Besides, there's a tradition in the way things is handled on Pony Penning Day. There's mounted men for the roundup and there's boatmen to herd 'em across the channel," he explained.

"Tide's out!" he called in clipped tones. "Current is slack. Time for the ponies to be swimmed across. Let's go!"

Suddenly the beach was wild with commotion. From three sides the roundup men came rushing at the ponies, their hoarse cries whipping the animals into action. They plunged into the water, the stallions leading, the mares following, neighing encouragement to their colts.

"They're off!" shouted Wyle Maddox, and everyone felt the relief and triumph in his words.

Trouble and Triumph

On the shores of Chincoteague the people pressed forward, their faces strained to stiffness, as they watched Assateague Beach.

"Here they come!" The cry broke out from every throat.

Maureen, wedged between Grandpa Beebe on one side and a volunteer fireman on the other, stood on her mount's back. Her arms paddled the air as if she were swimming and struggling with the wild ponies.

Suddenly a fisherman, looking through binoculars, began shouting in a hoarse voice, "A new-borned colt is afeared to swim. Wait! A wild pony is breaking out from the mob! Swimming around the mob! Escaping!"

An awed murmur stirred the crowds. Maureen dug her toes in

her mount's back. She strained her eyes to see the fugitive, but all she could make out was a milling mass of dark blobs on the water.

The fisherman leaned far out over the water. "It's the Phantom!" he screamed.

The people took up the cry, echoing it over and over. "It's the Phantom! She's escaped again!"

Maureen felt tears on her cheek, and impatiently brushed them away.

The fisherman was waving for quiet. "It's the Phantom's colt that won't swim!" he called out in a voice so hoarse it cracked. "The Phantom got separated from a bran'-fire new colt. She's gone back to get it!"

The people whooped and hollered at the news. "The Phantom's got a colt," they sang out. "The Phantom's got a new colt!"

Again the fisherman was waving for silence.

"She's reached her colt!" he crowed. "But the roundup men are closing in on her! They're making her shove the colt in the water. Look at her! She's makin' it swim!"

Grandpa Beebe cupped his hands around his mouth. "Can the little feller make it?" he boomed.

The crowd stilled, waiting for the hoarse voice. For long seconds no answer came. The fisherman remained as fixed as the piling he stood on. Wave after wave of fear swept over Maureen. She felt as if she were drowning. And just when she could stand the silence no longer, the fisherman began reporting in short, nervous sentences.

"They're half-ways across. Wait a minute! The colt! It's bein' sucked down in a whirlpool. I can't see it now. My soul and body! A boy's jumped off the scow. He's swimming out to help the colt."

The onlookers did not need the fisherman with the binoculars any more. They could see for themselves. A boy swimming against the current. A boy holding a colt's head above the swirling water.

Maureen gulped great lungfuls of air. "It's Paul!" she screamed. "It's Paul!"

On all sides the shouts went up. "Why, it's Paul!"

Grandpa leaped up on his mount's back as nimbly as a boy. He stood with his arms upraised, his fists clenched.

"God help ye, Paul!" his words carried out over the water.

"Yer almost home!"

Grandpa's voice was as strong as a tow rope. Paul was swimming steadily toward it, holding the small silver face of the colt above the water. He was almost there. He was there!

Maureen slid down from her mount, clutching a handful of mane. "You made it, Paul! You made it!" she cried.

The air was wild with whinnies and snorts as the ponies touched the hard sand, then scrambled up the shore, their wet bodies gleaming in the sun. Paul half-carried the little colt up the steep bank; then suddenly it found its own legs. Shouts between triumph and relief escaped every throat as the little filly tottered up the bank.

For a brief second Paul's and Maureen's eyes met above the crowds. It was as if they and the mare and her foal were the only creatures on the island. They were unaware of the great jostling and fighting as the stallions sorted out their own mares and colts. They were unaware of everything but a sharp ecstasy. Soon the Phantom and her colt would belong to them. Never to be sold.

Dodging horses and people, Grandpa Beebe made his way over to Paul.

"Paul, boy," he said, his voice unsteady, "I swimmed the hull way with you. Yer the most wonderful and the craziest young'un in the world. Now git home right smart quick," he added, trying to sound stern. "Yer about done up, and Grandma's expectin' ye. Maureen and I'll see to it that the Phantom and her colt reach the pony·pens."

Cherry TIME

Haiku
Wendy M. Harris

Burdened cherry limbs
Battleground of man and bird
Bucket against beak.

The Cherry TREES

Eileen M. Berry
illustrated by Del Thompson and Steve Mitchell

I remember the day I found out about Grandma. The bus had brought me home from school early because of the snowstorm, and Dad was sitting at the kitchen table holding Mom's hand. Dad never came home this early in the day. I knew that something had happened.

"Sit down, Charis," Mom said. She poured me a cup of hot cocoa, and when she brought it to me she stayed behind me with her hands on my shoulders.

"Sweetheart," Dad said, "we have some sad news for you." He looked down at the coffee cup in his big, rough hands. "Your grandma died today." For a moment he just sat without speaking. Then he looked up at me, and the crinkles around his eyes were back. "But the good news is, Grandma is with Jesus now."

Grandma had been in the hospital for a long time, but before that she had lived at our house. Mom and Dad told me about the things she had said in her hospital bed right before she died. Then they talked about funeral arrangements. Nothing could be

done until the storm was over, Dad said. I just sat and drank my cocoa and listened.

I didn't eat much for supper. Darkness came early, and I brought a chair to the kitchen window and sat where I could look out. In the dim light I could just see the snow falling on the cherry trees outside. Behind me on the table, a candle flame danced, making a bright spot of fire in the pane.

"If this storm keeps up," Dad said, "we could lose some of those trees."

I turned around. "Why?"

He leaned close to me, peering out the window over my head. "Their limbs aren't strong enough to hold the heavy snow," he said. "Much more of this, and the branches will crack beneath the weight."

I watched the snow, wondering how something so lovely and soft could be so deadly at the same time. Everything dies, I thought. And God just lets it happen.

"Remember how your grandma loved those cherry trees in the spring, Charis?" Mom said. "With all the white blossoms on them? If we do lose them, I'm glad she's not here to see it."

And then I tried to ask Mom why God would let the trees die, but I started to cry. Mom put her arms around me. She kept holding me even when the sobs made me jerk and tremble. When I was finally able to be silent, we just watched the snow together.

The next morning when I got up, the sun was shining on a clean, white world. I ran straight to the kitchen. Mom turned from the stove where she was frying eggs and smiled at me. "No school for you today," she said.

I looked out at the cherry trees. Just before I'd gone to bed the night before, I had prayed that God would not let the snow break the trees. And now here they were, all standing tall. Each branch was coated with a layer of snow like thick frosting on dark cakes. But not many branches had fallen—only a few of the smaller ones.

Dad was busy on the phone for most of the morning, calling my aunts and uncles and making plans for Grandma's funeral. I helped Mom sort through some of Grandma's things in the room where she had stayed. In the afternoon I went outside and built a snowman under the cherry trees. I used some of the fallen twigs for the snowman's arms. And I made him a smile with pieces of gravel from the drive.

sounding rushed. "Why did God let us keep the trees but not Grandma? I prayed we could keep both." I couldn't look up at him. I just kept staring at my snowman, but I was no longer smiling.

"I don't know, Charis," Dad said. "But I do know that God did what He knew was best."

He thought for a moment. Then he broke another twig off the cherry tree and handed it to me. "See how small that is—how fragile?"

I turned the little twig over in my mittened hands.

"We're like that sometimes," Dad said. "When we've had heavy burdens to bear, or when we've been in a lot of pain, we can grow pretty weak and frail. Grandma was like that."

I nodded, knowing what he meant. Right before she had gone to the hospital, Grandma could not even stand up without help.

"And sometimes when that happens," Dad said, "God decides it's time to release us from the suffering altogether. He takes the burden away."

"You mean dying?" I asked.

Dad came out after a while to see my snowman. "Good work, Charis," he said. He put an arm around my shoulders while we smiled back at my smiling white man. Dad reached over our heads and touched a cherry bough. "The Lord spared our trees," he said.

"Dad?" I shivered and took a deep breath. My voice came out

"Sometimes it's dying. And sometimes—like with the trees—God heals. Either way, He knows how much we can handle, and He knows when we've had enough."

"But how does He choose—dying or living, I mean?"

A whisper of wind stirred the cherry boughs above us, and a little dusting of snow sprinkled down. I looked up at Dad, and he smiled at me. "He chooses," he said, "because He *knows* what is right. That's why He's God."

I wanted to be able to smile too. But as I looked at Dad, I suddenly remembered the photograph of Grandma on the desk in my room, and the rocking chair by my bed where she had sat and read to me. The photograph was all I had of her, and the chair was empty now.

"What about the people who get left with the pain?" I asked. I felt tears prickling in my eyes. "What if God doesn't take it away?"

Instead of answering, Dad took the twig from my hand.

Stooping down in the snow, he used the twig as a pencil to write my name. *Charis*. "Do you remember what your name means?" he asked.

Of course I remembered. Dad had told me many times that he had named me after a Greek word in the Bible. "Grace," I said.

"That's right. And that's your answer. For the people who get left with the pain, God gives His grace."

"What is grace exactly?" I wiped my mitten across my eyes.

Dad looked far away for a moment, thinking. Then he looked back at me. "It's like little gifts of strength," he said. "Not all at once, just enough for each day. It means becoming like these tree branches when they're able to bend under the snow but not break. Do you understand?"

I looked at my name in the snow for a long time. Then I looked at him. And I suddenly found I could smile. "I think so."

Dad gave me a hug. Then he took my hand—just like he used to when I was very little—and led me back toward the farmhouse. "I guess we can thank God for leaving us the trees," I said.

He gave my hand a squeeze. "We sure can, Sweetheart. There'll be blossoms again in the spring."

I thought for a moment. "And cherry pies," I added.

I looked up at Dad in time to see his eyes crinkle when he grinned. "That's my Charis," he said.

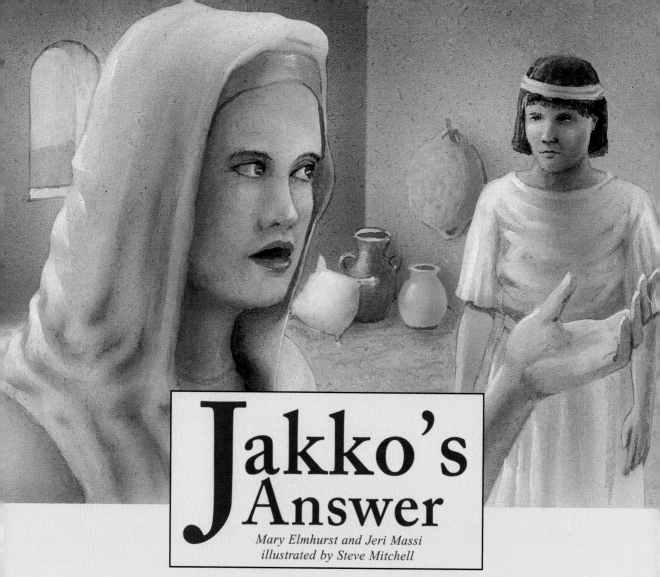

Jakko's Answer

Mary Elmhurst and Jeri Massi
illustrated by Steve Mitchell

This is a fictional story based on Judges 13-16. Its central character is only briefly mentioned in Scripture, but in this story he is given a name.

A Temple Boy

"Did you grind the corn yet, Jakko?"

"Almost," Jakko said, hurrying to the bag of corn in the corner.

"Almost?" His mother looked stern. "You mean you haven't even started yet! Lazy boy!"

"I'm sorry. I—"

"Don't do it now. You have to get up to the temple within the hour for the sacrifice. Change your clothes."

Jakko hurriedly found his working tunic.

"I suppose you and that blind man were blabbing again," his mother said. "If the priests found . . . Ah me, how am I supposed to keep track of you all the time? But mark my words, someday that Samson is going to snatch you up and give you a good lesson!"

Jakko couldn't help smiling. "Oh, Mother, he's chained."

"Chains! Hah!" She snapped her fingers. "He picked up the gates of the city of Gaza one time and carried them away on his shoulders. And he killed a thousand men once with some old bone he picked up off the ground. Chains won't hold him if he gets mad."

"Mother, poor Samson never gets mad at me. He's my friend. Besides, he's really not that strong. I've watched him turning the millstone, and sometimes he can barely move it."

"Mark my words, boy, if the priests find you making friends with that fiend, it will go hard for you—you, a temple boy!"

Jakko already knew that. The priests didn't tolerate very much at all. When Jakko had cried out because of their cruel punishments, the priests had only punished him again.

Temple boy! He hated the very name! When he had been afraid of the huge statues of Dagon, the priests had pushed him into the temple and made him stay through all the long, horrible ceremonies.

"Today," Jakko said softly, "Samson told me about the time he caught three hundred foxes."

His mother was interested. "What did he do with them?"

"He put burning wood between their tails and let them loose, two by two, to go wherever they wanted." He laughed.

"Ah!" She suddenly shook her head. "It was no doubt a trick of his to burn our crops. Isn't that so?"

"Well, yes," Jakko admitted. "They ran into the cornfields."

"Enough!" she said. "Not another word about Samson! Get to the temple! You'll get a whipping if you're late to help with the sacrifices."

Jakko hurried out. But his mind was full. Samson told him many things—and not all of them were funny. He said that Israel's God was greater than Dagon. Jakko wondered if it could be true. He was more afraid of Dagon than he was of the priests. But he knew he had to spend the rest of his life in service to the gods, for he was a temple boy, born and raised in the shadow of the temples.

But if there were another God—an all-powerful God—the thought of being free from the temples made Jakko's throat feel tight.

Jakko soon was busily sweeping floors, polishing silver, and doing other tasks at the great temple of Dagon in preparation for the sacrifice.

Jakko hoped that he would be chosen to work during the feast, waving palm branches over the tables to keep the flies away. Kitchen work always made him hot and tired, and helping at the temple rites before the feasts was even worse. The things that happened during the sacrifices frightened Jakko. The priests cut themselves when they prayed. They did worse things, too, that he couldn't bear to think about.

In the middle of the afternoon, Jakko was sent to watch the roasting meat that was slowly turning over the coals in the huge fireplaces. It was kitchen work, but he consoled himself: at least he didn't have to help with the sacrifices.

As the afternoon wore slowly away, Jakko thought about the things that Samson had told him. Was there really a God who was greater than Dagon? If there was, then why was Samson in prison and why were the Philistines having a feast to celebrate his cap-ture? It didn't make sense. How was he to know what to believe?

Jakko suddenly realized he was hungry. It was almost evening, and he hadn't seen a thing that was going on in the temple. The feasting had begun already. Finally, he was told that he could go.

Jakko hurried to the great hall to get something to eat. Mother would expect him to get his din-ner there. What he saw made him gasp in wonder. He had never seen so many people in his life. There must have been thousands!

The Answer

Jakko heard shouts of laughter from a group of splendidly dressed men and women and edged toward them. What he saw made his heart sink! There was Samson—he had been brought from the prison house—and everyone was making fun of him. Priests, soldiers, and even that beautiful lady they called Delilah. After a few moments Jakko heard one of the priests calling.

"Here, boy, lead him over there so the people on the roof can see him too." Jakko timidly edged forward through the laughing, pushing people and took Samson's arm.

"Samson, just go with me. I'll show you the way."

"Jakko, my boy." Samson's calloused hands touched Jakko's shoulders. "I forgot. You are a temple boy. Poor lad."

Jakko's eyes filled with tears. Somehow Samson understood what there was to fear and hate in the temples.

"Where are you taking me?" Samson whispered.

"To the middle of the hall. Where the pillars are." As they threaded their way through the crowd, Jakko decided that he had to ask. "Samson?"

"Yes, boy?"

"Samson, please don't be angry, but I must know. If your God is so powerful, why are you here in Dagon's temple with everyone laughing at you? And why did your God let them put your eyes out?"

Samson sighed and hesitated so long that Jakko was afraid he wouldn't answer. Finally he said, "Jakko, God is not just powerful; He is holy. He will not let His people do wrong without being punished. I disobeyed Him. I joined myself to the Philistines, even though I knew their wickedness."

Unseeing, he raised a hand and gestured around him at the people and priests. In the harsh light from the torches Jakko thought they looked twice as cruel. "And because of that, I am now suffering. Oh, how I am suffering!"

"But you told me that God loves you and all His people."

"He does. He does. And so He punishes us—not like the priests

180

punish you by being cruel. God drives us back to Himself. I was very far from Him, Jakko. He has had to drive me back very hard indeed to return me to Himself. Can you understand that?"

"Yes."

"I demanded in my heart to live among the pagan Philistines and be a part of them. And now I am. Now I know how evil I was." Howling and laughter rose around them again.

"And yet your God will accept you?" Jakko asked.

"Yes. And I have repented for my wrongdoing. Soon I will be with Him; all my blindness will be past." His big, rough hands patted Jakko's head. "God listens to those who truly ask His for-giveness. Someday He will send His Messiah who will be able to make us right with God."

By now the two had reached the center of the great feasting hall. Jakko shrank back from the eyes of all the people. They were looking, laughing.

"Are we in the middle of the hall?" Samson asked him.

"Yes." The words stuck in Jakko's throat. "I'm sorry, Samson."

But Samson wasn't listening.

"O Lord God, remember me, I pray Thee, and strengthen me, I pray Thee, only this once, O God, that I may be at once avenged of the Philistines for my two eyes." Then Samson clutched Jakko's shoulder.

"Jakko, take me to the pillars that support the roof, and then go home quickly. God is going to give me strength as He did in the past. I will show that He is alive and that He is the only true God. Always remember what I have told you about Him. And remember that He loves you too."

The look on Samson's face frightened Jakko; he dared not disobey. After leading Samson to one of the pillars, he hurried to the entrance of the hall and fled down the steps toward the road leading home. Then he paused and turned. What could one old, blind man do in the temple of Dagon? Suddenly he heard Samson's voice, loud above the noise of the festivities.

"Now let me die with the Philistines!"

Die? With the Philistines? Suddenly the great slab walls of the temple shook and then buckled with a terrific roar that knocked Jakko to the ground. The roof of the temple caved in. Jakko hid his head in his arm until the thunderous crash subsided. Then there was nothing but silence. He looked up and saw a cloud of dust rising over the mass of fallen stone where the temple had been.

Jakko had his answer about the God of Israel. Who but a living, all-powerful God could bring such defeat to His enemies? And through just one man—a man who wouldn't have to suffer anymore.

LITERATURE LESSON:

Biblical Fiction

"Jakko's Answer" contains many facts that you probably recognized. Yet it is a fictional story. Everything in the story about Samson is true and followed the scriptural account. But the main character of this story is the little boy who led Samson to the pillars in the temple. We don't know what that boy's name really was. And we don't know what he really learned from Samson's death. But the authors gave him a name and a personality. They wanted you to think about the story of Samson in a new way. They wanted to help you understand what life was really like in Philistia when Samson was there.

- **Plot That Builds an Understanding of Scripture**

Good biblical fiction is always true to Scripture. Every Bible fact that the story mentions is told the way the Bible tells it.

Other parts of the plot may depend on historical research. Jakko's job in the temple was a job that some boys had in Philistia in Samson's time. Suppose Jakko had used a tool or a weapon. The writers would have had to visit a museum or look in books to learn about that object. Suppose Jakko had visited the market. The writers would have had to know all about the products available in the markets of Philistia. Authors must do research in planning the story plot.

• Setting That Builds an Understanding of Scripture

Authors of stories set in Bible times must plan an accurate setting for their stories too. The writers of "Jakko's Answer" might have visited the ruins of a temple. Or they might have studied books with drawings and descriptions of temples. Suppose Jakko had taken a journey. The writers would have had to know about the roads. Were they paved with cobblestones? Were they dusty trails? And what kind of land did Jakko travel on? Did he cross mountains? Did he walk on grassy flatlands? Research for the details of the setting is a big part of the author's job.

Biblical fiction can be very exciting. It can help you feel as if you were actually there when some biblical event happened. A good story can take you right to the setting and help you live there with the characters. Someday you may decide to write a story like "Jakko's Answer." If you do, you may find that doing the research and writing will help you understand the Bible even better.

The Snow-White Robin

adapted by Karen Wilt
illustrated by Del Thompson and Noelle Snyder

The Birthday Gift

Many years ago a noble and just king ruled a kingdom surrounded by snow-capped mountains and azure blue seas. His people lived simple but happy lives. And the king himself lived a simple life with his queen and his daughter. As time passed, though, the queen fell ill with an incurable disease. Though doctors from countries far and wide treated her, nothing could be done, and she left the world, admonishing her husband to care well for their beloved daughter.

The king sorrowed greatly in his loss. But as his daughter Aurelia grew, her likeness to her dead mother charmed the king, and his heart grew tender. He surrounded her with beautiful gardens and peaceful forests. The palace walls abounded with wonderful paintings. Only the best foods were placed before the royal princess. Everything to make her life happy was lavished upon her.

But as the king spent more time with Aurelia, he spent less time on his throne. He began to turn the rule of the land over to wise counselors and ministers. They in turn allowed some of their own counselors to take charge of smaller matters. These counselors then allowed their secretaries to have some special duties, and so it went, until it came to pass that a single soldier was put in charge of the gate to the castle.

Most of the ministers, counselors, and secretaries acted on all the king's charges wisely. They tried their best to be fair and just.

But this guard of the castle gate was a wicked man. He flattered and praised his superiors until they trusted him completely. He allowed the rich people to pass through the gate without a murmur. But he was rude to the peasants of the kingdom, and he demanded money of them before they could see the king. The simple people could not pay the prices he demanded, so they could not get to the king to tell him of this unjust guard. They hoped that soon the king would start paying attention again to the affairs of the kingdom. Then he would realize how unfair this man was and dismiss him.

Meanwhile, the king breakfasted each morning with Aurelia, walked her to the royal tutors, lunched with her, read the chronicles of the kingdom with her, pondered several hours in his gardens, dined with Aurelia, and then returned to bed.

The wicked guard continued to demand money of the poor, the counselors and ministers continued to rule for the king, the king continued to seclude himself, and Aurelia continued to grow.

On Aurelia's tenth birthday the king asked, as he did every year, what present he could give to please her.

Aurelia's eyes filled with tears as she looked at her father. "I have learned that the things I desire most cannot be given."

Her father's eyes clouded. "Yes, my dear," her father replied. " 'Tis often so. But surely there is something I could give to please you."

"Then, Father," she said, "may I please have a snow-white robin to sing for us as we walk in our

The huntsman threw his tattered cloak over it and wrapped it in his arms. As the night deepened, he turned toward the city of the king.

Though the cold night wind chilled him, he remembered the king's noble spirit of years ago when the queen had reigned with him. He wondered why the king had secluded himself from his people. But his heart flew like the snow-white robin as he thought of the joy he would provide for the young princess.

By morning he reached the gate of the city. He held his precious bundle carefully, lest someone should steal it and win the prize. At last his eyes, heavy with sleep, beheld the palace. He knocked timidly at the gate.

Grumpily the castle guard opened the iron doors. "Begone," he snarled.

"I have come to see the king," the huntsman said.

"To see the king costs much more than one of your station and means can well afford," the guard said.

"I will see the king," the huntsman said. "I have brought him something of great worth."

"Anything brought to the king must be inspected by me, and of a certainty, you could not pay the fee for such a privilege."

The huntsman wrinkled his brow. "I must see the king. I have found the gift for the princess." A corner of his cloak slipped back, and a snow-white wing fluttered. The guard's eyes lit up.

"Give me that cloak!" he said, reaching for the huntsman.

The huntsman stepped back. "I will see the king," he said.

The guard lowered his eyelids until his eyes became as thin as silk threads. "You may see the king under one condition. Half of your reward must be given to me."

The huntsman nodded. "As you desire," he said.

The king's joy was boundless as he examined the pure white feathers and listened to the sweet morning song of the snow-white robin.

Then the king turned to the huntsman, and his heart gripped him, because he had not seen any of the peasants in many long years. "Whatever you wish shall be your reward," he said.

The huntsman bowed. "I desire only fifty lashes," he said.

The king's mouth opened in dismay. "Fifty lashes?" he asked.

Nothing could dissuade the huntsman from his choice. A strong soldier with a huge whip was summoned.

"Be gentle," the king murmured. "The man seems a loyal subject, though I cannot understand his ways."

As each strike was called, the king shuddered to see the huntsman suffer. "Twenty-two!" the soldier cried out. "Twenty-three! Twenty-four!" But when he reached twenty-five, the huntsman halted him.

"O king," he said, "the guard at your gate demanded half of the reward for the gift I brought you. He justly deserves the other twenty-five lashes."

The king gasped. Then he quickly motioned to the soldier to bring the guard. That wicked man's greediness was soon punished, and the huntsman received honor and riches from the king.

The princess trained the snow-white robin to sing in the palace to cheer her father. And once more the king opened his heart to his people and ruled wisely and justly on his throne.

WORLD WAR II

Jeri Massi
illustrated by Preston Gravely Jr.

In 1933 the country of France was still trying to recover from World War I. Some of the men who had been hurt in that terrible war could not get jobs. They had to stand on the street corners selling flowers or fruit. Food and clothing were expensive. Most people had to work very hard just to keep food on the table.

Meanwhile, across the border from France, a man named Adolf Hitler had become the ruler of Germany. His country was also poor and weak; many people did not have jobs, and food was scarce in many places.

Hitler promised his country that he would make Germany great. He turned it into a military nation. He told the people that loyalty to the military leaders would save them from poverty.

Many people believed Hitler and joined his military movement. He even appointed men and women to start clubs for children, called Hitler Youth. The children in the Hitler Youth wore uniforms and learned about military life. They were taught to be physically fit and self-disciplined.

Hitler soon began to take back lands that had belonged to

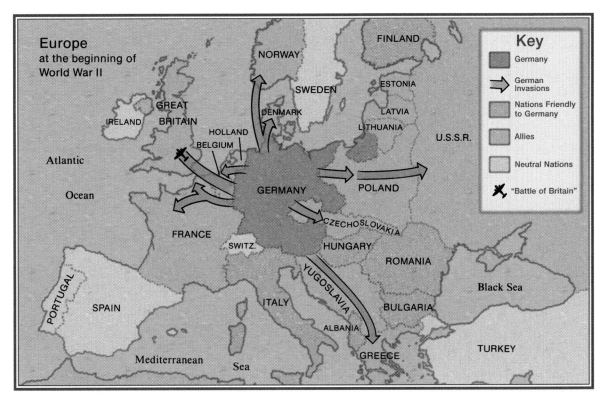

Key

Germany

German Invasions

Nations Friendly to Germany

Allies

Neutral Nations

"Battle of Britain"

FINLAND

NORWAY

SWEDEN

DENMARK

ESTONIA

LATVIA

LITHUANIA

U.S.S.R.

GREAT BRITAIN

IRELAND

HOLLAND

BELGIUM

Atlantic

Ocean

GERMANY

POLAND

FRANCE

SWITZ.

CZECHOSLOVAKIA

HUNGARY

ROMANIA

YUGOSLAVIA

Black Sea

PORTUGAL

SPAIN

ITALY

BULGARIA

ALBANIA

Mediterranean   Sea

GREECE

TURKEY

Germany in the past. He took part of Czechoslovakia. He put soldiers and ammunition along the border between Germany and France. Finally, he invaded Poland. The Polish people fought back and asked for help from the free countries. But at last they were conquered.

Leaders in France and England had not wanted to go to war. They knew that Hitler was making Germany a military nation. But they wanted all the countries of the world to stop making guns and ammunition. However, when Hitler invaded Poland, European leaders knew that they would

have to declare war on Germany or else Hitler would invade the rest of Europe too.

By that time it was too late for England and France to get ready for war. Germany was already fully prepared to fight. The Germans had thousands of soldiers, tanks, big guns, and fighter planes. They used armored vehicles that could move quickly into enemy territory and take over. These fast mobile units were called panzer units.

Germany invaded France in 1940. The French people in the north heard that the lightning-fast German panzer units were

coming. Quickly, the French people closest to danger packed their belongings and fled to the south. Many of these people were poor, so they had to walk, carrying whatever they could hold. These homeless people were called war refugees. The German planes traveled deep into France and attacked the refugees. The planes also bombed many of the quiet farms and villages.

The children of the refugees quickly learned what war meant. They faced starvation and death just as their parents did. Many of

them became orphans. They had to learn to survive.

France soon surrendered to Germany. Then the Germans took control of the French government. The refugees returned to their homes and tried to rebuild. But the Germans demanded food and valuables from France. Food grown in France was sent to feed German soldiers. Soon the French people did not have enough to eat.

The German-controlled French government started a process called rationing. Even if a French person had enough money to buy what he wanted, he could not buy farm products like eggs, vegetables, milk, and cheese. He needed a ration coupon. Only families with small children were given ration coupons for these items.

The people of France had to live through rationing and the hard German rule. But some French people were determined to be free again. Many secret resistance groups were started in France. The most famous group of all was the *Forces Francais d'Interieur,* or *F.F.I.* for short. This French name means "The Forces of the French Interior." The F.F.I. smuggled guns and ammunition into the country. It also spied on the Germans and reported German war plans to the British army. Sometimes the F.F.I. smuggled prisoners out of Germany.

The Germans suspected any French man or woman of being in the F.F.I. Because of this, many French children volunteered to help in the secret fight against Germany. A child could carry a piece of information in his pocket and walk right past a German soldier without even being noticed. After a while, the Germans realized what was going on. Some children were caught passing information for the F.F.I. They were punished just as if they were adults.

Finally, in 1945, America, Great Britain, and their allies defeated Germany. France was freed, but her government fell apart. The rationing and poverty continued in France for several years until the government became strong again. Only then could the French children return to childhood.

When the War Is Over

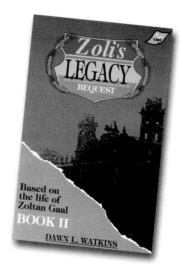

Adapted from Zoli's Legacy: Bequest
Dawn L. Watkins

Zoli Galambos, a young Hungarian, has been thrown out of his home for choosing to serve God. He arrives in the town where he once went to school to become the head of an orphanage.

A Little War of Wills
1937

Mrs. Toth gazed at me through the screen door of the orphanage.

"Yes?"

"Mrs. Toth, I'm Zoltán Galambos."

"Zoltán! I didn't know you. How you've changed! Come in. Please! Bring in your things!"

She swung open the door.

"My husband will be so happy to see you here already."

I set my books down by the threshold. I stepped inside the building that still smelled of fresh-cut lumber. Some of the windowsills were planed smooth but were yet unvarnished. The whole place was airy and clean.

I set down my parcel of books. "My baggage is all in."

She tilted her head. "Oh. Well, come along and let me find my husband. He has a thousand things lined up for you."

"Yes," I said.

"Zoltán!" The booming voice caught me just as a big hand closed over mine. Mr. Toth shook my hand vigorously.

Mrs. Toth said, "Let's show him to his quarters first." She leaned sideways toward me. "Once he gets to talking about the orphanage, you'll never get settled."

"Sure," said Toth. "Where are your things? I'll help you carry them up."

"I've only some books in the hall," I said.

We went into Komárom, and Mrs. Toth bought me a brand-new suit. I asked her whom I could pay back when I got the money, but she only waved her hand at me.

"The Lord provided," she said.

When the boys came from school that day, they had a new headmaster, all turned out in neat suit pants and a clean shirt.

Thirty boys, some as tall as I, rushed past me toward the upstairs. They threw down their schoolbooks by the stairs, yelling to each other and banging into each other.

"They're all yours," said Toth.

The kitchen vibrated with their shouts. Two women hurried to put down kettles on the table and lay out trays of bread. The boys plunged the dippers into the kettles and sloshed the stew into their bowls. The bread disappeared like snow in the April sun.

For a while, the shouting died into a slurping and jostling, and then it swelled again. The boys skidded back their benches. The spoons clanged into empty bowls and a few rattled onto the floor. The boys left in groups, twos and

The orphanage in Komárom, Hungary

threes and fours, and thundered up the stairs. I could hear them overhead, running and shouting.

The women began to take up the bowls and the glasses. I stood in the doorway, still expecting to find a reason for what had just gone on.

"Excuse me."

The women looked up.

"I'm Zoltán Galambos. I think I'm to be in charge here."

"Hello," said the older woman. "Everyone calls me Kis néni. The nanny. This is Greta."

"Let me help you," I said.

Kis néni nodded once and handed me a cloth.

"Is it always so noisy?" I asked.

"Yes," said Greta. "They run wild like pigs."

From the window I could see the boys playing soccer again, and some of the smaller ones wrestling on the sidelines.

"You are young," said Kis néni.

"That may come in handy," I said.

In the morning, before light, I heard tables being moved in the kitchen. I dressed quickly and went down.

"You're here early," I said.

Kis néni yawned and patted her mouth. She stood beside a lantern hanging by the wall. It still swung a little, and the shadows wavered back and forth around her.

An orphanage similar to Zoli's, but housing both boys and girls

"Yes," she said. "But much is to be done."

"What can I do to help?"

I tucked in my shirt and rolled up the sleeves.

"You could make sandwiches," she said. "The stuff is there." She pointed to a worktable by the sink. "And wrap each one in a paper. Here, I'll show you."

The first light began to come in the windows after perhaps the fifteenth sandwich. Upstairs no one had begun to stir.

"I'll call the boys," said Kis néni, "or do you want to?"

I went upstairs and down the hall, throwing doors open as I went and bellowing.

"Up, boys. The day's got the jump on you. Let's go!"

"Who are you?" The voice came from the dim lower bunk in the last room.

"The new headmaster."

The boy rolled out and stood up.

"Any boy not down in fifteen minutes is out of his breakfast."

Toth arrived amid the charge for the tables. Above the clamor of breakfast, he banged the sink with a metal ladle. All heads turned his way.

"Good morning, fellows."

"Good morning." The response was jumbled and feeble.

"This is Zoltán Galambos. He has come to be the headmaster here."

Thirty pairs of eyes looked me over.

He laughed his hearty laugh, too big for the small hour, I thought.

"Don't think you can slip anything by him, boys. He's an old hand at this."

In a while, the racket rose to its old level.

"I have been walking them to the school. But I expect you know where it is, yes?" said Toth to me.

I nodded and surveyed the company I would have.

The walk was not long, but I could see the wisdom of having a sheepdog herd the sheep toward the Gymnásium. The older boys made a sport of hijacking the younger ones for their sandwiches. And the younger ones had to be prodded to keep going toward their own school. Shirttails hung out from waistbands at every angle, and not one head of hair looked sufficiently combed. But the shoes, I noticed, were all shined.

"Mr. Galambos?"

I looked at the boy beside me. "Hello."

"You don't remember me, but I used to call you Zoli bacsi. A long time ago, up in Farna."

The face joggled something way back in my mind. Uncle Zoli, he called me.

"I'm Dani."

I suddenly remembered this face, smaller and fearful, looking to me for help. Four years before, my friend "Bootblack" and I had helped Toth at an orphanage in another town. I felt a pang at realizing Dani was still an orphan, still waiting to be wanted.

"Why sure," I said. "I hardly knew you. You're so big. What are you now? Nine?"

"Yes, sir."

He said nothing more, but just as before, he walked beside me, his chin tucked slightly, asking by his posture to stay with me.

I dispatched the older boys to the school lane I knew well. A little way on, I said good-bye to the younger fellows. I felt embarrassed at their ragged collars and their thin pants. A few waved to me, and I, but an older version of them, waved back.

At the orphanage upstairs, Kis néni and Greta were making beds. The hall had been swept

Zoli at the age he took over the orphanage

as far as the room they were in, the brooms resting against the doorjamb. The two women lifted the mattress together and snapped the sheet under it, and in the same motion, pulled the top of the sheet to the pillow. The washbasins were dry, the pitchers empty. I lifted the towel on the stand. It was dry as well.

"Kis néni," I said, "has everything been going about as usual around here? Last night and today, I mean?"

She straightened up from thumping a pillow into place.

"Pretty much."

"You always make the beds?"

"Sure."

She stared at me for a moment and then went past me and took up the sheets and broom.

"Let me carry that stuff," I said.

That afternoon when the boys came tearing in from school, I met them at the stairs. I stood three steps up, leaning on the rail.

They halted at the bottom and milled in the lobby.

"Good afternoon, gentlemen."

A couple of the smaller boys answered me.

I came down a step.

"I'm glad to see you home."

Still they said nothing.

"I've been just looking around," I said, "seeing how things go around here. And I've noticed a job or two that needs a man, but I haven't the time. I thought I might look over this group here and see if I could find a suitable worker."

"What jobs?" one of the tallest boys said.

"Well, for starters, splitting wood and carrying water."

"Mr. Toth did that," said a boy with wavy black hair.

I ignored the rustle among the troops.

"And shining shoes."

"Ahh," the first boy said.

I sat down on the second stair. "Kis néni does that now, doesn't she? Every night while you sleep.

Well. That's no job for women. They haven't got the arm for it. A man can get a real shine on leather when he wants to."

I slid my foot out and leaned back on the third stair. A few eyes went down to my gleaming shoe and back to me.

"But," I said, "maybe there's no one here to do it but me."

There was no volunteer, but neither were there any deserters.

"And," I said, "men have to learn to look after themselves. Kis néni and Mrs. Greta won't always be around. What I like is independence. Don't you?"

I waited. At last, Dani spoke up.

"I'll do it, sir."

A bigger boy said, "You? It'll take you a week to learn how."

The tallest of them spoke again. "Can't you idiots see what he's doing? He's tricking you into doing his work."

I stood up slowly and glowered down on him. "No, boy, I'm trying to trick you into doing your own work. But if you won't be coaxed, there are other methods."

By the end of the next week, there was a new order at the Komárom orphanage. Every boy made his own bed and carried his own plate to the sink after meals. The shining of shoes and the splitting of wood were rotated among the privileged older few. Younger boys watched as though from the sidelines of a soccer game and begged for something important to do.

"Please, Zoli bacsi," they said, "we'll do a good job."

"Well, I don't know," I said. I rubbed the back of my neck. "This sweeping is tricky."

"Show us how," they said.

I drew my hand across my chin as if in deep thought. "I guess we could try it for a week. But if it starts to look shabby in here, I'll have to take the job back myself."

I did not have to take the job back.

Every night after supper, I read from the Bible. At first I chose verses from the Proverbs about the value of hard work and obedience. I watched the faces, some smooth with innocence, some already cloudy with bitterness and rebellion. The tallest boy, Gab, had eyes like stones. His chin jutted out in constant defiance of all the world.

"Now," I said, closing the Bible, "I think we should talk about homework. I haven't seen any being done around here. Surely you all have some."

"No," said Gab, "they don't give orphans homework because they don't have homes to work it in."

The boys looked to me with wide eyes, expecting perhaps a sermon or punishment for Gab. Gab balanced his chair on the two back legs.

"Boys," I said, "when your parents died, God gave you many mothers and fathers in their stead. You have Mrs. Greta and Kis néni and Pastor and Mrs. Toth and me. And as your papa, I'm asking you, where is your homework?"

Gab's chair slammed down. "You are not my father!"

"Suit yourself. But where is your homework?"

His eyes blazed at me.

"Get it or I go with you to the Gymnásium tomorrow."

The other boys looked at him cautiously. He finally stood and cast his chair backward and strode out. The others looked again to me, waiting.

"From now on," I said, "you will do your homework and show it to me."

The eyes went down to the tables and plates.

"You have to learn to work. Knowing how to work makes you enjoy your life. Don't you want the pleasure of being able to do many kinds of things?"

"Yes." The replies put all together made but a feeble response.

Gab returned and threw the notebook down in front of me so that it spun to a stop just beside my hand. "Very good. Now I'm going to put a note to the teacher here, asking him to write the assignment out so that I can check on it."

Kis néni smiled over from her chair by the stove and nodded.

"And before you do any chores tonight, I want to see everyone's notebook. And if you don't have a notebook, we'll send a piece of paper to your teacher."

I gave Gab his book, looking at him directly.

"The rest of you can go," I said. "Bring me your notebooks."

They piled out of the kitchen. I had not taken my eyes from Gab.

"Gab, the handwriting in this book is terrible. Now, I know you can do better. I suspect you are the smartest boy in your class. Why do you make an effort to hide it?"

"You think you know all about it, don't you?"

"More than you think," I said.

"What do you care about my handwriting?"

"I care about your handwriting because I care about you. If you have the right heart, you'll have a better hand. Laziness has many witnesses."

He shoved away from the wall he had been leaning on and, looking at me as he might at a growling dog, went out.

Kis néni said, "You're not as young as you look."

Seven years later, Zoli is still running the orphanage.
He is married now with two sons. Throughout World War II
Zoli has been an officer in the reserve army.

Riding Out World War II
April 1944

"A major to see you, sir."

I nodded and stood up. My desk was strewn with papers, by which I was trying to stretch short rations and medicine further than they would go.

The major was Bootblack, my friend from school days.

I saluted the rank and took the hand of my friend.

Zoli and Ilona on their wedding day

Ilona (right) before she was married

Bootblack said, "How's Ilona— and Henrik?"

"They're well." I motioned to a chair. "Henrik has a brother since you were here last. Kalman."

He smiled widely and shook my hand again. Then he sat down, and I followed his lead.

He passed his hand over his mouth and then dropped his hands, gripping his knees.

"I am here officially to order you to take the reserves out of Komárom immediately."

"The war is over then."

He sighed. "The Germans are retreating. The Russians are advancing. They will occupy Hungary within the week."

"Where do we go?"

"Try to get the supply unit west to Austria or Germany. Take what supplies you can. Don't leave anything for the Russians. Burn stuff, if you have to."

"How long do I have to move out?"

"Three days. Advise the citizens to get out as well. But you can't take the time to force them."

He was standing again.

"Can I take Ilona with me?"

"Your privilege, Zoli. Do what you think best there. Move at night as much as you can. The Russian airplanes are always overhead."

* * *

Ilona's face was white. She held Kalman asleep in her arms.

"Henrik," I said, "come sit down."

He came and stood by his mother. The boys were there, waiting with sober faces. Gab and eight others had already left to join the army. But twenty-one were still in my charge.

"We have to evacuate the city," I told them. "I have to go with the reserves. But Pastor Toth will be here in the morning to take you with him or find you a place to stay."

Destruction of war in Eastern Europe

A little boy, about eight, put his head on his knees and sobbed. Ilona went to sit beside him and stroked his hair.

"Any of you who are sixteen," I hesitated and then went on, "can do what you will."

"Can't we go with you, Zoli bacsi?" said Dani.

I shook my head. "I'm sorry. I can't take you."

He looked as though he might cry as well.

"I love you, boys, but God loves you more. And I must trust Him to look after you. I want you to trust Him too."

* * *

"Where are we?" Henrik asked.

He sat in the front of the wagon.

I reined Alexander near.

"Somewhere west of Bratislava, I think," I said.

We made such little headway, traveling slowly in the dark, hiding in the woods all day. Two months of this dodging, and still no Hungarian fighting units had appeared.

I held Alexander in and let the next wagon come abreast of me.

The driver said. "Yes, sir?"

"I'm going to take a blanket off the wagon and ride to that farm over there and see if I can make a trade for our breakfast."

He nodded.

"Keep moving. I'll catch up with you."

The farmer's wife gladly parted with some eggs and milk for the heavy wool blanket. It hardly would feed twenty-seven men and my family. But it was the best deal I could make.

There was another farmhouse in the distance. I could still see the wagons to the left. I turned Alexander to the house. A stout woman there looked me up and down.

"What do I want with eggs?" she said. "I have chickens myself."

"Please," I said, "I have children with me."

"No soldier has children with him."

"If I bring my son here, will you believe me?"

"I might."

I looked at the sky. The sun was nearly full up.

My assistant, Pataki, took the eggs gingerly, and then the milk. I reached for Henrik, and he came flying. He took his place in front of me and grabbed into the mane.

"Let's go, Papa."

"Pull off in that woods over there," I told Pataki. "We won't be long."

Alexander snorted to a halt in the farmyard. The woman leaned out the window.

"Well, I'll be," she said.

"Hello," said Henrik. His blond hair shone in the early sun.

"Hello yourself."

He laughed. "Papa and I rode over from the wagon. Alexander is one good horse."

She came out of the house then and up to Henrik. She looked at me. "I might have some extra around here," she said.

She returned with a sack of bread and vegetables and cheese.

I offered her money.

"What good does that do anybody? Just see this little one gets out of this."

Evacuating a city

Zoli and his men were stopped by American soldiers but were released because the war was nearly over. Zoli and his family go home to Hungary where Dani has been waiting for them near the old orphanage. But the Russians are taking Hungary by force, and once again Zoli must flee an enemy. He, Ilona, their sons, and Dani pretend to have a picnic near the Austrian border. Then they must decide if they will make a run for freedom through a farmer's fields.

A Run for Freedom
1947

The corn rustled around us. I gathered Ilona, Henrik, Kalman, and Dani to me.

"I love you," I said to them. "Remember that."

We started down the rows, planted so as to lead those who dared to freedom.

"Just keep walking straight down the corn rows. Follow the row, Henrik."

I picked Kalman up and carried him.

The lifeless stalks rattled in the rain and with our passing. The darkness deepened. The searchlights from the guard towers at the end of the field switched on and passed over the corn.

"Papa, look at the lights!"

Zoli and his family escaped through a field like this.

"Shhh."

"Why?"

"Shhh."

The lights came over us and we froze. The white beams flowed on by, and we moved again. The rain was like silver needles in the lights.

Water ran down my face, down inside my shirt. Dani, a gray movement just two rows over, held his hand over his eyes to block the flow. My heart pounded now—not from the walking, but from the last terror I had not told them of.

The leaves of the corn scraped by my face, rasped on my ears. Kalman fell asleep on my shoulder.

Suddenly I was aware that Henrik was not beside me.

"Stop!"

I thrust Kalman into Ilona's arms. I started back through the row, looking with more than normal sight into that black and muddy world.

"Henrik!"

I ran then, beating the stalks away from me.

"Son!"

Between my gasps for air, I heard, "Papa, Papa."

I went across the rows toward the sound.

"Henrik! Call to me!"

Suddenly he was ahead of me, running toward the station again. I overran him and grabbed him.

"Henrik, what are you doing?"

"Oh, Papa," he said, "I was running after you!"

I held him to me until thought I would crush him. "You got turned around, son."

"I fell, Papa."

His tears were heavier than the rain.

"It's all right now. Papa found you. Papa found you."

We went on again. I carried Kalman and held Henrik's hand. At last the corn thinned out, and we were at the edge of a great plowed field. On the other side was the wire—the flimsy, terrible border.

We crouched in the corn. They waited for me to speak. The rain drove down on us, splattering and rattling on the stalks. When the lights passed over a second time, I drew in a deep breath.

"Some borders have land mines. Some don't."

There was no answer from anyone. Finally, Ilona's voice came to me, hardly above the noise of the rain.

"How do we know?"

"We don't."

Again there was no speaking.

At last Dani said, "As God wills, I say."

"Yes," said Ilona.

I felt for their hands, one then the other.

"When I say to go, we all go together. Henrik, do you understand?"

"Yes, Papa."

Dani said, "I've got him."

The rain was pounding now. We were soaked, the water running into our shoes. The army kept the ground plowed smooth, to look for footprints, but I was sure this rain would take our secret to the streams.

I watched for the lights to pass once more.

"Now!"

We ran. The mud caked to our shoes and our legs, slowing us down. Ilona struggled, and I took her by the arm and lifted her. The lights arced on the far end of the field and started back for us. We were but seconds from the border.

"God," I cried out, "help us!"

The lights swept through again, but this time we were behind their range. We were over the wire, all of us.

I dropped to my knees in the Austrian soil, holding my sons to me. And in the pouring rain, I wept.

The Gaal family in America

Encyclopedias

The word *encyclopedia* literally means "many feet." A person has to "walk through" all the sciences to know everything. Ancient scholars thought that anything encyclopedic would contain all knowledge. Today, books that provide general information are called encyclopedias. Most encyclopedias list their information alphabetically.

• Using a Keyword

You might want to learn more about the war that changed the lives of the children in "When the War Is Over." An encyclopedia could help you. First you would have to decide what keywords to use. You might try *World War II* or *Hungary*. The letter on the spine of each volume tells the part of the alphabet that it contains. *World War II* would be in the *W* volume.

• Using Titles and Subtitles

Some subjects are so broad that encyclopedia writers organize them with subtitles. Usually major subtitles appear in the center of the column or are capitalized. Minor subtitles are usually in dark print, but they are of normal size and are not centered.

• Using Illustrations and Captions

Illustrations give you an idea of how a certain person, place, or event looked. The sentence underneath an illustration is called the caption. It explains what is going on in the picture. Captions provide an idea of what the article will cover. A careful reader can skim through an encyclopedia article by reading the captions.

• Using Computers

Computers offer a quick and easy way to access information. Once you load your program, you can type in your keyword. This will take you to the encyclopedia article. The article may offer a variety of media-pictures, sounds, or videos relating to the topic. Also,

Back   **Forward**   **Stop**   **Search**   **Tools**   **Print**

Address: | www.WWII.edu

The Axis Powers

Leaders of the *Axis*. Tojo of Japan (left) and
Hitler of Germany with Mussolini of Italy (right).

World War II
Formation of the Axis

The *Axis* was the name given to a group of nations that banded together during World War II. In 1936, Germany and Italy agreed to support each other's foreign policy. They called their alliance the Rome-Berlin Axis. When Japan signed on in 1940, the alliance was known as the Rome-Berlin-Tokyo Axis. Eventually, six other nations joined, bringing the total to nine. The complete list included Albania, Bulgaria, Finland, Hungary, Romania, and Thailand.

Political Reasons—The governments in the Axis were military dictatorships. The nations who joined faced similar problems after World War I: people were hungry, their homes were destroyed, and money was scarce. Politicians saw that people felt hopeless and insecure. In these nations there had never been a democracy. People looked to government to meet their needs. Dictators promised to provide a stable government and a return to prosperity. When dictators seized power, they used secret police and brute force to silence any protests. During the 1930s, Hitler in Germany,

Mussolini in Italy, and Tojo in Japan, convinced their nations that they must conquer more land. They chose weaker countries to invade. The people of Germany, Italy, and Japan had been taught that building a strong military was the only way for their countries to survive.

Historic and Economic Reasons—At the end of World War I, officials from the victorious nations met in Paris in 1919 to write treaties for the defeated nations. The many treaties were called the Peace of Paris. As part of the agreement, Germany was forced to accept blame for starting the war and was required to make reparations (payments for war damages). As a result, the nation was deeply in debt, and the German people resented the provisions of the peace plan. Thousands of German citizens rallied behind the radical, nationalistic Nazi Party and its leader, Adolph Hitler. Under Hitler, Germans hoped to regain their national honor and leadership.

Nationalism (devotion to the interests of a nation or culture) was also growing among the

next

keywords in the article may be highlighted. By clicking on them, you will be able to access corresponding articles.

If you have Internet access, your encyclopedia software may

have a Web link to take you to related information on the Web. Some companies offer an online encyclopedia. This would give you current information about your topic.

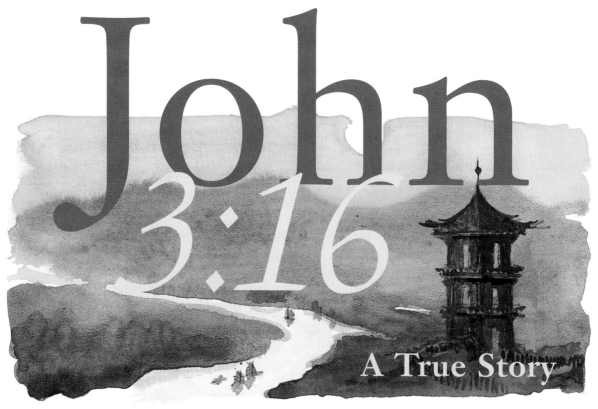

John 3:16

A True Story

Milly Howard
illustrated by Roger Bruckner

A biography of Gladys Aylward, These Are My People, *written by the author of this story, ended as the English missionary escaped from a war-torn area of China with many Chinese children. This is the story of an experience that Gladys had later in her life.*

A Place on the Map

Gladys Aylward got out of bed and pulled on her robe. Quietly she walked to the doorway and stood still, listening. There again was the sound that had awakened her. She moved slowly down the hall and stopped at an open door. Inside, a group of fifteen Chinese students knelt around a map. The sound of praying had awakened Gladys.

Gladys waited as student after student prayed for a town or village on the map. When the meeting was over, she approached the leader of the group.

Softly they began an old hymn. Then their voices became stronger as the words rolled out into the clear mountain air. When the notes faded away, they began another song. Suddenly Dr. Huang stopped.

"There he is!" he shouted.

"What? Who?" Gladys peered into the dusty distance.

But Dr. Huang had already raced off down the path and was soon out of sight. Gladys sat on her pack, feeling very alone in the sudden silence.

Finally she saw two tiny figures moving toward her across the rocks. She shaded her eyes. As

John 3:16—A True Story   219

they came closer, she recognized Dr. Huang. The two figures stopped above her, and she realized they were on a higher trail.

"Come up here," Dr. Huang called. "This is the man!"

Gladys looked at the steep, rocky slope and shook her head. "I can't," she said. "I'm too tired."

Dr. Huang scrambled down the slope. When he reached Gladys, he said, "Leave the packs here. I'll help you up."

Together they struggled up to the other trail. A Tibetan lama, or monk, was waiting. He stood patiently beside a large rock.

Gladys stared. "Did you tell him I was a woman?"

she asked, knowing that the monks had nothing to do with women.

Dr. Huang nodded. "Yes, but he still invited us to spend the night in the lamasery."

"Me? In a lamasery?" Gladys hesitated. "Why would they invite a woman into their sacred building?"

Suddenly the monk spoke. His accent was strange, but Gladys could understand him. "We have waited a long time to hear about the God who loves."

The God Who Loves

Without another word, Gladys followed the two men. They crossed the mountain ridge, and Gladys gasped in amazement. The other side of the barren mountain they had been climbing was lush and green. Thick grass grew along the slopes, and water ran over the rocks. Brightly flowered vines drooped from the walls of a beautiful temple on the crest of a slope.

Gladys and Dr. Huang followed the monk down a trail to the temple gates. As the huge carved gates closed behind them, Gladys stared in amazement. They were standing in a large courtyard. Sunlight patterned the cool shadows of the courtyard and gleamed off golden statues in recesses along the walls. A movement in the shadows caught Gladys's attention. A group of yellow-clad lamas came forward and bowed. They led Gladys and Dr. Huang to rooms that had been prepared for them. Gladys rested comfortably on tiger rugs and silk cushions as water and dish after dish of delicious food were brought to her.

Later, two monks escorted Gladys and Dr. Huang through several courtyards to a large room near the center of the lamasery. Nearly five hundred lamas were seated there in half circles. Gladys and Dr. Huang were taken to the front.

"Whatever shall we do?" Gladys whispered.

"You must sing," Dr. Huang said.

Gladys began to sing.

When she finished, there was a deathly silence. She looked at Dr. Huang.

Dr. Huang stood up and began to speak. He told about the birth of Jesus, of His life, and how He died on the cross at Calvary.

Gladys sang again, and then she talked. When she finished, Dr. Huang spoke again. Gladys sang another song and talked; then it was Dr. Huang's turn. And so it went.

Gladys couldn't see the faces of the lamas. The silence was unbroken except for the sound of Dr. Huang's voice as he spoke. Finally Gladys said, "I must rest. I'm afraid I'm going to fall off this seat."

"Then we will finish," said Dr. Huang. They rose and walked straight out into the hall. Behind them they heard the first sounds of movement since they had entered the room.

They reached their rooms, and a tired Gladys began to prepare for bed. A knock sounded at the door. When she opened it, two monks stood outside. "Woman, are you too tired to tell us more?"

"Are you allowed to enter?" Gladys asked.

"If there are two of us," they answered.

"Then come in."

Far into the night more lamas kept on coming. They sat around the room, listening. They accepted without question God's creation of the world, the virgin birth, the miracles. It was God's love that amazed them. Over and over they asked to be told about Calvary.

Gladys and Dr. Huang stayed for a week, answering questions. On the last day of their visit, Gladys was taken before the head lama. She sat on a stool beside him and listened as he told her his story.

"For many years," he explained, "the monks of this lamasery have collected an herb that grows on the mountainside. The herb is much desired in the cities and has always brought a good price. Some years ago, after the herb had been harvested and dried, it was taken to the city as usual. As the monks passed through a village on the way, a

man stood on the side of the road waving a piece of paper."

"Curious, a monk stopped and took the piece of paper. He tucked it inside his robe and brought it back after the herbs had been sold."

The lama interrupted his story and pointed to a worn piece of paper stuck on the wall behind him. Leaning closer, Gladys saw an ordinary tract on which was written in Chinese the words of John 3:16: "For God so loved the world that he gave his only begotten Son, that whosoever believeth in him should not perish but have everlasting life."

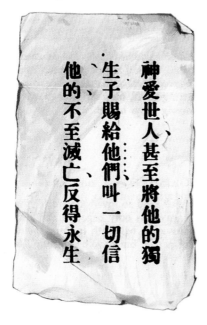

"The God who loves . . ." Gladys murmured softly.

The lama nodded. "Yes," he said as he continued his story. "When we sent the herbs to be sold the next year, the men were instructed to find out more about the God who loved the world, but for five years they heard nothing. Finally, one year they decided to keep going until they found someone who could tell them more about this God. When they reached the city of Len Chow, their persistence was rewarded. They found a man who told them to go to the building that had 'Faith, Hope, and Charity' carved above the door. In that building they found someone who told them more and gave them the four Gospels, Matthew, Mark, Luke, and John.

"The men hurried back to share their news. Eagerly we read the Gospels and believed what we read. However, there was much that was not clear to us. Over and over we read the verse, 'Go ye into all the world and preach the gospel.'

"At last we realized all we had to do was wait. This God would send a messenger to tell us more. So for another three years we waited.

"Last week two of our lamas were out on the hillside, gathering sticks. They heard you sing. Believing that only those who know God will sing as you did, they knew that God's messengers had arrived. One hurried back to the lamasery with the news of your arrival, and we began preparations for you as our guests. The other hurried down to meet you and bring you back to us."

Gladys listened to the end of the story in awe of God's power, knowing she was listening to an account of the working of the Holy Spirit. "Truly, Lord," she thought as she remembered the tracts, the mission, and the young

Christians who had been so faithful in their prayers, "it is as Paul said, 'I have planted, Apollos watered; but God gave the increase'!"

Gladys and Dr. Huang began their long trip back, enriched in mind and spirit. Years later, Gladys learned that the Communists had destroyed the lamasery and driven the lamas away. She never discovered what happened to those five hundred lamas. Gladys trusted the Lord, knowing that He could finish what He had begun in His own way, in His own time.

unit **4**

CREATURES

Cat

Mary Britton Miller
illustrated by Mary Ann Lumm

The black cat yawns,
Opens her jaws,
Stretches her legs,
And shows her claws.

Then she gets up
And stands on four
Long stiff legs
And yawns some more.

She shows her sharp teeth,
She stretches her lip,
Her slice of a tongue
Turns up at the tip.

Lifting herself
On her delicate toes,
She arches her back
As high as it goes.

She lets herself down
With particular care,
And pads away
With her tail in the air.

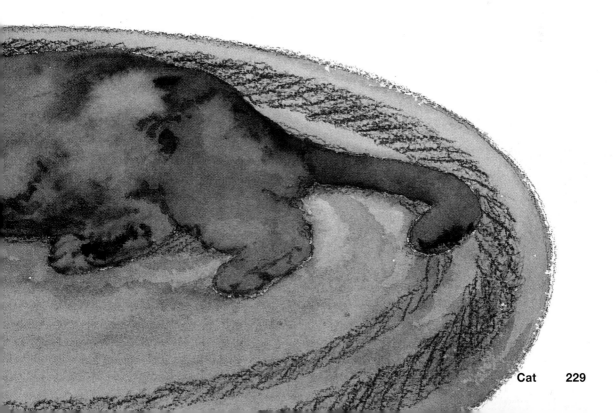

Dick Whittington and His Cat

adapted by Karen Wilt

*illustrated by Dana Thompson
and Dyke Habeggar*

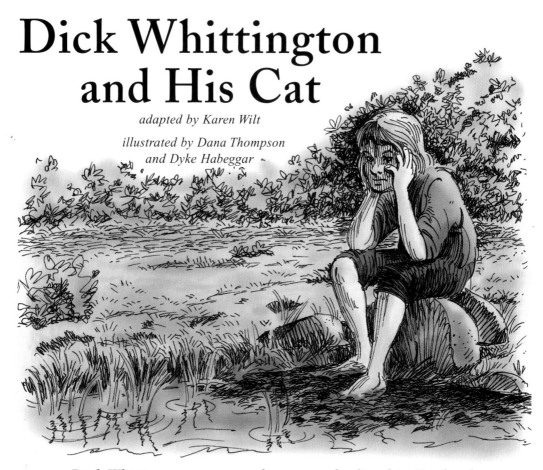

Dick Whittington was a real person who lived in England during the fourteenth century. He started out as a poor boy and then earned an education and wealth for himself. He was Lord Mayor of London three times. The people loved him, and many stories sprang up about his rise to fortune. The following story is a folktale from England about Dick Whittington. Today it is a popular story throughout the English-speaking world.

To Find a Fortune

Dick Whittington dunked his blistered feet in the cool mud along the banks of the Thames River. His stomach growled at him, but his tattered pocket didn't have even a crumb of bread left from the crust he had saved and eaten for breakfast.

"A job is what I need," he muttered. "But who would hire a starving urchin like me?"

He shuffled through the thin grass along the shore until most of the mud had wiped off, though some of it stuck and dried.

He remembered the words of the muffin man in Colchester. "London streets are built of gold brick," he had exaggerated. "The windows are cut diamonds. And no one goes hungry there."

"Then I'm off to London to find my fortune," Dick had said.

But the horses and carriages riding out of London didn't boast the riches the muffin man had told of. Dick Whittington had begun to wonder.

Now he walked under London Bridge, tired and hungry. Buildings towered above him. Bells in church spires rang. People hurried by, nearly trampling the boy in their haste.

At last Dick Whittington collapsed on a doorstep. He rested his whirling head on the smooth marble bannister.

"Off with you," a red-faced maid said, opening the door and brandishing a wet mop in Dick's direction.

"And where should I be off to?" he asked.

The maid leaned against her mop and sighed. "No mum or dad?" she asked.

"Both killed by the Plague."

"For shame," the maid said. "Well, come in. Me master is looking for a boy, but you're more than a bit scrawny."

"Oh, but I'll grow. I know I will. My dad was a great giant of a man, and everyone says I'm exactly like he was."

The maid squinted her eyes. "Sure, but giants eat a lot, and such as that we can't be feeding."

"But that's what we were saying; I'm just a scrawny bit of a lad."

The maid burst into a fit of laughter, turning her face an even brighter shade of red. "Such a wit as you've got is just what we may be needing in a solemn house as we have."

And so Dick Whittington became the errand boy for Merchant Lockharte. From morning till evening he ran about London, buying this, or ordering that, delivering messages, or doing whatever the merchant required.

Life would have been more than enjoyable except for two small problems. One was Alice, the merchant's beautiful daughter. Alice made Dick stutter whenever she bid him good day and made him blush to the roots of his hair whenever she glanced his way from under her long, black eyelashes. His heart turned somersaults whenever she smiled her two-dimpled smile.

The other problem was the attic where he slept. It had rats.

Every night the rats raced beneath his cot and chewed the corners of his blanket as he slept.

Dick took care of the rat problem. On the day Merchant Lockharte paid him his first penny, he hurried to the market and bought a fine cat. This cat was no ordinary mouser. It had six toes on each paw, weighed at least twenty-five pounds, and had eyes that could spot a flea on the tip of a mouse's ear.

Every night the mouser caught two fat rats and left them outside the doorsteps to show his master what a fine job he could do. Dick Whittington grew very fond of the cat and even let him follow him as he ran errands. The cat pleased Alice too. She combed the mouser's fur until it shone, and Dick could hear him purr for her.

"If I weren't just a pauper, I should some day ask for her hand in marriage," he thought to himself.

Best Mouser in London

One day Dick brought the message of the return of Merchant Lockharte's ship to port. Merchant Lockharte clasped Dick's hand. "Good news, indeed, lad," he said. " 'Twill be the making of riches for me this year." Then he rubbed his hands. " 'Twas the quickest passage she's ever made. I'll have her outfitted and ready to leave port again in less than a month. Dick, my boy, 'tis good news indeed. And you shall be rewarded." He scratched his head. "How would you like to send something on my next ship to Barbary? Do you have anything of value?"

Dick's eyes grew wide. Then his look of excitement changed to a look of disappointment. "The only thing I own is my cat," he said. "He's the best mouser in London, but I'm afraid he's of no true value."

Merchant Lockharte shook his head. "No, a cat has little value, but we'll send him and see."

Dick trudged home, dragging his heels. His cat lay on the stone wall that surrounded Merchant

Lockharte's house. Alice skipped rope inside the gate. Just then the bells in the church spires began to ring, and Alice sang and jumped to their rhythm, smiling at Dick.

"Turn again, Whittington,
Lord Mayor of London."

Her eyes were teasing. Dick felt his face grow warm. He knew he was blushing.

He picked up his cat and trudged to his attic room. "Oh, I

wish I could tell you to behave yourself in Barbary," Dick said.

The cat rubbed his head against Dick's chin.

"If ever I can, I'll come visit you there," he said.

The cat started to purr.

"Oh, I'll miss you, you old cat," Dick said, and he buried his head in the cat's thick fur.

The next day Dick watched the ship sail down the Thames and out of sight. The captain's boy had promised to care for the cat. All the sailors had admired his six-toed feet. They had gasped at his weight, all twenty-five pounds, when they had lifted him on board. And they saw from the shine in his eyes that he truly was a good mouser.

The months passed slowly. Dick had been to the market to search for another mouser, but none matched his old cat. Still Alice teased him and sang:

"Turn again, Whittington,
Lord Mayor of London."

Dick blushed, but no quick wit came to his head to return to her. He knew he would never have enough money to marry Alice and care for her as a good husband must.

Then one rainy morning Dick could bear it no more. He packed his meager belongings in a scrap of material and slung it over his shoulder. London was no city of riches for him to find fortune in.

Slowly his feet carried him out the door and down the cobblestone streets. Great London Bridge loomed over the Thames River. Dick remembered the day he had squished his toes in mud. A flock of ravens flew by, and their dark feathers reminded him of Alice's long black curls and her teasing eyes under long, black eyelashes. The bells in the church spires began to ring, just as Dick had heard them ring that first day in London. But this time, maybe because he was thinking of Alice, or maybe because he had left without eating breakfast, they seemed to say,

"Turn again, Whittington, Lord Mayor of London."

Dick heard it again as the bells pealed out the hours across London town. Slowly his feet turned around, and Dick found himself walking back. The fog had lifted as he crossed London Bridge again, past churches and looming buildings, down the cobblestone to the marble doorstep of Merchant Lockharte's. As he reached the bottom step, the door flew open and Alice and her father dashed out.

"Dick, my boy, where have you been?" Merchant Lockharte asked. "You have just become a rich man."

Dick blinked his eyes. "Me?" he asked.

The merchant thumped him on the back. "Yes, Dick. It seems the royal palace of Barbary was infested with rats. The captain of my ship sold your cat for a king's ransom."

Alice smiled from behind her long, black eyelashes, and her dimples laughed at Dick.

Dick smiled back. "I knew he was the best mouser in all of London," he said.

Can You Tell the Difference?

Marilyn Elmer
illustrated by Paula Cheadle

"Mom, look at the butterfly I just caught. It was flying around the porch light. I'm going to find out what kind it is."

Cindy was making an insect collection, and this was the largest insect she had caught so far. A few minutes later she returned to her mother and said, "This isn't a butterfly at all. It's a moth—a cecropia moth. But it does look like a butterfly, doesn't it?"

Have you ever had an experience like Cindy's? Do you ever get the names of certain animals mixed up because the creatures are so much alike?

Moth

Antennae: *Moth (left), Butterfly (right)*

Take the butterfly and the moth, for example. They are both insects with velvety wings. They both go through four life stages: egg, larva, pupa, and adult. But they are different in several ways. The butterfly's body is slender, while the moth's body is fat and soft. The butterfly's antennae are like threads with little knobs on the ends. But the moth's antennae are feathery and do not have knobs. Butterflies normally fly in the daytime, whereas moths are active at night. These two insects rest in different positions, too. Butterflies fold their wings together while resting, but moths spread their wings wide open.

Butterfly

Alligator

Two other animals that are often mistaken for each other are the alligator and the crocodile. Both of them are reptiles, and both of them have tough, bumpy skin and webbed feet. They both live in tropical regions where the water stays warm all year.

The best way to tell these two animals apart is to look at their heads. The one with the broader head is the alligator. It also has a rounded snout. The crocodile's snout is quite pointed. There is another difference, but you may not want to get close enough to check it. The fourth tooth of the lower jaw of a crocodile fits into a groove on the side of the upper jaw. This tooth arrangement makes the crocodile seem to smile.

Crocodile

Toad

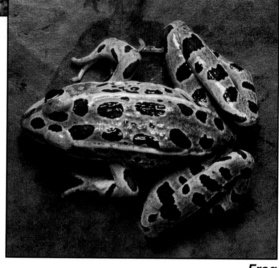

Frog

Here is another pair of creatures that some people confuse—toads and frogs. Both are cold-blooded, and both are about the same size. They both jump, and they both hatch from eggs as tadpoles. But they are different. Put them next to each other and do some comparing. One has dry, rough skin. That's the toad. The frog is smooth and moist. One is broader and flatter and has a darker color. That's the toad again. Most frogs are more slender than toads.

If you have ever seen toads' or frogs' eggs, you will be able to recognize another difference. Toads lay eggs in long strings that look something like chains in the water. Frogs' eggs form jellylike clumps as they are laid.

There is one more difference between these animals. Frogs always live close to water. Toads can live anywhere as long as they can get to water to lay their eggs.

Some people think that monkeys and chimpanzees are the same, but they are not. There are

Chimpanzee

Monkey

If there is no tail, it is a chimp. Also, monkeys' arms are generally shorter than their legs, but chimps' arms are longer than their legs.

When it comes to the duck and the goose, you can hear one difference. Ducks quack, but geese honk or hiss. These birds look just a little bit different too. Ducks have short necks and large, flat bills. Geese have long necks and pointed bills.

several ways to tell these animals apart, but perhaps the easiest way is to look for a tail. If you can see a tail, you are looking at a monkey.

Goose

Duck

Dolphins

Some people use the names *dolphin* and *porpoise* interchangeably, but it is possible to tell the difference. One of the quickest ways to tell is by looking at the snout. A porpoise's snout is short and round. But a dolphin's snout is long and looks a little bit like a beak on the end. The trained animals in shows at aquariums are usually bottle-nose dolphins.

Cindy watched her new moth resting on a leaf inside her jar. "I'm glad God made this moth just the way He did," she said. "Aren't its wings beautiful?"

Mom peered into the jar. "God made everything with a wise, perfect plan in mind," she said. She put her arm around Cindy. "Including you."

Ingersoll

Gail Fitzgerald
illustrated by Tim Davis
and Noelle Snyder

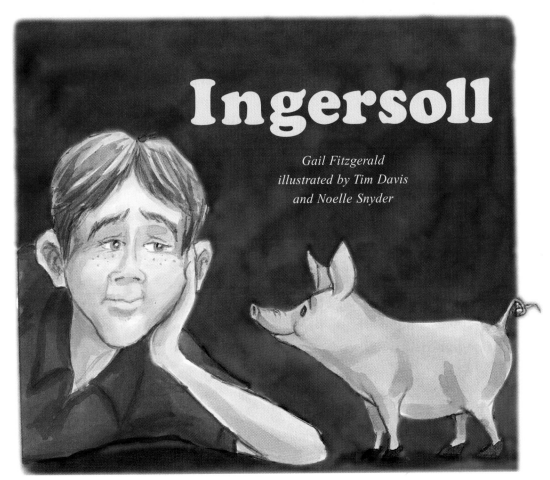

Pint-sized Pig

Believe me, it certainly wasn't my idea. I am not, by any stretch of the imagination, an animal lover. My mother assures me I came into this family by birth. But I'm convinced I must have been adopted. You'll understand when I tell you about my family.

My father grew up on a farm and is constantly talking about the good old days of horses, mules, chickens, and geese. My mother has four cages of birds on the sun porch, a turtle over the kitchen sink, and a little black "mop" named Fifi. My brother's bedroom is wall-to-wall horse posters, and he reads horse books every spare minute. He even makes models of horses and paints them.

Then there's me, Harold J. Otis. The only way I like animals is on the table—fried chicken, barbecued pork chops, and hamburgers.

So you see, it could not have been my idea to welcome that pint-sized piglet into the house. It was more likely that one of my father's childhood memories got tangled up with reality the day we visited an old friend in the country.

"Yes sirree!" Mr. Elroy had nodded his balding head and scratched the little piglet he had under his arm. "This little critter is the result of years of research and breeding. As an adult, she'll weigh only one hundred twenty pounds."

Right then we should have known. Who raises pigs to be small? The more bacon, the better, I always say. But I didn't.

Instead my mother gushed, "Why, that's only the size of a large house dog! How nice. It would be fun to have a house pig!"

"Yeah!" My brother's eyes grew big. "We could take her in the car on vacation with us."

The thought of sharing the back seat of the car with a pig didn't excite me at all. Pigs belonged on the back of trucks headed for the market, not in the cars of respectable people. But my family wasn't thinking about respectability.

"We'll take her!" said Dad, with a note of finality ringing in his voice. I knew better than to argue with that.

I stayed my distance during that ride home. I even managed to stay out of the way for the first couple of months that Ingersoll lived in our house. She stayed in her box in the garage, and I spent most of my time as far away as possible. But that fateful day finally came.

Mom had gone to the store; Dad was at work, and my brother, of course, was at the library, getting another stack of horse books.

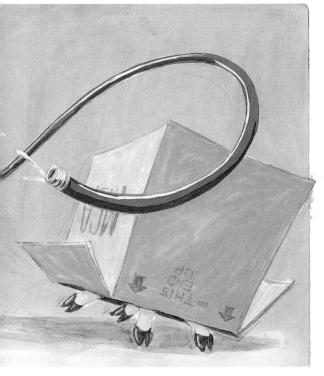

That meant just Ingersoll and I were at home. Now I was minding my own business and hoping Ingersoll would do the same. But a series of high-pitched squeals from the garage told me that Ingersoll's business was about to become mine. I raced to the garage, wondering what calamity had set off such a racket.

I nearly split my seams laughing when I saw what had happened. Ingersoll had turned her box—newspapers, dishes, and all—right over on herself. Now she was dashing around underneath the box, squealing like the frightened pig she was. The box crashed into a stack of flowerpots and then went scurrying through the wound-up garden hoses. After banging into the wall and knocking over some garden tools with a clatter, the box headed for my new bicycle.

"Oh, no!" I choked on the laugh that had been in my throat. I knew then that Ingersoll and I could no longer keep our distance. I headed toward the bike, hoping to be in time to catch the box.

I wasn't. Box, pig, papers, dishes, and I flew into the air. The bike crashed behind us. I grasped blindly for the pig and succeeded in grabbing a hind leg. Holding on tightly, I noticed how big the hind quarter had gotten—almost big enough for pork chops, I thought.

Then came the first time we took Ingersoll in the car with us. It was a disaster. She did not behave like the clean, intelligent, well-bred pig she was supposed to be. Instead she got nervous and then frantic. She dashed from one back window to the other, pulling a big thread in my sweater and knocking my brother's book out of his hand.

Mom became excited too. "Oh, dear. I guess Ingersoll isn't a car pig." She leaned over the back seat and tried to calm her by patting her head.

Meanwhile Dad turned the car around, and we headed back home by the shortest and quickest route possible.

"Do you think we ought to take Ingersoll to the vet to get her calmed down?" That came from my brother, who always talked about becoming a vet.

I just rolled my eyes. Maybe riding in the front seat would have helped her. I wasn't going to suggest it, though. I still thought pigs belonged in pickup trucks. That was the first and last time Ingersoll rode in the car.

It was also about that time that Dad had to start parking the car in the driveway instead of the garage. Ingersoll was getting just too big. Maybe we fed her too much. Or maybe the researchers were wrong. But Ingersoll soon left the 120-pound mark far behind. Secretly I was glad. Sausage for breakfast—mmm!

Dad built a run like a dog run for Ingersoll in the back yard. Proudly he showed his finished project to Mom.

"See, I chose the grassiest spot in the lawn."

Mom clapped her hands. "Oh good! Now Ingersoll won't get dirty. She's getting too big to bathe every day, you know."

Evidently Dad had never raised pigs. It didn't take Ingersoll more than a couple of hours to root up every blade of grass inside the fence.

Ingersoll just kept growing and growing. She grunted and groaned, wallowing in her mud hole that now took up half the yard, but we all thought she was doing pretty well in her backyard home.

Pig-Sized Problems

Then one night during dinner Dad got a phone call. Later the phone rang again, and Mom took the call. The neighbors had begun to complain. Apparently they could hear Ingersoll grunting all the way down on Park Lane. We held a family council.

I was about to suggest that maybe it was time to take Ingersoll for a visit to the butcher's when I noticed Mom dabbing her eyes.

"She's such an affectionate animal," she said, folding up her tissue.

"And she's so much smarter than the average family pet," Dad added. "I just don't know how we can keep her from grunting so much."

"Maybe she's bored," my brother chimed in. We looked at him questioningly. "You know, sometimes smart kids get bored in school, and then they cause trouble."

"So you think Ingersoll needs some additional activities?" I asked.

Dad snapped his fingers. "That's it. Ingersoll needs to be taken for walks to see the countryside."

It sounded like a simple solution. Dad would walk Ingersoll before breakfast; Mom would take her turn at lunch time. I would have the privilege after school, and my brother's turn came after dinner.

Dad was the first to try the exercise routine. He arrived home from work with an extra-large dog collar and leash. Before breakfast the next day he headed out into the frosty air with Ingersoll. All went well until he got down to Park Lane. Just as he was rounding the bend, walking briskly to keep up with our eager pet, he met a group of early-morning joggers.

Dad is usually a pretty friendly fellow, but that morning he tried to avoid looking at the men approaching. Ingersoll, however, was feeling much more friendly. She took off running in their direction, with Dad clutching the leash tightly and trying to keep up with the friendly pig. Still trying to avoid looking at the joggers, Dad tripped, let go of the leash, and watched helplessly as Ingersoll headed across the field toward home. When Dad arrived back at the house, Ingersoll was waiting for her breakfast in the garage. I don't know who the joggers were or what they said to my Dad, but he refused to walk Ingersoll after that.

Then my brother suddenly came down with an overload of homework. He said he couldn't possibly spare time to walk the pig.

Mom tried to keep her part of the agreement. For several days Ingersoll was content to wait while Mom stopped to look at wildflowers or listen to birdcalls. Then one day Mom decided to give Fifi a walk at the same time. Fifi isn't used to a leash, but Mom ventured down the lane with a leash in each hand. I don't know who saw the rabbit first, Ingersoll or Fifi, but those two animals must have taken off on some run. Mom is certainly no runner, but you have to give her credit—she never did let go of the leashes. I helped get the burrs out of Fifi's fur and cleaned the mud off Mom's tennis shoes, but needless to say, that was the last time Mom got involved in Ingersoll's exercise program.

Guess who was left to do the walking?

So I walked her and tried not to complain. At least, I reasoned, it gave me a chance to get out in the fresh air. I even got to where I enjoyed it sometimes. And Ingersoll got larger and larger.

The official-looking letter was in the mailbox when I came up the drive with Ingersoll one late afternoon. As I closed the garage door on the big gal, she looked up from her dinner long enough to grunt what sounded almost like a thank you. I reminded myself that no pig would ever show any sign of gratitude.

Mom opened the letter and started reading it while she made supper. Then Mom dropped her spoon right into the gravy.

"Oh, honey," she cried, waving the letter toward Dad. "They say we have to get rid of Ingersoll . . . something about zoning."

"What!" cried my brother. "Now what are we going to do?"

Several months ago I could have told them exactly what to do with an oversized hog. Now I started to say something but found a strange lump forming in my throat. I wiped a tear on my shirt sleeve, hoping no one noticed. What was I crying for? I certainly was not an animal lover. But somehow, to think of Ingersoll on the table was just plain . . . well, unthinkable.

"Don't worry, dear," Dad patted Mom on the arm. "I'll call Mr. Elroy. I think he'll be glad to see what has become of his experimental pig. Surely he'll be willing to come with his pickup truck."

So that's what we did. And that's what happened. Life in the Otis household returned to normal. The back yard is nearly all green again, but we have reminders of the Ingersoll days. My bike still has a dented fender, and I couldn't bring myself to get Mom to fix that pull in my sweater. Some of the horse posters in my brother's room have been replaced by pictures of prize pigs. And we never eat bacon anymore.

Last week we visited Mr. Elroy. He had called Dad to tell us there was something special to see. Mr. Elroy nodded his balding head and scratched the little piglet he held under his arm. Nearby Ingersoll sprawled happily with the other eight piglets in her first family.

"We can't take her!" said Dad with a note of finality ringing in his voice. I knew better than to argue with that.

Rabbit Preschool

Elizabeth Abbott
illustrated by Preston Gravely Jr.

To one just out of the warren
Everything must seem foreign:
The meadow,
The hawk's shadow,
The maple tree,
A honey bee.
Everything's a surprise–
And way oversize:
You standing there,
Big as a bear;
A leaf is a bedsheet;
The forest is–wheat.

A hop or two
Is all he can do.
Why, just tugging a clover
Can topple him over.
Everything is wondrous,
And thunderous,
And brisk–
And a risk.
His mother must remind him
To be watching behind him,
Till he gets in the habit
Of being a rabbit.

Just an Albino Squirrel Kit

Karen Wilt
illustrated by Paula Cheadle

Robert Curtis McRae carried the pink-white huddle of an albino squirrel kit into his home. He had carried it miles across the mountains, smoky blue now in the distance. It had curled up in his hunting cap, and he had buttoned the bundle inside his flannel shirt.

In the kitchen it lay in a stupor, shivering as Robert Curtis drew his hand across the downy fur of its forehead and between its little bits of ears, each no bigger than a kernel of dried corn.

"Gimme; gimme bunny," Travis hollered.

"Nope," Robert Curtis said. "This'n is special for Lydia Joy, to cheer her up."

Ma sighed. "That one needs a heap more than cheerin' up to set her right. Healing of the soul comes slower than healing of the body."

"Me hold," Travis interrupted.

"Let him get a look, Robert Curtis," Ma said.

The little boy's eyes grew large and round. "Careful," Robert Curtis said. "You have to be gentle."

"You heard your brother, Travis," Ma said. "Now you just get on out in the yard and play."

"Thanks," he whispered almost reverently before backing out the door.

Robert Curtis unlatched the door of worn leather and scrap

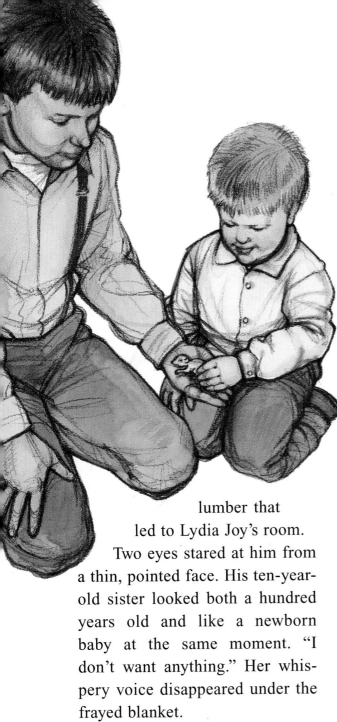

mean, it's not just an ordinary tree-climbing, acorn-stealing squirrel. It's an albino. Pure white from nose to tail. And it's an orphan. Elwood shot its ma by accident." He dug his toe into a knothole in the floor, trying to think of excuses. "Besides, I can't take care of it. I have to be in school all day. But you can. I'll get a little eyedropper from Doc and put it by your bed where you can reach. Ma will give us some milk for it. It'll die if you don't care for it. Looky, its eyes are barely opened yet."

He set it on Lydia Joy's pillow with its fluffy duster of a tail touching her ear.

"I'm too tired, Robert Curtis," Lydia Joy said. "When it grows up and runs around outside, I'll still be lyin' in this dreary old bed, 'cause I'll never be walking again."

Robert Curtis rolled Lydia Joy over and set the squirrel kit gently in her arms. "Don't you talk that way, Lydia Joy. You will walk. No polio germs can stop a McRae."

lumber that led to Lydia Joy's room.

Two eyes stared at him from a thin, pointed face. His ten-year-old sister looked both a hundred years old and like a newborn baby at the same moment. "I don't want anything." Her whispery voice disappeared under the frayed blanket.

"Sure you do," Robert Curtis said. "This is somethin' like you've never seen, Lydia Joy. I

Lydia Joy shook her head slowly, and Robert Curtis saw the tears glisten in her eyes.

"I'll ask Ma to bring in some milk. Try to get the kit to lick some drops off your finger while I run to Doc's for an eyedropper. I'll be back in less than an hour."

When Robert Curtis returned, the squirrel lay asleep in a cornflakes box with Lydia Joy's hand draped over the side.

"What are we gonna call you?" he whispered as he tweaked its ghost-white tail.

"Puff," Lydia Joy said.

Robert Curtis felt his heart rise in his chest. He wanted to shout or cry or light off a whole box of firecrackers. Lydia Joy had forgotten herself and her useless legs. Like the pond that the spring winds had begun to melt, the cold that had chilled Lydia Joy to the bones had begun to warm. A laugh of relief caught at his lungs.

"Don't you be using him for a powder puff," he said, but behind his back he counted off the weeks she had been sick and silent. This was the ninth week. "Maybe the last," he thought to himself. He'd be out of fingers to count on soon. "It has to be the last."

Ma hummed as she dished up supper. She scooped up two dumplings for Robert Curtis.

"Puttin' your mind to somethin' takes it off yourself," she said quietly.

After school the next day, Robert Curtis dropped his books on the table. In Lydia Joy's room the patched curtains in the windows fluttered up and down, making the sunshine advance and retreat in a battle to reach the pillow she rested on.

"I had to let Puff get some fresh air so he wouldn't forget that he's really a wild thing," she said, twirling his tail around her little finger.

Robert Curtis caught the squirrel by the scruff of the neck. "Is this how your mammy used to hold you?" he teased.

He glanced out the window and thought of the miracle Christ had performed—daubing mud on the blind man's eyes to make them see. If He could use mud to heal a blind man, then He could use a squirrel kit, too, for a little miracle. At least, if He chose to do it.

Robert Curtis turned back to his sister. He winced as he looked at the dark circles under Lydia Joy's eyes. The frail hand that held the albino kit blended in with the kit's pale white fur, but Lydia Joy's brown eyes glowed, almost as brightly as they had three months earlier, when she had been a whole little girl with two strong legs. "Legs as quick as Ma's weaving shuttle," Pa used to say.

In the next few days, spring swept in, wiping away the blanket of winter frost and waking up the trees to turn them a thousand shades of green. Robert Curtis started carrying Lydia Joy to the kitchen every morning. As spring grew bolder, Lydia Joy asked to be carried to the doorway and then to the porch. The dark circles under her eyes faded. Pink roses began to bloom along the trellis and in Lydia Joy's cheeks.

The squirrel kit became more lively. It climbed the porch railing, the trees, the mailbox, and Lydia Joy's hammock to perch on her shoulder and peer at the world from behind her golden-brown hair. It chased Lydia Joy's yarn and the chicks and the puppies and Ma's laundry and its own tail.

It also played hide-and-seek, hiding its eye-dropper feeder, Ma's clothespins, Travis's diaper pins, acorns, Pa's carpenter nails, and anything else it could find. And Ma did the seeking, warning Lydia Joy that she had better know every nook and cranny Puff used.

Slowly Lydia Joy awoke. Robert Curtis sensed it was happening, but Travis discovered it first. It was her laughter. When Travis had first learned to talk, he had promptly nicknamed Lydia Joy Laugh-Laugh, but everyone had forgotten that name during the long, dark winter months. As Puff batted her nose with his paws and Lydia Joy's voice rippled like the brook, Travis sang out "Laugh-Laugh" again.

Doc came out less and less to check on Lydia Joy. He spent more time giving Ma and Pa advice about exercises and leg braces. Robert Curtis helped his sister do the exercises faithfully, and Puff chattered instructions from Lydia Joy's stomach.

Then Pa brought the braces home. Puff chewed the cardboard package open during dinner. While Ma cleared the table, Pa fitted the braces on Lydia Joy's thin legs. Her tears made dark splotches on the leather holders.

"Where do they hurt?" Pa asked.

Lydia Joy shook her head. "They're . . . so . . . ugly," she sobbed.

"But Lydia Joy," Robert Curtis said, "they'll help you walk."

"Take 'em off; take 'em off!" she cried.

Puff jumped onto the chair and chattered loudly in agreement.

Pa unbuckled the braces and propped them up on the porch. He carried Lydia Joy solemnly to bed.

Robert Curtis tried to get Lydia Joy to try them again after exercising the next day. But she balanced precariously and wouldn't hold the crutches. Tears streamed down her cheeks.

"I want to walk on my own," she cried.

Robert Curtis unbuckled them.

Lydia Joy sat in her chair and played forlornly with Puff, ignoring the braces as they lay on the porch, an arm's length away.

School was dismissed for the summer, and Doc hired Robert Curtis to collect mountain herbs. The summer days passed, and Lydia Joy fanned away the afternoons, watching Travis from the shade of the oak tree beside the porch. Puff usually slept in the hollow of the tree to keep Travis from pulling his tail, but one afternoon a wild squirrel started chattering at a blue jay from the edge of the yard. When squirrels had come before, Lydia Joy had always taken Puff inside the house, but this time Puff scampered off to investigate. Travis

pounced on him as he paused at the chicken house.

"Chrrr, chrrr, chrrr," Puff screeched.

"Travis!" Lydia Joy called.

Travis jumped up, and Puff scampered into the woods.

"You leave him be," Lydia Joy said. "Here, Puff, come on," she called.

The woods were silent.

"Puff," Lydia Joy called louder. "Puff!"

She pulled herself up on the porch rail. "Puff! Puff!"

"Puff!" Travis echoed.

Lydia Joy scanned the trees for a blur of familiar white fur. Nothing. "Puff!" she screamed. She pulled herself to the far side of the porch. Splinters cut the palms of her hands, and she scraped both elbows. Her legs caught on the crutches and sent them sprawling.

Lydia Joy grabbed the braces and wrenched them onto her legs. She propped herself up again and raised the crutches.

Robert Curtis, coming in from the fields where he had been digging roots, saw his sister hobbling across the yard. "Robert Curtis!" she called. "Puff went in those woods. Get him!"

He stood still for a moment. Then he jogged toward the woods. "Puff?" he called. He paused and listened, but the only sound he heard was the wind stirring the leaves. He shrugged and turned back.

Lydia Joy was standing in the middle of the yard, watching. He walked slowly toward her.

"You didn't even try!" she said, her voice breaking. As Robert Curtis came closer, he could see tears sparkling in her eyes.

Gently he put a hand on her shoulder. "You know he had to go back to the wild things," he whispered. "Puff had too much heart in him to stay cooped up forever. Just like you, Lydia Joy."

Lydia Joy stayed quiet, staring at the ground. Finally she drew in a shaky

breath. "You think he's happier this way?"

"Sure as my name's Robert Curtis."

Lydia Joy leaned on her crutches, biting her lip for a long moment. Then she stood taller, raised her chin, and looked her brother in the eye. "Walk with me around the yard once, Robert Curtis," she said. She tightened her hands on the crutches. "I've got just as much heart as an albino squirrel kit— maybe more."

The Tales
of Beatrix Potter

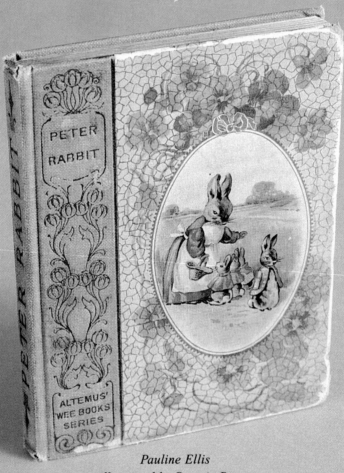

Pauline Ellis

illustrated by Beatrix Potter

The maid handed Beatrix a letter that had come in the morning post. With trembling fingers Beatrix tore it open. Maybe this time . . . but no, the seventh publisher in a row had rejected her book. She opened the cardboard cover of the manuscript and studied it again. The tiny pages had only a sentence or two on each of them, just perfect for a child's small hands. And the pictures! Had the men in the publishing office studied the miniature pictures?

She had titled her book *The Tale of Peter Rabbit*. The book written years ago for little Noel Moore had been a letter. Noel had been sick for months, and keeping a five-year-old quiet for that long had been hard for his mother. Beatrix decided to help. She knew she could write a story to cheer up Noel. Each part of the story could have a picture. The pictures would be just the kind a five-year-old would love to look at again and again. And so the story started as a special get-well letter to Noel.

"My dear Noel,

"I don't know what to write to you, so I shall tell you a story about four little rabbits whose names were Flopsy, Mopsy, Cottontail, and Peter.

They lived with their mother in a sandbank under the roof of a big fir tree.

" 'Now my dears,' said old Mrs. Bunny, 'You may go into the field or down the lane, but don't go into Mr. McGregor's garden.'

"Flopsy, Mopsy, and Cottontail, who were good little rabbits, went down the lane to gather blackberries, but Peter, who was very naughty, ran straight to Mr. McGregor's garden and squeezed underneath the gate.

"First he ate some lettuce and some broad beans, then some radishes, and then, feeling rather sick, he went to look for some parsley; but round the end of a cucumber frame, whom should he meet but Mr. McGregor!

"Mr. McGregor was planting out young cabbages, but he jumped up and ran after Peter, waving a rake and calling out, 'Stop thief!'

"Peter was most dreadfully frightened and rushed all over the garden, for he had forgotten the way back to the gate. He lost one of his shoes among the cabbage and the other shoe amongst the potatoes. After losing them, he ran on four legs and went faster, so that I think he would have got away altogether, if he had not unfortunately run into a gooseberry net and got caught fast by the large buttons on his jacket. It was a blue jacket with brass buttons, quite new.

"Mr. McGregor came up with a basket, which he intended to pop on the top of Peter; but Peter wiggled out just in time, leaving his jacket behind, and this time he found the gate, slipped underneath, and ran home safely.

"Mr. McGregor hung up the little jacket and shoes for a scarecrow to frighten the blackbirds.

"Peter was ill during the evening, in consequence of overeating himself. His mother put him to bed and gave him a dose of camomile tea, but Flopsy, Mopsy, and Cottontail had bread and milk and blackberries for supper.

"I am coming back to London next Thursday, so I hope I shall see you soon, and the new baby. I remain, dear Noel, yours affectionately,

Beatrix Potter"

But Flopsy, Mopsy, and Cotton-tail had bread and milk and blackberries for supper.

Naturally, each rabbit in the letter looked like a real rabbit you might meet while out on a stroll in the woods, but each one had a little jacket or apron to wear.

Noel had looked at the letter again and again, enjoying the pictures and remembering the story his mother had read to him. He loved it so much that eight years later he still had the copy Beatrix had written for him. When Beatrix told Noel that she wanted to make the story into a book for other children, Noel gladly lent it back to her. But now, after all the work of redrawing the pictures and making the story just right, another publisher had turned it down. Well, Beatrix Potter would not be stopped!

Beatrix withdrew money from her savings. Then she paid a printer to print her book. Of course, her relatives bought copies. They showed the little books to their friends, and the friends bought copies. Soon the friends' friends bought copies, and before Beatrix knew it, she had sold all two hundred copies, and she had made money—fourteen pounds. Before she could get it reprinted, one of the publishers who had turned down her book wrote to ask her if he could publish it.

Finally, all the studying Beatrix had done of animals and all the ideas she'd been storing up began to burst out. She had many stories to tell and hundreds of pictures to draw and paint.

Her book *The Tailor of Gloucester* grew partly out of her memory of the tamed mice the butler had caught when she was only six years old. She had also seen a tailor's shop in Gloucester, all cluttered with scraps of leather and tools. This shop would be the background, and the mice would be perfect helpers for

the tailor. In a museum she found embroidery designs that were just right. She could paint those for the work the mice would do at night while the tailor slept. The story grew and grew in her mind. At last she wrote it, telling the story of mice that acted almost human and finished the Lord Mayor of London's coat for the poor tailor and his wife.

By this time the children of England began to ask for more stories about Peter Rabbit. Beatrix wrote a sequel called *The Tale of Benjamin Bunny.* All winter in 1904 Beatrix worked on the pictures. She drew over seventy sketches until she had exactly what she needed. The children loved the book—and they asked for still more.

Beatrix wrote *The Tale of Two Bad Mice.* She needed a doll-house to use as a model for her drawings. And the bad mouse, Hunca Munca, was named for the very first pet mouse she had ever owned.

Then the stories tumbled over one another to fill page after page of the little books Beatrix Potter became famous for writing. *The Tale of Jeremy Fisher* told the story of a bullfrog. *The Story of a Fierce Bad Rabbit* and *The Tale of the Flopsy Bunnies* gave the children more rabbit stories. Then Beatrix wrote *The Tale of Jemima Puddle Duck, The Tale of Mrs. Tittlemouse, The Tale of Johnny Town-Mouse,* and many more. She even wrote a book of poetry called *Appley Dappley's Nursery Rhymes.* If you listen closely, you will hear the old poems everyone knows.

You know the old woman
    Who lived in a shoe?
And had so many children
    She didn't know what to do?
I think if she lived in
    A little shoe-house
That little old woman was
    Surely a mouse!

And so the children fell in love with Beatrix Potter's stories and pictures. When children had to leave London during the bombings of World War II, they clutched the little books of Beatrix Potter as they boarded the trains. Today a child in a bookstore in France can buy a copy of *Pierre Lapin;* a child in Germany can buy *Die Geschichte des Peterchen Hase;* a child in Italy can buy *Il Coniglie Pierino;* and all of them can go home with a tiny book that we know as *The Tale of Peter Rabbit.*

Publishers learned from Beatrix Potter that children are good customers. Soon more authors and illustrators became interested in writing good books for children.

Today the little books that began as a letter to Noel Moore can be found in most libraries and bookstores. You can even find toys, dishes, and china characters fashioned after the animal characters of Beatrix Potter's books. Her beautiful work will not be forgotten.

ELETELEPHONY

Laura E. Richards
illustrated by Dana Thompson

Once there was an elephant,
Who tried to use the telephant—
No! no! I mean an elephone
Who tried to use the telephone—
(Dear me! I am not certain quite
That even now I've got it right.)
Howe'er it was, he got his trunk
Entangled in the telephunk;
The more he tried to get it free,
The louder buzzed the telephee—
(I fear I'd better drop the song
Of elephop and telephong!)

THE PONY EXPRESS

Beki Gorham
illustrated by Stephanie True and Roger Bruckner

Suppose you are living in New York in 1860, more than one hundred twenty years ago. Your brother lives in California, where he is panning for gold. You miss him and would like to talk to him. But how do you get to California? You'd have to take a stagecoach or ride in a horse-drawn wagon through deserts and rugged hills. That would take too long. And you can't call your brother. The telephone hasn't been invented yet. The only way you can talk to him is to send him a letter by stagecoach or boat. But even a stagecoach or boat travels so far out of the way that your letter won't get to California for six weeks.

"That's too long!" you think. "In six weeks I'll have a hundred million other things to tell my brother!"

William H. Russell and several business partners felt the same way in 1860. "News is old after six weeks," they thought. "Suppose the letters could travel straight to

California without having to go so far out of the way. Then the mail would get there sooner. Let's get some fast horses and good riders to cut straight through. Then we could get the mail to California in two weeks. Maybe even ten days!"

Russell and his partners went ahead with plans for a fast mail service. One hundred ninety stations were made ready along the route. They stretched from St. Joseph, Missouri, to Sacramento, California. These relay stations were spaced from ten to fifteen miles apart.

The partners bought five hundred horses for one hundred fifty dollars each. This was ten times the amount usually paid for a horse. But these were special horses. They were small, fast, and tough. They were able to travel rough country, carrying both rider and mail swiftly and safely.

A special saddle was designed for the horses. It was flat and very light. Over it was a leather covering, called a *mochila*. It had four pockets to hold the mail.

As the relay stations were being made ready, the partners advertised for riders. The riders had to be skilled horsemen. Also, they couldn't weigh more than one hundred twenty-five pounds. That meant the riders had to be extremely small, thin, or young.

Finally the equipment was in place. The relay stations were ready. The horses were waiting. Now everything depended on the riders.

On April 3, 1860, the *mochila* was flung over the saddle of a nervous pony. A boy in buckskin britches jumped into the saddle. He kicked his spurs into the pony's flanks. The crowd cheered!

A cannon thundered! And the first pony express rider was off and galloping!

On he raced to the next relay station. There he hopped from his horse, slapped the *mochila* onto a

fresh mount, and took off for the next station, fifteen miles down the trail. Then in relay-race fashion, horses and riders traded off. On and on the trail stretched. On April 13, 1860, the people of Sacramento lined the streets to cheer the last rider. The mail had arrived in ten days!

From then on the mail usually did arrive in ten days. But there was trouble on the trail. Sometimes riders arrived at burned relay stations to find that Indians or thieves had stolen the horses. During one Indian uprising, "Pony Bob" Haslan rode past one destroyed station to another and another. He rode a total of three hundred eighty miles before he found a station where he could stop.

"Buffalo Bill" Cody was another who rode past burned stations for three hundred twenty miles. Another rider found a pass blocked by Indians. But he charged on through, yelling and firing his pistol. Others were chased by Indian warriors and managed to escape. Some were wounded. A few were killed.

Weather was as much an enemy as were warring Indians. Blizzards could cause a rider to lose the trail. One rider found his way only by following a river flowing in the right direction. In winter, the horses plowed through deep snow in the mountain passes. In summer, they raced over hot plains.

Often people in wagon trains waved to the riders as they passed. People in the settlements would gather to cheer the heroic riders on.

The pony express riders had been galloping bravely from East to West and back for nearly a year. Finally the riders began passing crews stringing telegraph wires. In 1861 the telegraph line was completed. Then the telegraph lines took the place of the pony trails. The pony express lasted only eighteen months, but it will forever remain an exciting part of the history of our growing country.

If you had lived in 1860, you might have sent your brother a letter by the pony express. Or maybe you would have been a pony express rider yourself!

Directions on a Map

illustrated by Preston Gravely Jr.

• The Compass Rose

The pony express riders always had to know which way they were going. Sometimes they had to travel across the desert where there were no regular roads. A wise pony express rider might have carried a compass with him. A compass needle is magnetic and always points north. Suppose the rider wanted to go west. He would face the way the compass pointed, turn left, and head in that direction.

A compass rose on a map works much the same way. It shows which direction is north on the map. The main points of the compass are north, south, east, and west. Between main points there is another direction. *NE* stands for northeast, *SE* for southeast, *SW* for southwest, and *NW* for northwest. By using north as a starting point, you can tell what direction to travel.

• Reading a Map

A pony express rider might have ridden on a path much like the one shown on the next page. Look at the compass rose. Then you can see which directions the trail winds.

Use your finger to trace the trail on the map as you read the following description.

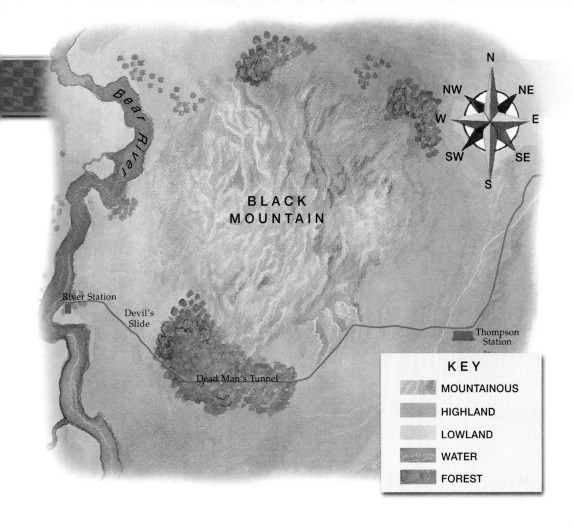

The station keeper is sitting on the porch of the Thompson Station watching for a pony express rider. He is facing north. The rider will come, and he will start out with a fresh horse. He will head west for a few miles. Because of Black Mountain, the trail goes southwest. Then it seems hidden in a wooded area that the riders call Dead Man's Tunnel. The trail through Dead Man's Tunnel heads west. Finally, coming down Devil's Slide toward River Station, the rider is traveling northwest.

Suppose the rider could go back from River Station to Thompson Station "as the crow flies." Then what direction would he travel?

Night Ride to River Station

Milly Howard

illustrated by Del Thompson,
Noelle Snyder and John Bjerk

In the early days of the 1860s, boys dreamed of being pony express riders. This fictional story tells of ten-year-old Seth Thompson. Seth had these same dreams, but he was closer to his dreams than most boys. His family ran a relay station on the pony express route. On a spring night in 1861, Seth got his chance for a wild ride he would never forget.

Night Shadows

"Easy, now." The bay mare twisted and backed away from Seth. He slipped the reins up and thrust the bit into Copper's mouth. He pulled the reins tight, coaxing the horse toward him. The mare flung her head up. Quickly Seth pulled down hard as he had seen his father do, forcing the mare's head back down. Talking soothingly, he led the dancing mare to the post at the front of the log cabin. When she was safely tied, he gave a sigh of relief. "You need to be ridden more, Copper," he said. "But Pa won't let me ride you express horses. Not yet, anyway."

The express horses were kept separate from the rest of the horses and exercised only by Seth's father. "These horses aren't to learn on," Mr. Thompson had said. "Don't want to teach them bad habits that might cost a rider his life someday. Learn to ride your pony well. Your time will come soon enough."

Seth looked up at the mountains that were casting night shadows on the little valley. Nothing moved on the trail leading down to the cabin. "Pete'll be here soon." He patted the fidgeting horse. "Then you'll get a good workout."

Seth knocked the mud off his boots and stepped into the one-room cabin. He sniffed the beans simmering in a pot hung over the fire. Seth had been smelling them most of the afternoon as he worked outside. Chores seemed to take forever when he was working alone. Now it was late, and his stomach felt like it was tied in a knot from hunger.

He walked quietly across the room to the quilt that divided off the sleeping area. "Ma?" he said softly.

The edge of the quilt lifted, and a small, thin woman stepped around it, holding a barely touched bowl of broth.

"The horse is saddled and waiting?" she asked.

"Sure, Ma. I tied her to the post outside, just like Pa always does. All Pete will have to do is throw the *mochila* on and ride." He looked at the bowl. "Pa didn't eat?"

"He's no better," Mrs. Thompson put the bowl on the rough table. "Not so much as a mouthful for two days."

Seth gave his mother a questioning look. "He's had the fever before—"

"He'll be all right," she said. "It just takes time. Don't you go fretting now. You have enough to do without that."

they raced, half a mile, a mile. Suddenly the scream of a mountain lion split the darkness. Seth's heart froze. He loosened the reins and yelled.

Copper leapt forward, muscles bunching. Down the trail and around the bend she ran. Trees flashed past. Alarmed, Seth pulled back on the reins, but the frightened horse only ran faster. He jerked harder, fear growing again. Copper had the bit in her teeth! She was gripping it so hard Seth couldn't turn her head.

Branches slashed at them as the horse swung wide around a bend in the trail. Seth pulled on the reins, trying to get the bit from between Copper's teeth. He ducked as an overhanging branch snatched at his hat. When he pulled again, one end of the bit came loose. Seth sighed with re-

lief. Only one end left. Steadily he pulled on the reins, not allowing Copper to get a grip on the loose half. On they raced, Seth gasping for breath, Copper's sides beginning to heave. Around the next bend they swept. Seth's heart leapt. There was a glimmer of cold light ahead. They were nearing the end of the tunnel. Ahead was Devil's Slide! Seth pulled harder, forcing Copper's head back. She shifted the bit in her teeth, trying to get a better grip. Seth felt the bit move, and jerked. The bit fell into place, and Copper's headlong pace slackened. Seth gently eased his grip. They passed the thinning aspens and came out into the open, slowing to a steady lope.

At the top of Devil's Slide, Seth pulled Copper to a stop. He ran his hands lightly along her neck and flanks, checking for the telltale foam of a too-hard run. "It wouldn't do to turn up with a worn-out horse," he thought.

Stretching his tired arms, he looked down the slide. "Pa says you're as surefooted as a goat," he spoke quietly to the bay mare. "I sure hope so, 'cause tired as we both are, we're going down the slide."

Gently urging the horse on, Seth headed down the steep trail. He held his breath as Copper picked her way past the first boulder. A rush of gravel slid behind her hooves, but Copper didn't falter.

Here on the moonlit slope she was more sure of herself. She moved slowly and easily past the rocks. Sensing her confidence, Seth loosened his grip on the reins and let her pick the way. From time to time a spattering of gravel below them made him catch his breath, but Copper walked on carefully. At the bottom of the slope, she stopped and tossed her head.

Seth burst into laughter, in response to tension as much as anything else. "You horse." He laughed. "You knew you could do it! It's funny, though; the part I thought would be the hardest was the easiest. That'll teach me to worry ahead of time."

Seth patted Copper's shoulder. "Come on; I know you're as tired as I am, but we have some time to make up."

Urging Copper into a gallop, he headed toward the broad river. Beside its silver waters stood the next relay station.

"Ho, Station Master!" Seth galloped into the station yard. Two young men came running with a fresh horse. Seth peeled the *mochila* from Copper and flung it across the fresh horse.

"Hey, you're not Pete!" One of the men grabbed Copper's bridle.

"Pete's been shot," Seth answered. "And Fort Sumter's been fired on. War's started!"

The man gave a sharp whistle and called back to the station house. "Ma! Pa! It's Thompson's boy!"

As the others came running, he turned to Seth. "You've ridden enough tonight. I'll finish the run."

Seth nodded wearily. He let himself be led to the station door and then stopped to watch the rider disappear into the night.

"He'll get the mail through." The other man smiled. "You've done a night's work to be proud of, Seth Thompson!"

A Narrow Fellow in the Grass

Emily Dickinson
illustrated by Preston Gravely Jr.

Emily Dickinson was born on December 10, 1830, in Amherst, Massachusetts. The people of the quiet town thought it strange that as she grew older she preferred to stay at home and see only her family and a few friends. She wrote over 1,700 poems during her life, none of which she wished to have published. Ten were published without her permission while she was alive. After her death, her sister-in-law discovered most of Emily's poems—tied up in packets at the bottom of her dresser drawers.

Emily Dickinson frequently broke the rules of punctuation as she wrote her poetry. She capitalized often and used dashes more than other punctuation, yet she is considered one of the greatest American poets. Her poems about animals and nature are detailed and beautiful.

In this poem she describes a young boy's reaction to almost stepping on a snake. Do you agree with his feelings?

A narrow Fellow in the Grass
Occasionally rides—
You may have met Him—did you not
His notice sudden is—

The Grass divides as with a Comb—
A spotted shaft is seen—
And then it closes at your feet
And opens further on—

He likes a Boggy Acre
A Floor too cool for Corn—
Yet when a Boy, and Barefoot—
I more than once at Noon
Have passed, I thought, a Whip lash
Unbraiding in the Sun
When stooping to secure it
It wrinkled, and was gone—

Several of Nature's People
I know, and they know me—
I feel for them a transport
Of cordiality—

But never met this Fellow
Attended, or alone
Without a tighter breathing
And Zero at the Bone—

Goliath

Beki Gorham and Jeri Massi

illustrated by
Mary Ann Lumm

Friends

Goliath was David's dog. Or perhaps David was Goliath's boy. Goliath was a big, flopping giant of a dog. He probably had some St. Bernard in him—and a little something else too. No one was sure. All anyone really knew about Goliath was that one winter day he had turned up on the porch all alone.

Mr. Brooks put an ad in the newspaper to find Goliath's owner.

And one Saturday David and his friend Eric walked all the way into town, asking at every house. Nobody had ever seen Goliath before.

Meanwhile, life on the farm was never quite the same with Goliath around.

When David went out to milk a cow by hand, Goliath followed him. The steam rose in the cold air as warm milk filled the pail. At first David shoved the curious dog away to keep him from tipping the milk pail over. When David realized he was doing more shoving than milking, he aimed a long shot of milk right into Goliath's mouth. Goliath jumped back, licking his face and snapping his teeth. After that David milked in peace while Goliath inspected the rest of the barn or stood guard at the door.

When spring planting began on the Brookses' farm, Goliath tried to help. He replowed the new furrows and unearthed the seed corn. He ripped new bags of fertilizer and scattered the fertilizer on the ground. He also chased the noisy crows right over the newly planted fields. Scolding didn't help, and scolding didn't make up for lost time. Goliath was locked in the barn until the planting was finished.

Later in the spring, he had to be tied to keep him from chasing David down the long rows of green corn. But every day after school, David did his chores and then untied Goliath, and both of them raced to the creek down in the south pasture. As the days became hotter, David and Goliath lay in the thick pasture grass to dry off after their swim.

The only thing better for David than swimming with Goliath was swimming with Goliath and Eric. All during the summer Eric came over nearly every day.

Eric lived on the next farm with his aunt and uncle. He was an orphan. At first David had felt a little shy whenever Eric talked about that, but Eric seemed to be more occupied with Goliath than with anything else. "I sure do like your dog," he would say. "I had a real St. Bernard when my parents were alive."

Once David asked Eric how he felt about living with his uncle. "Oh, Uncle Henry's great," Eric said. "He takes good care of me."

"Do you think about your parents?" David asked.

"I miss them, and sometimes I feel sad. But I know they're in heaven," Eric said quietly.

In late summer the barn was full of hay. Most of it was baled, but below the loft rose a mountain of loose hay.

Eric and David climbed up to the loft, held their breath, squeezed their eyes shut, and leapt out, yelling the whole way down. They sank deep into the sweet-smelling pile of hay, rolling and tumbling as Goliath charged in after them.

That's how life went until the summer David turned ten. One night, close to the end of school, David heard his father and mother talking quietly in the kitchen.

Mr. Brooks was saying something about low milk prices, about the drought that had gotten this spring off to a scorching start, about big corporate farms and little independent farmers. As the days went by, the looks on his parents' faces made David uneasy. He noticed that his father didn't joke around as much as he usually did. And sometimes at night he could hear his parents' voices across the hall, praying.

When Mr. Brooks came to David's bedroom the last week before summer vacation, David wasn't surprised. He had known something was wrong; he just hadn't known what. Mr. Brooks sat down on the bed and patted the mattress beside him for David to sit too.

"David," Mr. Brooks said seriously, "you know we've been having some trouble here on the farm. There's not enough money to pay the bills. Your mother and I have been praying about what to do."

David nodded, remembering the peanut butter sandwiches instead of the hot school lunches, the carefully patched jeans, and the oatmeal for breakfast.

Mr. Brooks paused and looked straight ahead at David's wall. "I've found a job in Atlanta, Son." He breathed deeply as if he were tired. "So we'll be moving soon—and we'll have to sell the farm. You understand?"

"Moving?" David's voice sounded strange even to him, and his stomach felt a little queasy. "I don't want to move!"

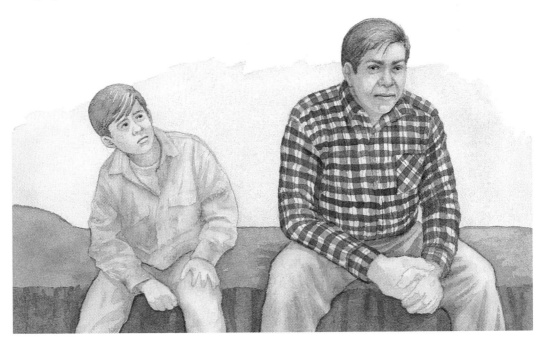

His father nodded, looking at him again. "The Lord has given me a good job, David, and in a time when it's hard to get a job. I know you love the farm. You were born here, and it's only natural that you would want to stay. But try to understand—"

"I don't understand!" David said. His eyes stung. "It isn't fair!"

Mr. Brooks frowned. "Don't talk that way, Son. Listen to me. In three weeks we'll move to a little apartment until we can afford another house—which brings us to another matter." Mr. Brooks tried to put his arm around his son's shoulders. David shrugged it off. "We're going to have to find another home for Goliath. Maybe—"

"For Goliath!" David stiffened. "We're not taking Goliath? Why not?"

"We can't take a dog that big to the city," Mr. Brooks tried to explain. "The apartment will just barely hold us."

"We can make him a place in the yard. We can build a fence or tie him up or something." David's words ended in an anguished sob.

"We have to take Goliath! I can't go if we don't take Goliath!"

His father shook his head sadly. "I know what Goliath means to you, Son, but he's a farm dog. He wouldn't be happy in the city."

David shoved away from the bed and jumped up. "He would be happy! We'd be together. That's what counts!"

Mr. Brooks stood up too. "This is hard for all of us, David, but it's God's will. It's for the best." He put his hand on his son's shoulder. "Would you like me to pray with you about it?"

David didn't answer. Mr. Brooks turned and walked away, but at the doorway he stopped. His voice sounded tired. "Please do pray about it, Son," he said.

When his father was gone, David threw himself on the bed. Moving was bad enough, but losing Goliath too? Surely the Lord wouldn't let that happen! He tried to pray for God to show him a way to keep Goliath. But he had a hard, cold feeling in his chest. God's will. It seemed like everything sad and hard was God's will. Why had God allowed the drought and low milk prices? He had taken Eric's parents away too. Didn't God ever try to make people happy?

"I'll teach Goliath to be a city dog," he thought. "Then we can take him with us." He sat up, wiping his wet face. "Yes, that's what I'll do. I'll teach him!"

David's Choice

The next morning David was awake and dressed before the sun was up. His father was sitting at the kitchen table, reading the morning paper. He looked up quickly as David charged in. David's mother turned from the stove with a questioning look in her eyes.

"I can do it, Dad!" David exclaimed. "I know how we can take Goliath!"

Mr. Brooks put his paper down. "How, David?"

"I can teach Goliath to behave in an apartment. I can check out a book on dog training from the library and teach Goliath to behave like a city dog. Okay, Dad?"

Mrs. Brooks gave him a doubtful smile. "That might be hard to do, David. Especially in three weeks."

"He deserves a chance to try," Mr. Brooks said slowly. "I'll stop by the library when I go to the hardware store. But you do understand that it might not work, don't you, David?"

"Oh, it'll work, Dad," David said confidently. "Goliath is smart!"

In the barn David found an old rope just long enough to use as a leash. He tied it to Goliath's collar and said, "Let's go, Goliath!"

Goliath went. He leapt happily out of the barn, ready to play this new game. David lost his footing on the loose hay and slid outside on his stomach, still holding on to the rope. "No, Goliath, no," he screeched. "Stop!"

Goliath stopped beside the horse trough long enough to lap up some water, giving David time to scramble to his feet. For the rest of the morning, the lesson continued in much the same way. When David said, "Go," Goliath went. When David said, "Stop," sometimes Goliath stopped, and sometimes he didn't. When Mr. Brooks's car rolled into the driveway close to lunch time, Goliath was trotting beside David.

Mr. Brooks handed the library book to David, trying not to grin at the burr-covered dog and mud-streaked boy. "Been out in the fields, Son?" he asked.

"We've been all over this farm," David gasped, trying to catch his breath. "But look at him, Dad! He's doing much better! "

"So I see," Mr. Brooks replied. He ruffled David's already-tousled hair and said, "Come on in; it's time to eat."

After lunch David called Eric and asked him to come over and help. Eric came over every day. Still using the rope as a leash, they took turns walking Goliath through the fields. After the first few minutes of affectionate pawing and licking, Goliath was content to walk beside the boys.

The problem was the rabbits—or the gophers, or the birds, or anything else that moved. Eric was walking Goliath the first time the big dog scented a rabbit. As serious as David was about training Goliath, he had to laugh at the sight of Goliath charging through the grass with Eric bouncing behind, yelling, "Whoa! Stop! Wait!" When Goliath dashed through the blackberry bushes, the shouts turned to "Ouch! Help!" There were a few shrieks and a final "You big ox!" as both boy and dog ended up in the creek.

By the time Eric and Goliath had climbed out of the creek, David was there to help.

Goliath shook himself, showering both boys with water. David said, still laughing, "The first day, he dragged me all over this farm!"

Eric grinned. "If I didn't love that old dog—"

"Yeah, me too," David said, giving the wet dog a hug. "Since we're already wet, how about a swim?"

Shrieking and yelling, the boys dived in, Goliath right behind them.

After that day Goliath settled down to work, or maybe the boys did. They avoided areas where Goliath was sure to catch the scent of a rabbit, and the wild dashes became fewer in number. By the end of the next week, both boys were ready to try Goliath inside.

Goliath trotted to the kitchen door happily, but when the boys tried to get him to enter, he began to whine. "Come on, boy," Eric coaxed. "It's all right. Come on."

David tugged on the rope leash. Goliath took a few steps onto the polished kitchen floor and tucked his tail between his legs. "Come on, Goliath," David said, tugging again.

Eric pushed from behind. Goliath gave up and trotted in, still whining deep in his throat. Eric stumbled over the threshhold and closed the door, grinning at David. "Well, we got him in, anyway."

Goliath dashed for the door, sending David sprawling. The frightened dog slammed up against the closed door and then, yelping in pain and fright, charged for the living room.

"Get him! Get him!" David yelled to Eric.

"I'm trying!" Eric yelled. Goliath brushed against a small table. A lamp toppled, crashing to the floor. Goliath slid around the doorway into the hall and bumped into Mrs. Brooks. The basket of laundry she held spun across the room as she tumbled to the floor. Shirts, socks, and towels showered the hall. Goliath dashed on, his head covered by one of Mr. Brooks's white shirts. Another lamp crashed. The hall table tilted.

"Out! Out!" gasped Mrs. Brooks. "Get him out before he gets hurt!"

Goliath charged past the boys and back into the living room. There was a crash, the sound of glass breaking, and then the boys heard Mr. Brooks's voice. "What's going on—"

A ripping sound muffled the rest of his words. When Mrs. Brooks and the boys reached the kitchen, Mr. Brooks was holding the kitchen door open and staring through the demolished screen door. Goliath had shed the white shirt and was disappearing into the barn, yelping at the top of his lungs. Eric, David, and his parents followed him.

David sat on a bale of hay and braced his head with his hands. "I guess I didn't think about what Goliath would like," he said slowly. "Now I know what you meant when you said he's a farm dog."

"Goliath is a grown dog," Mrs. Brooks said, sitting down beside David and putting her arm around him. "I wouldn't mind trying to keep him in the house, but I don't think Goliath really wants to be an indoor dog, do you?"

David shook his head slowly. "I almost hurt him, trying to make him do what I wanted him to do. But what will we do with him?"

"Can't he stay with me?" Eric asked quietly.

David looked up in surprise. "Eric! Why didn't I think of that?"

"I guess because you were just thinking about taking him, not leaving him," Eric said. "And I didn't want to ask about keeping him for the same reason. I knew you wanted Goliath to go with you."

David agreed. "I just wasn't thinking of anybody else but myself." His voice trailed off. Goliath looked from Eric to David and back to Eric. "I prayed for a way to keep Goliath and not lose him. If he stays with Eric, I'll get to see him sometimes, won't I?"

"Sometimes," Mr. Brooks said. "The Lord wants us to see that trusting Him, even if it means sacrifice, is always good."

David patted Goliath's head. "Maybe I had to learn to give," he said softly. "I guess that's why God did it."

Later Eric and David took Goliath to the creek for another swim. As they walked along, David said, "Goliath has always been as much your dog as mine, Eric. Now he'll be as much my dog as yours!"

LITERATURE LESSON:

Characters

- **Characters and Plot**

When you read about a character in a story, you are often reading about somebody make-believe. Yet you usually expect make-believe characters to behave like real people. In "Night Ride to River Station," Seth does not pull out a laser gun to shoot the mountain lion. He behaves just like a boy from the Old West. You come to know Seth by the way he reacts to everything that happens. He helps during his father's illness. He tries to calm Copper's fear. And he recognizes the need to get the mail through.

In "Ingersoll," you come to know the narrator of the story by the way he reacts to all animals and especially to Ingersoll, the pig. The plot of a story helps you to know the characters. Each one reacts to the events in his own way. Authors plan their stories carefully to help you get to know the characters.

• Characters That Change

In "Ingersoll," Harold J. Otis begins the story by explaining his dislike of animals. At first he just endures Ingersoll. But by the end of the story he almost cries when she is given away. You can see that he has changed his opinion of animals. A story is always more interesting when a character you know changes in some way.

In "Just an Albino Squirrel Kit," Lydia Joy changes. At first she doesn't want to do anything to help herself. But by the end she is willing to use her crutches. And in the story "Goliath," David changes from being selfish to being kind. He shows it by giving his dog to his best friend.

• Characters That Do Not Change

You know that the brother in "Ingersoll" likes horses. At the end of the story he still likes horses. He does not change. The character Mr. Brooks in "Goliath" is firm but kind. You would expect him to be honest about giving up the dog. You would expect him to tell David what must be done. By the end of the story he is still firm and kind. He has not changed.

Good authors are talented people, but they are also people who work hard. They write and rewrite their stories. They use interesting information to make their stories hold your attention. A good author also chooses colorful words. And each good story that you read has just the right combination of changing and unchanging characters.

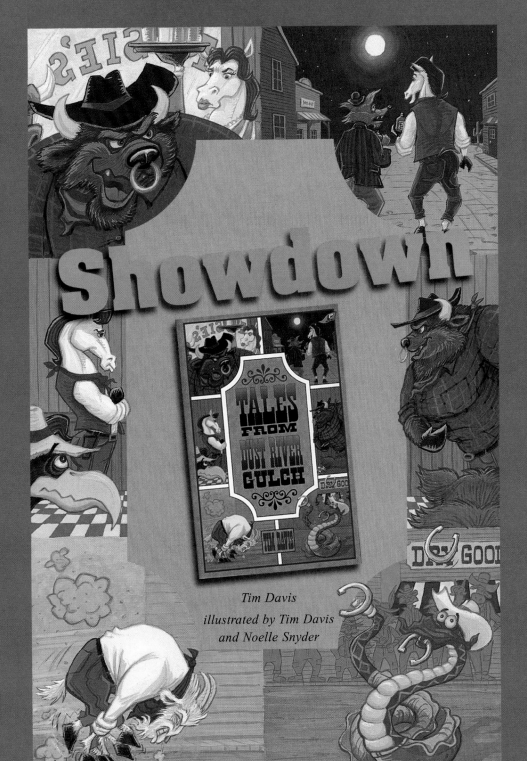

Showdown

Tim Davis

illustrated by Tim Davis
and Noelle Snyder

Dust River Gulch

Now don't git the notion that the folks in Dust River Gulch were a bunch of softies. Nothin' could be further from the truth. Dust River Gulch was inhabited by some of the wildest characters west of the Mississippi. Few human-type outlaws would test a town whose sheriff was a thoroughbred mustang. But this here Gruffle O'Buffalo—now there was a different sort of outlaw. He was wanted in seventy-eight counties an' half a dozen zoos. It was no wonder the folks of Dust River Gulch were feelin' a mite queasy when they heard he'd be passin' through.

It wasn't that folks didn't have confidence in Sheriff J.D. Saddle-soap. No doubt about it, he was an awe-inspirin' figure—a mighty good lawman an' a fine-lookin' horse to boot. Many's the wild an' woolly outlaws he'd driven out of town. But, ya see, this was different. This was Gruffle O'Buffalo.

Well, seems as if it was old Tumbleweeze McPhearson that mostly started stirrin' up the townsfolk. Over at Rosie's Restaurant, he was a-gobblin' down some grub when he leaked out the rumor.

"Yep, 'bout this time tomorrow, I reckon most folks'll be sittin' in their houses with the doors bolted up."

Old Bo, the lizard, leaned over from the next table. "Whatcha talkin' 'bout, Weeze?"

"Nothin' other than Gruffle O'Buffalo an' his gang of bum steers," replied old Tumbleweeze with a snort.

"Gruffle O'Buffalo!" Old Bo got so startled that he dropped his spoon—*perclunk.*

Well, the murmurin' started up mighty quick-like all through the restaurant. 'Fore long every ear in the house was tuned in to old Tumbleweeze. (It was the usual way news got around in Dust River Gulch.)

The old weasel continued, "Yep, word has it old Gruff an' his gang are comin' to town tomorrow."

"Tomorrow?" squealed Rosie, who kept the restaurant as tidy as her own kitchen. "Somebody go git J.D.!"

While a wild-eyed prairie dog went a-scamperin' after Sheriff Saddlesoap, Old Tumbleweeze kept on a-stirrin' up the folk.

"I heard the last town old Gruff an' his gang passed through, the folks haven't nearly recovered yet."

While some folks were tremblin' an' whisperin', Bo asked, "Why haven't they?"

"Well, he an' his gang done humiliated the sheriff an' his deputies so bad that they hightailed it outta town. So then the folks were so scared they just did whatever old Gruff asked 'em." Tumbleweeze paused to munch a spell. "Nearly stole the town blind, they did."

A scrawny buzzard asked, "You think Sheriff J.D. can take 'em on?"

Tumbleweeze shrugged. "I don't know. Gruff's ruined plenty of sheriffs in his day."

Well, at that comment, the mutterin' an' murmurin' got near a deafenin' pitch there at Rosie's Restaurant. Some folks were sayin' they'd been a-plannin' to be out of town the next day anyway.

An' the rest started makin' such-like plans.

But Miss Rosie, she wouldn't have none of it. She started a-scoldin' an' a-shamin' those folks fer not trustin' in Sheriff J.D. like they should've. 'Course, everybody knew she had a sweet spot in her heart fer J.D., but they took the scoldin' to heart anyways.

The little lady kept on a-going. "Why, he's the finest, bravest sheriff you'll find in any county, anyplace! No outlaw's gonna run him outta this town! No, not J.D."

Then the doors swung open. In walked none other than Sheriff J.D. Saddlesoap himself. "Why, thank ya, Miss Rosie. That's mighty sweet of ya."

Miss Rosie turned sorta pink-like as J.D. smiled over at her. "Well, it's true, isn't it, J.D.?" she said. "You're gonna stand up to that there Gruffle O'Buffalo an' his gang, aren't you?"

J.D.'s smile looked a mite strained, an' he swallowed mighty hard. But he said he would. If nothin' else, he wouldn't make Miss Rosie into a liar.

Well, tomorrow came a mite sooner than Sheriff J.D. was a-hopin'. Seemed like most folks decided to stay in town after all, seein' as how Sheriff J.D. was a-gonna stand up to Gruff an' his gang. They weren't about to miss that, now were they?

Round about noontime, old Tumbleweeze was out in the street with his ear to the ground. Lots of folks was a-watchin' real quiet-like. Perty soon he spoke up. "They's a-comin'! I kin hear the rumble!"

Everybody cleared the street an' waited. They was a-lookin' out winders an' peerin' 'round barrels. Rosie's Restaurant was jammed with folks, eatin' an' strainin' their necks to see 'round each other outside.

No doubt about it, that cloud of dust on the horizon was gittin' closer every second.

J.D. was a-waitin'. He wouldn't start no trouble—but as sure as he'd promised Miss Rosie, he wouldn't stand fer none either.

So into Dust River Gulch they came—old Gruffle O'Buffalo an' his gang of bum steers. They did a little hootin' an' hollerin' an' then they headed to Rosie's.

Everybody was actin' as calm as they could inside—but most folk were sweatin' like it was two hundred degrees. Then in sauntered Gruff an' his steers.

"We's hot!" rumbled the big, mangy buffalo. He turned to Rosie, standing behind the stove. "You there, give m' boys some milk shakes."

Rosie went right to it an' served those five bum steers real quick-like. They started a-slurpin' an' a-sloppin' it like the no' count critters they were. Meanwhile, ol' Gruff, he was a-saunterin' 'round the place like he was king. He plucked the cherry right off the top of one buzzard's sundae. Gruff smiled an' rubbed his straggly-lookin' beard whiles he ate that cherry.

The buzzard didn't say nothin'. Fact is, the only sound in the place was the slurpin' an' sloppin' of those bum steers, startin' in on their second round of milk shakes.

Finally, Gruff seemed 'bout strutted out, an' he found a table to his likin'. So old Gruff, he took a seat. Poor old Bo, the lizard, he was already a-sittin' at that same table. Gruff sorta gave him the eye an' rumbled, "I prefers a private table, myself." An' Bo, he pert near melted to the floor an' slithered over to the next table whiles Gruff chuckled to himself.

"Hey, gal," Gruff yelled out real sudden-like. "I's ready to order." So Rosie, she hustled on over to his table. "Give me a gallon of the sourest, smelliest, most curdled-up milk ya got," growled the shaggy outlaw.

There was some quiet-like oohin' and ahhin' at that, an' Gruff sat back in his chair with a satisfied snort.

Then Rosie said, "Only *one* gallon, sir?" in a smart-alecky sorta way.

Gruff, he raised himself up and rumbled out, "Nah, make it *three* gallons, gal! An' quick-like!"

Perty soon Rosie came back with the sourest milk you ever smelt! Gruffle sorta chuckled an' drank it all down like it was nothin' to him. Course, everybody at Rosie's couldn't hardly believe it.

The old buffalo let out with a hiccup an' yelled over to his gang of bum steers (still a-slurpin' an' a-sloppin'), "C'mon, boys! We's a-goin'!"

So the whole bunch of 'em started fer the door. Most of the folks started breathin' normal-like again—that is, till Miss Rosie spoke up. She said, "Sir, you an' your boys haven't paid your bill."

Then Old Gruff turned around real slow-like an' looked Rosie in the eye. An' it got quiet—terrible quiet. Then the bum steers started a-laughin' an' a-snortin' like nobody's business, an' out the door they went. And Gruffle, he started a-saunterin' out too.

Then Rosie (she was a mighty plucky lady) said flat out, "Sir, you haven't paid."

The bum steers couldn't hardly take it, they were laughin' so hard. Old Gruff strutted over to poor old Bo an' picked him up by the kerchief an' set him on a table by Rosie. He blew out some sour milk breath and said, "My friend here says he'll pay." An' the bum steers started a-howlin' with laughter.

But the laughin' didn't last long this time. 'Cause who do you think came through the swingin' doors? None other than Sheriff J.D. Saddlesoap.

Gruffle smiled an' said, "Well, if it ain't the sheriff!"

J.D. just looked at Rosie an' asked, "What's the trouble here, Miss Rosie?"

Rosie told him, whiles Gruffle sorta snickered an' rubbed his mangy beard. The bum steers, gettin' mighty interested in the goings-on, sauntered back into Rosie's. One of the mangiest of 'em spoke up. "Whatcha gonna do about it, Sheriff?"

J.D. puffed up his chest an' replied, "Gruffle, you're not gittin' away with anything in Dust River Gulch. Pay up an' git outta town."

Gruff sauntered over till he was 'most in J.D.'s face an' breathed out sour-milk breath. "Who's gonna make me, Sheriff?"

"You're lookin' at him."

Well, Gruff, he started smilin' an' rubbin' that mangy beard of his.

"Maybe we can make a deal with this here sheriff, eh, boys?"

The bums a-snorted an' a-snickered. "Yeah, boss. Maybe."

"You boys want a little entertainment?"

"Yeah, boss!"

Gruffle smiled real mean-like an' said, "How 'bout we have ourselves a little rodeo, Sheriff, just you an' me?"

"What're you sayin', Gruff?" asked the sheriff, and the steers commenced their laughin' again.

"We'll have a rodeo. You ride me an' I ride you. An' the one who stays on the longest is the winner, see?"

Well, now, that mangy buffalo musta had nearly a thousand pounds on J.D., but one glance in Miss Rosie's direction, an' the sheriff figured he'd accept the challenge. "If I win, you'll pay up an' git outta town, right?"

Gruffle snorted his approval. "Gladly, Sheriff. But now, if you might just happen to lose, you'll do the same?"

J.D. nodded.

"That is, if you kin still walk." At that, the bum steers started a-snickerin' an' a-snortin' like nobody's business again.

"Let's go, Sheriff," grunted Gruff.

So out went the outlaw an' the lawman, followed real close-like by the snickerin' steers. An' then 'most the whole town gathered 'round in front of Rosie's Restaurant.

Face-Off

Gruffle and J.D., they stood on opposite sides of the street, a-loosenin' up an' eyein' each other real fearsome-like. They decided old Tumbleweeze would keep time, along with one of the smarter bum steers (or at least one of the less dumb ones, that is). J.D. would ride Gruffle first, then vicey-versey.

Gruffle, he had a sneaky, sly sorta smile on his face like he was up to somethin'. An' wouldn't you know it—he was. When nobody was a-payin' no mind, he slipped one of the spurs off his boot an' hid it in the thick, mangy hair on his back, real secret-like. He whispered what he'd done to his no 'count steers, and they started some fearsome snickerin'.

Meanwhile, J.D. was developin' a perty sizable lump in his throat. He hadn't never ridden no buffalo before. Specially not when it counted fer so much.

Miss Rosie, she musta sensed it, 'cause she ran over to him an' planted a big, sweet kiss on the end of his nose an' said, sweet as anything, "Whup him, J.D.!"

With a spark in his eye, Sheriff J.D. Saddlesoap called out, "I'm ready, Gruffle! Are you?"

Gruffle O'Buffalo, he smiled an' snorted out, "Yep." An' there he stood, ready to be ridden.

All the folks held their breath. Then J.D. galloped over an' hopped onta Gruffle's back.

"Start a-timin', Weeze," called Miss Rosie. An' he did.

The mangy outlaw started a-buckin' an' a-snortin'. He ran 'round in a circle front-wise an' back, sendin' some folks fer cover. Up he reared an' down he tramped, whiles J.D. was a-bouncin' 'round on his back like a jackrabbit.

"Ride'm, J.D.!"
"Yahoo!"

"Whup'm, Sheriff!"

"Ride him right outta town!"

Meanwhiles, the bum steers was a-snickerin' a mite less. But Gruff was a-snortin' up a storm. He was a-twistin' in contortions an' a-kickin' like a mad billy goat.

J.D. was a-feeling like a sack of pataters that's been bounced downstairs, but he was still a-holdin' on. Then he hit that spur.

"Yee-ooowww!"

The spur sent J.D. up past the roof of Rosie's, an' down he landed in a cloud of dust. But one glance in the direction of his favorite gal, an' he claimed he was just feelin' a mite sore.

316

some black and white paint in a hurry."

Mr. Akers scratched his head. "Don't know as I've ever seen a can of black and white paint. A person has to buy one can of each and keep them separate, or he'll come out with gray."

Beanie sighed. He didn't have time for one of Mr. Akers's long-winded discussions. "Okay, give me a can of black and a can of white."

"Now Son, don't get your horses going too fast." Mr. Akers shuffled over to a distant shelf. "Do you want oil-based paint or water-based paint?" He peered over his glasses at the two boys.

Beanie looked at Freighter with raised eyebrows. Freighter shrugged his shoulders. Beanie turned back to Mr. Akers. "What's the difference?"

"Well, now, the two are just not the same. Quite a bit of difference, I'd say." Mr. Akers rubbed his chin. "In the first place, the water-based paint is much cheaper. In the second place—"

Beanie didn't give him a chance to finish. "We'll take the water-based paint and a large brush and a small brush."

Beanie counted out the money on the counter, standing first on one foot and then on the other as Mr. Akers bagged the paint and brushes. The boys grabbed the bag and headed out the door.

Mr. Akers stood shaking his head. "Youngsters are always in a hurry."

Walking briskly down Main Street, Beanie went over the plans with Freighter. "You take the first sheet of paper and start painting a

white block on the curb in front of each customer's house. Meanwhile I'll go to the door and collect the money. When we're done with this street, I'll go back and paint the house numbers in black on the white block while you go on to the next street.

"Sure thing!" Freighter agreed readily. He had been given the easier job. He wondered if Beanie's usually sharp mind had been dulled by all the excitement and missed that detail.

He didn't wonder long. "And then, when we're halfway through, we'll switch jobs," Beanie continued.

Freighter sighed. Work had tightened its noose around him again. "Okay, where do we start?"

Beanie looked at his sheets. "Pine Street—the next block over. Come on!"

Mix-Up Fix-Up

Business went well for the two boys all morning. Both were working so hard that neither one noticed the slow disappearance of the sun or the approach of black thunderclouds. Not until they sat down under the big oak tree for lunch together did they notice the first pinhole in their dream bubble.

"My shadow," Freighter mumbled, his mouth full of baloney and bread.

"What about it?" Beanie asked.

"It's gone. And look at the sky! It's all clouded up!"

Beanie looked up. Then he jumped to his feet. "Oh, no! The newspaper was wrong! It's not going to rain on Friday; it's going to rain this afternoon!"

Freighter stuffed the last of his sandwich in his mouth and grabbed a handful of papers. "Let's get moving!"

The two boys worked feverishly for the next three hours, running from house to house and curb to curb, slapping on white paint and then black paint. At one point Freighter, somewhat annoyed, stopped Beanie in the middle of the street.

"You know, some of these people act like they never even heard of our service before. I have to explain everything to them all over again. This must be one of the streets you canvassed. I've never seen these people before."

Beanie waved him aside. "Don't get so upset. You know how adults are; they only half listen to you the first time. Come on, we've got to finish before it rains. We'll meet under the big oak tree when we're done."

Freighter started to say more, but just then a large raindrop hit him on the nose. He took off running towards the next house.

It was 4:07 P.M. when Beanie and Freighter met under the large oak tree in the center of the town park.

"We did it!" Freighter cried, slapping a paint-spotted hand on his knee.

Beanie grinned. "The drug store has a triple-decker fudge sundae just waiting to be eaten. Beat you there!"

"Whoopee!" Freighter shouted. And down the street the boys raced as the first trickles of rain began to fall.

Later, after eating his sundae, Beanie darted home through the pouring rain, singing at the top of his lungs. After all, he had fifty dollars in his pocket for two days' work. Nothing could dampen his spirits.

Nothing, that is, until he opened the kitchen door at home and saw his mother.

"Samuel Jedidiah Haskins!"

Beanie knew right then that he was in trouble for something. It took a serious occasion for his mother to remember his full name. But the telephone rang, and Mrs. Haskins dashed off to answer it. By the time she came back into the kitchen, Mr. Haskins had come into the room.

"Now Dear," he began, "nothing could be that bad . . ."

Mrs. Haskins straightened her apron, seized a potato, and began peeling furiously. Beanie was glad it was the potato and not him that she had gotten her hands on. Then the story began to come out.

"It's not just me; all of Briar Cliff is angry with Beanie. The phone has been ringing off the hook." Mrs. Haskins thumped a potato on the counter. "Beanie has painted all the wrong house numbers on all the curbs. A lot of guests have arrived for the anniversary celebration, and they've been driving around town for hours!"

Beanie sank slowly into a chair. How had it happened? He had planned everything so carefully. Where had the plans gone wrong?

"Son?" Dad's one word asked the questions already jumbling around in Beanie's mind.

Beanie shuffled through his sheaf of papers, as if the names and addresses hid a secret. Then he began to study the papers more carefully.

"Oh, no," he groaned. "Somehow the papers have gotten out of order." He kept shuffling the papers in disbelief. Suddenly the bright scribbling caught his attention. "The papers must have gotten mixed up when the baby colored on them!"

Beanie lay in bed that night listening to the drip, drip, drip of the raindrops. Their dismal tune matched his spirits all too well. He sighed. His father was right. He was responsible for the mix-up, and he was responsible to fix it up.

Early the next morning Beanie and Freighter set off for the hardware store again, making a detour to behold the damage they had done the day before.

"This must not be one of our streets," Freighter said. "There aren't any numbers or white blocks." Beanie didn't even look. "I guess we started with the next one."

The two boys trudged on to the next street.

"Nope, not this one either," Freighter exclaimed. "No blocks and no numbers."

On and on the two boys went. On street after street they found no blocks and no numbers.

"This is strange," Freighter said. "Did we dream the whole thing yesterday?"

Beanie didn't answer right away. Little bells were beginning to ring in the back of his mind. Then, with a tug on Freighter's arm, he shouted, "Come on! I think we need to find out from Mr. Akers what the other differences are between oil-based and water-based paints!"

Of course, once inside Mr. Akers's store, the two boys discovered the secret of the disappearing house numbers. And this time they bought oil-based paint, both black and white.

Friday turned out to be a perfect day for repainting house numbers on curbs. And on Saturday both boys joined the Briar Cliff celebration activities with sunburned arms and money in their pockets.

Strange Fire in the White House

Steffi Adams

*illustrated by Stephanie True and
Preston Gravely Jr.*

*Benjamin Harrison was elected president of the United
States in 1889. In 1891 electric lights were installed in the
White House. President Harrison was so afraid of being
shocked by this new invention that he would never use the
lights unless one of the servants switched them on and off.*

Changes

Eleven-year-old Ebenezer Tate lowered himself into the cane-backed wheelchair as the carriage creaked away down the graveled path. He felt awed as he sat looking at the front of the huge house. It was hard to believe that he would be living in the White House for the next few weeks.

Mrs. Tate smoothed the scratchy wool lap robe around Eben's legs. "Now don't be nervous, dear," she said, ringing the doorbell. "Just because the Harrisons are in the White House now doesn't mean they're not our friends anymore."

The bell was still ringing when the door opened.

"Yes, ma'am? May I help you?" asked the doorkeeper.

"I'm Mrs. Tate, and this is my son, Ebenezer."

"Please come in," the door-keeper said, opening the door wider. "The president and Mrs. Harrison are expecting you."

Mrs. Tate rolled Eben through the doorway while the doorkeeper rang for the other servants.

"What lovely stained glass!" said Mrs. Tate. "Don't you think so, Eben?"

"I guess."

The doorkeeper glanced at the sparkling colored panels that covered the far end of the vestibule. "Mr. Tiffany built that for President Arthur to separate the public and private quarters. The Blue Room is just beyond those panels," he said to the Tates while the servants gathered around him. "Now if you will follow Annie, she will show you to your room."

"Don't mind about your baggage," said Annie, the friendly young maid. "We'll take the elevator. It'll be easier for the young master." She pushed Eben's chair toward the two strange-looking doors.

As the elevator doors closed behind him, Eben squirmed in his chair and pulled his cap over his ears. He tried to hide from the maid's curious eyes.

"Oh, my!" said Mrs. Tate when the elevator jerked to a stop. "That was quite a ride. What will they think of next?"

"A body can't keep up with the changes these days, mum," Annie agreed. "Now, if you two will just follow me."

When the baggage had been delivered and the servants had gone, Eben lifted himself out of the wheelchair and onto the smaller bed. "Did you see how they looked at me?" he asked. "They pitied me just like every-one at home does."

Mrs. Tate sat on the edge of Eben's bed. "Hold your head high, dear," she said, taking off his cap and smoothing his flyaway blond hair. "Only a pitiful man can be pitied."

There was a knock on the door. Before Eben could blink,

Mrs. Harrison was smothering him in her plump arms. "Oh, poor boy," she said. "I was so sorry to hear about your accident. It seems like just yesterday that you were running to the market for me back in Indianapolis. We are in quite a disarray around here with all the repairs going on, but you are comfortable in this room, aren't you?"

"Yes, ma'am."

"I've instructed the servants to take care of your every need," she said. "The doctors here are very good."

While his mother and Mrs. Harrison talked about all their friends back home in Indianapolis and the redecorating of the White House, Eben turned his face toward the wall and closed his eyes. "I wouldn't complain about running to the market now," he thought.

When the two ladies finally left the room, Eben pulled a dog-eared copy of *Treasure Island* from his coat pocket and began reading as the shadows lengthened. His eyes began to close in spite of himself.

Eben opened his eyes suddenly. "Why is it so dark?" he

wondered. His heart pounded against his chest like a blacksmith's hammer on an anvil. As he tried to calm himself, a small hand touched his shoulder.

"Who's there?" he shouted into the shadows.

"Me and Ike turn on the lights," a small voice answered. "Who are you?"

"Go away," said Eben.

The door opened wider, and a beam of light fell across the small bed. A tall man stood framed in the doorway.

"Benjy McKee, you mustn't disturb the guests," said the man to the president's four-year-old grandson. "Mr. Tate, I'm Irwin Hoover, better known as Ike, the White House electrician. Would you like electric lights this evening?"

"Electric lights?" asked Eben, propping himself against the feather pillows.

"Yes, they've just been installed," said Ike. "The president and his family won't touch the lights, so I turn them on every evening and off again in the morning."

"Are they afraid of the lights?"

"Most people are afraid of new things, especially things they don't understand," said Ike. "The president and his family fear a deadly shock, although I've told them that these lights are safe. Still, they allow no one to touch them except me."

"Mama calls them 'strange fire,'" Benjy added.

The word *fire* was enough for Eben. "I don't want the electric lights anywhere near me," he said.

Ike obediently left, leaving Benjy alone with Eben.

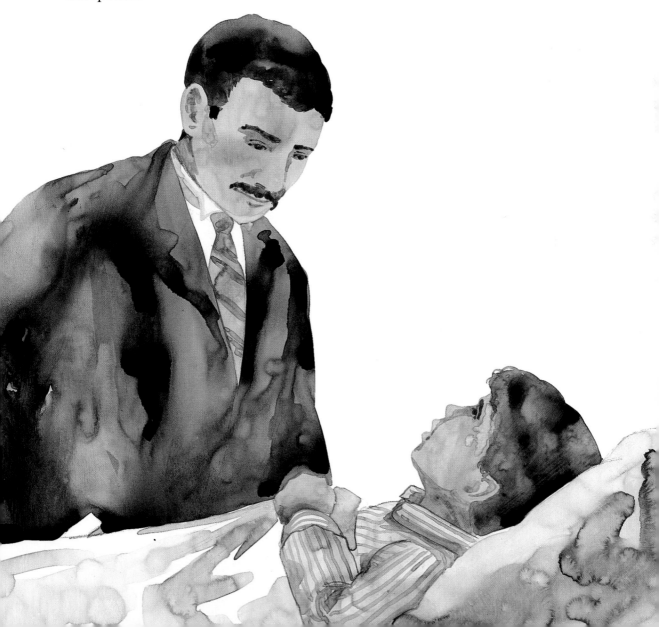

Before long, bright white gas light filled the room. Benjy touched the ugly red scar on Eben's forehead. "Does that hurt?" he asked.

Eben shrugged away from Benjy's touch. "No, not any more."

"I got one too," said Benjy, pointing to a small scar on his left knee. "I fell out of my goat cart." Then, tugging Eben's sleeve, he added, "Let's play with my soldiers."

Eben decided he liked Benjy. "Where are they?" he asked.

"In the nursery down the hall," said Benjy.

Challenges

Benjy prattled on as Eben slowly wheeled himself along. Suddenly Eben asked, "Are you the one they call Baby McKee?"

Benjy nodded shyly. "Some people do," he said.

Eben nodded. "I remember reading about you in the newspapers," he said. It seemed that almost every day the newspapers were printing another story about the pranks of "Baby" McKee.

All through the rest of that evening, Eben felt happier than he had in a long time. Playing with Benjy was almost like having a little brother of his own.

The next morning as he laid his breakfast tray on the table, Eben's spirits were as bright as the morning sun. He could hardly wait to see Benjy again.

"Benjy, let's go outside," said Eben as he wheeled himself into the nursery. "Benjy?"

"He's downstairs," said Ike from the hall. "The Harrison family always has Bible reading and prayers after breakfast. Your ma is with them, I believe."

"Oh," said Eben sullenly, turning the wheelchair around. "Push me back to my room."

"Why should I?" asked Ike. "You've got two strong arms, haven't you? Anyway, you shouldn't stay closed up in that room all day. Come with me while I turn off the electric lights. I'll give you a personal tour of the White House."

A faint spark of excitement flickered in Eben's brown eyes. "Will you show me the president's office?" he asked.

"We'll take a peek in there," said Ike as he strode down the hall toward the East Wing.

"Wait!" said Eben. "You forgot me."

"You're right behind me, aren't you?"

Sullenly Eben began to push himself after Ike. Ike showed him room after room, so grand and glorious that Eben soon forgot that he was pushing his chair along by himself. Ike showed him the marvelous electric light switches that went on and off with only a flick of the finger.

Finally Eben rolled to a stop just outside the second-floor library. "Did you enjoy the tour?" asked Ike as he snapped off the hall lights.

"Benjy has a grand home." Eben sighed. "I'd love living here except for that strange fire. How can you touch it?"

"I've been trained," said Ike.

"Yes, but before that. Weren't you afraid?" Eben insisted.

Ike sat down carefully on a plush velvet chair. "Thinking back, I guess I was a little fearful at first. But then I said to myself, 'Irwin, get on with this. Don't let fear keep you from learning something new, especially in the line of duty.' I had to try to learn. Even if I failed, I had to try."

"But what if you had failed?"

"Why, if I had never tried, that would have been a failure in itself," said Ike. "Not trying is worse than failing."

Eben stared at the rug. "I couldn't touch that electric switch even if I tried," he said. Before he knew it, he was telling Ike about the fire that had destroyed his home and left him scarred and crippled.

"When I woke up, well, it was almost like being in the hell that Pa preaches about," said Eben. "If I hadn't jumped out of my bedroom window, I would have burned up with the house. So you see why I'm afraid of fire."

"Seems to me that you should be counting your blessings," said Ike. "You still have your pa and ma."

"I am happy about that," Eben agreed, "and I'm glad to be alive. But sometimes I get so tired of just sitting in this wheelchair while everyone makes a fuss over me."

"Can't the doctors do anything?" asked Ike.

Eben shrugged. "I'm supposed to see a special doctor tomorrow. He wants me to have an operation to help me walk again."

"Surely that makes you happy," said Ike. "Just think. You'll soon be out of that wheelchair."

Eben twisted his cap in his hands. "The operation is just the beginning. It will hurt for a long time."

"But you will try, won't you?" asked Ike.

Eben lowered his head and did not answer.

"Eben! Eben!" Benjy called. "Our Bible-reading time is over. Come outside with me and see my goat!"

Eben's eyes lit up. "I'm coming, Benjy!" he said.

Eben rolled into the bedroom late that afternoon. "Ma, you should have been with us. I got to see the goat and acres of flowers in the greenhouses. I even saw a fly-catching plant!"

"That's wonderful, dear," Mrs. Tate said. "President and Mrs. Harrison are taking me to a formal dinner. We won't be back until late." Leaning over, she kissed Eben. "You have a big day tomorrow, so be in bed by eight o'clock."

"Yes, ma'am," Eben promised, wondering how he would stay awake through supper.

Eben was nodding when the supper tray slid off his lap. Dishes, silverware, and the metal tray hit the floor and woke him suddenly. Darkness had crept into the room.

Carefully, Eben rolled out into the hall. He paused for a minute, trying to see. Something was wrong. A faint smell of smoke came from somewhere down the hall.

"Ike! Annie! Fire!" yelled Eben as he tried to remember the way to the elevator. "Benjy! Benjy! Where are you?"

Eben became frantic. If "Baby" McKee was up to one of his pranks again . . . he could be in a dangerous spot.

Quickly, Eben crossed the hall. Even in the darkness he could tell that the library door was ajar.

"Benjy!" called Eben, opening the door wider. He felt as if someone had kicked his stomach.

A fire crackled in the wastepaper basket. Soon flaming tongues could spread to the draperies nearby!

"Benjy? Where are you?" shouted Eben, ignoring the pounding in his head. "Oh, if I could only see!"

The electric lights!

Eben's hand fumbled along the wall. There it was, just as Ike had shown him this morning.

Taking a deep breath to steady his trembling hands, Eben flicked the switch. Instantly the room was filled with harsh, yellow light.

When his eyes had adjusted to the sudden brightness, Eben saw Benjy lying behind the desk near an overturned chair. An open box of matches lay on the desk.

I have to smother the fire, thought Eben. He looked around for anything that he could use. That's it! My lap robe is just the thing.

Eben quickly rolled his chair across the room and tossed the wool cover over the flames. Then, when he was certain that the fire had died out, he pulled the dazed child up into his lap.

"Eben, you're here," said Benjy as he weakly patted Eben's flushed face. He burst out crying.

Eben was examining Benjy when Ike rushed into the library saying, "I smell smoke."

"Benjy was playing with the matches," Eben said. "He fell off the chair, but he's all right now."

Then Ike noticed the lights. He relaxed a bit and rubbed his chin. "What about you?" he asked. "Weren't you afraid? What if you had failed?"

Eben smiled. "I guess you answered that question this morning."

"And what about tomorrow when you see the doctor?" asked Ike.

"I can only try," said Eben. "It might hurt to try to walk, but if I do my best, I won't be a failure."

Wind Song

Lilian Moore
illustrated by Doug Young

When the wind blows
The quiet things speak.
Some whisper, some clang
Some creak.

Grasses swish
Treetops sigh
Flags slap
and snap in the sky.
Wires on poles
whistle and hum
Ashcans roll.
Windows drum.

When the wind goes—
suddenly
then
the quiet things
are quiet again.

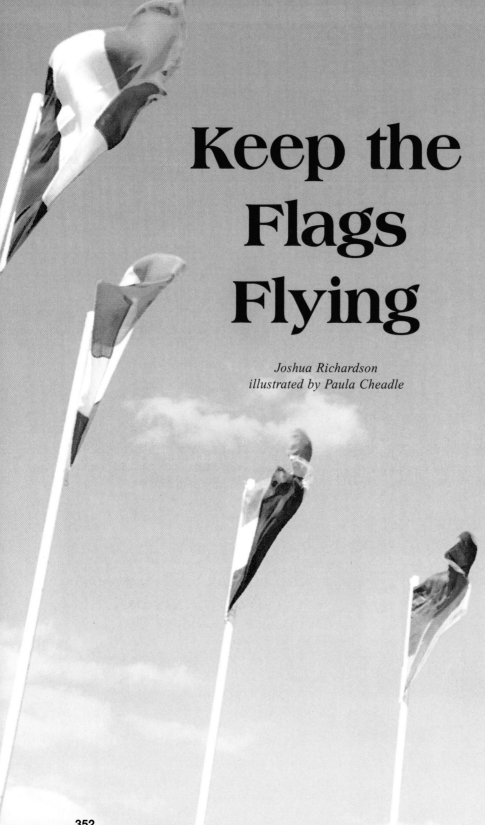

Keep the Flags Flying

Joshua Richardson
illustrated by Paula Cheadle

Just about everyone has heard the legend about Betsy Ross sewing the first American flag. You may have heard the story of how Francis Scott Key wrote the "Star-Spangled Banner." And when astronaut Neil Armstrong became the first man on the moon, people everywhere watched as he planted the American flag there.

Flags have played an important role around the world for centuries. Men from many nations have followed their flags into battle and died for what their flags symbolized. Patriots everywhere still hoist flags to show their loyalty to their nation. But how did people start using flags in the first place?

Actually, flags were never invented. They just developed out of simpler objects. Most people who have studied flags believe that the very first "flags" were used in battles. The dust and confusion in battle made it hard for soldiers to recognize their leaders. So some ancient captains in Egypt, Persia, and Greece started tying a piece of colored cloth onto the end of their spears. That way they could guide their men more easily.

Years later, the Roman cavalry used a square cloth banner called a *vexillum*. At first the *vexillum*

hung straight down from a crossbar on the end of a spear. In time, though, soldiers discovered that they could attach the banner to the side of the spear. In this position it could wave in the wind. It was also easier to handle.

As flags became more popular, people began trying out new designs. Many flags remained square, but others became rectangles or triangles. Some people even created swallow-tailed flags—flags that taper off in two or three points, or tails. In 1206 the Mongol invader Genghis Khan used a battle flag that had so many tails that it looked like tongues of flame streaming behind a spear! As time passed, though, most flags became rectangle-shaped.

Later in history, flags became common symbols for cities, and even some individuals. In the Netherlands each city still flies its own flag. A flag with waterlily leaves represents the city of Friesland. Many noblemen created their own personal flags and flew them over their castles.

Friesland flag

Some pirates even flew a "Jolly Roger"—a black flag with a white skull and crossed bones—to show that they were pirates!

"Jolly Roger" flag

Today, most flags show loyalty to countries or states. But there are still many other jobs for flags to perform. For instance, a solid red flag warns of danger. A solid white flag raised in battle means surrender. And an American flag flown upside-down becomes a distress signal, a cry for help.

At sea, ships use flags to identify themselves and to send messages. International code flags are brightly colored flags that stand for letters and numbers. By flying certain groups of these code flags, sailors can pass signals to other ships. But they must be careful to use these flags properly.

During World War II, some British soldiers escaped from the Japanese in a small sailboat. After many days at sea, they finally spotted an Allied ship. So they excitedly raised what they thought were the signal flags to ask for help. The captain of the ship was astonished when he read the little boat's message: "Preparing to attack!" He shouted that the soldiers had better take their signal flags down or be blasted out of the water. The embarrassed soldiers quickly followed his advice!

Flags may have had simple beginnings, but they certainly have become important parts of our lives. But what of that first ancient captain who invented a flag by tying a strip of cloth to his spear? What would he have said if someone had told him that his idea would someday be used around the world and even on the moon? He probably would have laughed!

The Christian Flag

A Choral Reading

by Sharon Wintermute and Ron Shields

Readers

Chorus One: light voices

Chorus Two: dark voices

Reader One

Reader Two

Reader Three

Reader Four

Reader One: A pledge. What does it mean?

All: A pledge—

Chorus One: A pledge is a promise—

All: A pledge—

Chorus Two: A pledge is a promise given by me.

All: A pledge—

Choruses One and Two: A pledge is a promise given by me

All: to the flag of my faith.

Reader One: I pledge—

Reader Two: I pledge—

Reader Three: I pledge—

All: We pledge allegiance to the Christian Flag, and to the Savior for whose kingdom it stands.

Reader One: From His kingdom in heaven God sent His beloved Son

Reader Two: To die on the cross, God's will to be done.

All: We pledge allegiance to the Christian flag, and to the Savior for whose kingdom it stands, one Savior—

Reader Three: Christ is the only Savior of man.

All: Crucified—

Reader One: He submitted to God's divine plan.

All: Risen—

Reader Two: On the third day Christ arose from the tomb. He ascended into heaven where we'll meet Him soon!

All: And coming again—

Reader Three: When the Lord returns, the dead in Christ He will receive and gather up those who are alive and believe.

All: One Savior, crucified, risen, and coming again, with life and liberty to all who believe.

Reader Four: When I see the Christian flag in many lands—

Reader Two: *(quietly)* red cross, blue band on a field of white—

Reader Four: I think of our Christian faith for which it stands.

Reader Two: A red cross, a blue band, and a field of white remind me of my Savior for whom we fight.

Reader One: I pledge—

Readers Two and Three: I pledge—

All: I pledge allegiance to the Christian flag, and to the Savior for whose kingdom it stands, one Savior, crucified, risen, and coming again, with life and liberty to all—

Reader Four: To all!

Readers One, Two, and Three: To all!

Readers One, Two, Three, and Four: To all!

All: With life and liberty to all who believe.

The American Flag

A Choral Reading

arranged by Becky Henry

Readers

Reader One

Reader Two

Reader Three

Reader Four

All: A pledge—

Reader One: A pledge to our country—

Reader Two: A pledge to the flag that represents our country—

All: A pledge of allegiance—

Reader Three: But what is allegiance?

Reader One: Allegiance is loyalty; allegiance is love—

Reader Two: A desire to serve, a desire to stand—

Reader Four: Allegiance is the bond that makes us stand up for our country—to work or to fight.

All: I pledge allegiance to the flag of the—

Reader One: United States. When Thomas Jefferson wrote the Declaration of Independence in 1776, he declared that the thirteen states were—

All: "United States."

Reader Four: They were united in their desire to stand together, without the tyranny of a king!

All: I pledge allegiance to the flag of the United States of America, and to the Republic for which it stands—

Reader Three: Republic? What is a republic?

Reader One: When the United States became a country, it was one of the first republics ever established.

Reader Two: Our Founding Fathers wanted to guarantee that every citizen would be able to have a say in the government.

Reader Three: That's what a republic is—government that belongs to the people.

All: I pledge allegiance to the flag of the United States of America, and to the Republic for which it stands, one nation—

Reader One: Standing together—

All: Under God—

Reader Two: Seeking Him as our Guide—

All: Indivisible—

Reader Three: Never to be divided—

Reader One: With liberty—

Reader Two: And justice—

All: For all! I pledge allegiance to the flag of the United States of America, and to the Republic for which it stands, one nation, under God, indivisible, with liberty and justice for all.

LITERATURE LESSON:

Similes

Trip: San Francisco

Langston Hughes

I went to San Francisco.
I saw the bridges high
Spun across the water
Like cobwebs in the sky.

illustrated by
Kathy Phlug and Noelle Snyder

Did you like the picture that "Trip: San Francisco" made in your mind? It's funny to imagine bridge cables being like cobwebs. Yet suppose the author said, "The cables looked thin and silvery." Then the picture probably wouldn't have lasted as long in your memory.

• Reading Similes

When a writer compares two things that are really different by using the keyword *like* or *as,* the expression he makes is called a *simile.* "I saw the bridges high / Spun across the water / Like cobwebs in the sky" uses the keyword *like.* It compares bridge cables and cobwebs, two things that aren't really similar. These are the two ways you can know that this expression is a simile.

When you come across a simile in your reading, notice it. First, make sure that it really is a simile. "Allison looked like she was angry" is not one. Why not? "The dandelion leaf was like lions' teeth" *is* a simile. Why? Next, try to decide if it is a good simile or not. Does it make a new picture in your mind, or is it an old expression that you've heard many times before? Does "She was as quiet as a mouse" give you a new picture or an old one? What about "The cat acted as wild as a winter storm"?

• Writing Similes

The best way to learn how to write good similes is to pay attention to the good similes that you read. They can help you think of new word pictures to liven up your writing. And practice writing similes too. Your teacher can help you make your similes better. Then you can write expressions that will last a long time in someone's memory.

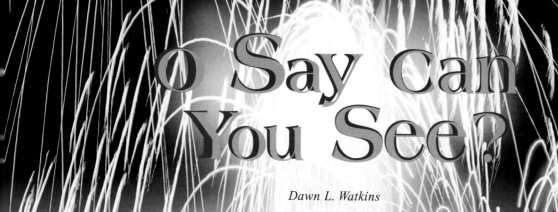

O Say Can You See?

Dawn L. Watkins

Searing whistle, sizzle and
Ripping pah-poom, pah-pum—

Like guns from some far-off battle
Rattling over fife and drum—

A moment's lull and then

Out burst bouquets of light
Shimmering down petals
That glimmer and melt on the night.

Pah-poom, we throw more stars into the sky

Where they hold,
       and drizzle to the ground.

Below we gasp and ah!
Wait for another thunder round.

Story About
George Washington

illustrated by Kathy Phlug

Almost two hundred years ago, when the pioneers were moving farther and farther west, William McGuffey was born. He grew up on the Ohio frontier, worked his way through school, and then became a teacher.

As a teacher he had some good ideas about education. First, he believed that a teacher could not separate God's truth from education. Second, he used shorter words for small children and used pictures to help students understand the stories. He put these ideas together and wrote the McGuffey readers. Because his books were interesting, easy to understand, and faithful to Scripture, they were used for many, many years. Most children in the 1800s were raised on the McGuffey readers.

The story that follows was taken from an early edition of a McGuffey reader. The sentences were numbered to help the teacher and the students as they answered questions and read aloud.

LESSON LXVII

1. One fine spring day George Washington's father prepared a bed of earth in the garden near a walk George was known to favor.

2. In the bed he lettered, with a small stick, the name of his son, "George Washington," in its full length, and filled the letters with cabbage seed.

3. After he had completed his task, he carefully smoothed over the bed, and waited for the seed to come up.

4. In due course, tiny plants appeared, and there was to be seen, in living green—in nature's own penmanship—the name of "George Washington."

5. As George was playing in the garden, either trundling his wagon or riding his prancing horse, his eyes fell upon the wonder.

6. He halted and studied—he spelled the name—he hesitated and puzzled, and read again. He never saw such a splendid thing before—he never heard of any such thing—he could not believe his eyes, yet it was so.

7. He didn't stay long but bounded away towards the house, and soon stood in the presence of his father.

8. "Father!" exclaimed he.

9. "Well, George, what distresses you?"

10. "Why, Father, I've seen such a sight!"

11. "What? Where, my son?" inquired Mr. Washington.

12. "In the garden, sir."

13. "And what have you seen strange in the garden?"

14. "Oh, come and see—come and see, Father; something I never heard of before," said George.

15. Mr. Washington went with unusual readiness to the spot, well convinced what the strange sight would prove to be. George led the way by some rods.

16. "Here, Father, here it is; did you ever see such a strange sight before?"

17. "What is it you see that you find so strange?" said Mr. Washington, now drawing close and appearing somewhat astonished.

18. "Why, here, Father, don't you see these?" said George, stooping down and gently passing his little fingers over the letters of his name in the bed.

19. "What, George?"

20. "Why, my name, Father—here—growing in this bed, so green. How did it happen?"

21. "Is it anything strange?" Mr. Washington asked.

22. "Why Father, I never heard of any such thing before, did you?"

23. "Why—George—well—" said Mr. Washington, hesitating at the unexpected query, "it certainly is curious."

24. "But, Father, how did it get here?"

25. "Perhaps, by *chance,* George."

26. "No, no, Father. It could not have come by chance. I never heard of such a thing."

27. "Well, and why may it not have come by chance?"

28. "I don't know, Father, but I don't *believe* it did."

29. "There are many things we don't believe, George, which nevertheless are true."

30. "Yes, yes, Father, but I never *saw* any like it before."

31. "That may be, and yet it may have come by chance."

32. "Well, I never *heard* of any such thing."

33. "True, and yet might it not happen, although *you* never heard of it?"

34. "Ah, but Father, how should little plants grow up just so to make the letters of my name—*all* the letters—all in exact order? Why was it not your name? Ah, Father, why was it anyone's name?"

Questions—1. What is the story about? 2. What did Mr. Washington plant? 3. How did he plant them? 4. How did George feel when he discovered his name? Was it a very novel sight?

said	such	here	full
earth	query	rather	never
exact	fingers	doubted	prancing
strange	favorite	prepared	unexpected
all	high	what	your
green	heard	letters	relieve
father	garden	bounded	trundling
appearing	hesitated	exclaimed	nevertheless

1. "It is *rather wonderful*," Mr. Washington admitted.

2. "Ah, Father, I perceive," said George, looking up inquisitively.

3. "Well, and what do you perceive, my son?"

4. "Why, I perceive somebody did this. Yes, I've just thought, somebody sowed the seed to make my name. I perceive *you* did it Father, didn't you?"

5. "Well, George, for once you are quite right in your guessing. I *did* do it."

6. "What for, Father?"

7. "What for! Why, does it not look beautiful?"

8. "Yes, but you had some design, Father. What did you mean by it?"

9. "I meant, George," Mr. Washington expounded, "by means of it to teach you an *important lesson*."

10. "What, Father, to plant seeds?"

11. "More important than that. I want to prove to you that there is a great and mighty God."

12. "Why, I believe that now, Father. Mother has often told me about that."

13. "Well, but, George, how do you *know* that there is a God?"

14. "Because Mother says there is."

15. "But what I mean, my son, is how you would *prove* that there is a God?"

16. "I never studied that, Father, and I don't know."

17. "Well, that is the very point I wish you to understand. Listen and I will explain."

18. "A short time ago, you discovered these letters in this bed. They appeared wonderful to you; you called me; you wished to know how they came to be. I told you that they might have come by chance, but this explanation did not satisfy you. Can you tell me why?"

19. "Because it seemed as if somebody must have sowed the seed here just so," said George.

20. "True, it does appear so. Now, can you tell, my son, *why* it appears so?"

21. "Because," said George. "I think somebody had a *design* in it, and indeed you told me that you had some design in it, Father."

22. "Just so, George, I *had* a design in it, and the marks of design prove that the plants did not grow that way by chance, but that some agent, or being, was concerned in them. Is it not so?"

23. "Yes, sir."

24. "Now then, George, I entreat you to look around. Observe this beautiful world. See how nicely all things are planned, what marks of design there are! We have fire to warm us when we are cold, water to drink when we are thirsty, teeth to eat with, eyes to see with, feet to walk with. In a thousand things we see design. There must, then, have been a *designer*—some one who formed these things for a purpose—for some end."

25. "Ah!" said George, "I know whom you mean, Father."

26. "Whom, my son?"

27. "God Almighty. Do you not?"

28. "Yes, I mean Him. It was He that created all the beautiful and convenient things which you see around you. I mean Him who is God the Lord, and owner of all things, and Who should be worshiped by us all."

29. "But, Father, is not this garden yours alone, and the house, and all things around us here?"

30. "No, my son," replied Mr. Washington. "They are not mine. True, I call them mine, and they are mine to use, rather than my neighbor's; but they are only entrusted to my care. All things belong to God. He created them, and they are His. He has given the care of them to His creatures here, and will one day require an account of them."

31. "But Father," said George, "you built your house, didn't you? Do you not own it, then?"

32. "Yes, George, but if I did build it, did I create the materials of it? Who made the trees, from which the timber, the boards, and the shingles were obtained? From what source did the iron come, from which the nails were made? God formed all. It was He, too, who formed the oxen, and the horses, and the sheep, and everything which you see on the farm."

33. George now became silent, and appeared for a time lost in reflections on his father's remarks. A good impression had been made on his mind and heart. From this time, it is believed, George Washington never doubted that there is a God, the Creator and Proprietor of all things.

Questions—1. Who did George Washington think placed the seed in the ground? 2. What did Mr. Washington intend to teach George by it? 3. Do we not see the evidences all around us, that there is a Great Being who has made the world? 4. Aren't the things which are made, well adapted to our happiness? 5. What should this teach us of that Great Being? 6. If He is good, should we not love Him? 7. What other and surer evidence have we that there is a God, than what we find in nature?

perceive	worshiped	reflections	looking
marks	chance	Creator	entreat
guessing	sowed	wild	Washington
convenient	beautiful	appear	observe
once	impression	appeared	expounded
lesson	some	Proprietor	materials
Almighty	design	world	important

Uncommon Names

Morgan Reed Persun
illustrated by Sam Laterza

Aunt Mergatroid is picky
Over what we call her plants!
And though she's always fussing,
She's the best of all our aunts.

"Don't call that yellow foxglove!
It's *digitalis grandiflora!*"
"But Auntie, I can't thay thoth wordth,"
Says little Lindsey Laura.

"And this," says our Aunt Mergie,
"Is a *rosa polyantha.*"
"It sure looks like a rose to me,"
Says my sister Nell Samantha.

"And this one here," Aunt Mergie says,
"Is a fine *Bellis perennis.*"
"It's not a daisy, then?" say I—
Her nephew Bradford Dennis.

We do that just to rile her—
Use the wrong names for her flowers;
For though she calls them all by name,
She can't remember ours!

A Tale of Chanticleer

Geoffrey Chaucer
retold by Eileen M. Berry
taken from The Canterbury Tales

illustrated by Brian Johnson and John Bjerk

Once upon a time, a poor widow lived in a little cottage beside a grove of trees. She had a garden which she managed wisely to support herself and her two daughters. She had three hogs, three cows, and a ewe. She also had a little yard enclosed with a wooden fence in which her rooster, Chanticleer, lived with his seven hens.

A more beautiful cock than Chanticleer could not be found in all the land. His comb was redder than fine coral and rose above his head in thick spires like a castle tower. His bill was shiny jet black, and his legs and toes were azure blue. His claws were the purest lily white. His neck and back were the color of burnished gold in the sunlight.

But lovelier by far than all of these was Chanticleer's voice. Merrier than the church organ and timely as the abbey clock, his crows rang out each morning just as the sun ascended.

One morning just before dawn, Chanticleer and his hens sat on their perch overlooking the yard and the fields beyond. Chanticleer sat next to Madam Pertelote, the fairest of all the hens. As Chanticleer sat dozing with closed eyes, he began to moan in his sleep.

Fair Pertelote nudged him with her bill. "My own dear heart, what is wrong?" she asked. Her tail feathers bristled up in alarm. "Why must you groan so, as though you were having a terrible dream?"

Chanticleer awoke, and a shiver went through him from his comb all the way down to his claws. "Ah, a dream. Was it only a dream? It seemed so real that my heart still quakes with fear. I dreamed that I was here in our yard, walking up and down, when a frightful beast approached me."

"What sort of beast?" Pertelote drew back and gave her wings a little flutter.

"Rather like a hound, but smaller—a light tawny color, gold mixed with red. His ears and tail were tipped in black, his snout was sharp and pointed, and his eyes sparkled with malice. I know he would have seized me and put me to death if my dream had continued."

"How faint-hearted you are!" Pertelote cried. She lifted her beak and looked sideways at Chanticleer. "Truly, I cannot love a coward. Your dream was probably caused by something you ate. I know some herbs and berries right there in the widow's garden that will cure you in a matter of minutes." She spread her wings as if to hurry off to the garden.

"Madam," said Chanticleer, "your advice is wise indeed; but I have read that such dreams are often warnings of danger to come. I don't want to take such a thing lightly." He gazed off into the distance for a moment. Then he looked at Pertelote. "Ah, it matters not," he said. "I have the

fairest hen in all the land beside me. I defy my dreams!"

The first rays of sun shone above the hill, and a soft May wind began to blow. Before long, Chanticleer was singing in the dawn as he did every sunrise.

Little did Chanticleer know that a very sly fox had broken through the hedge the night before and found his way into the bed of cabbages in the widow's garden. About nine o'clock, when the sun was bright and the chickens were scratching busily about in the dust, Chanticleer noticed a butterfly flitting among the cabbages. "How beautiful!" he sang out. "I must go for a closer look at the creature!"

At that moment, he noticed the fox lying low under a green cabbage leaf. It was the face he had seen in his dream! Chanticleer felt himself trembling from comb to claws. He flapped his wings wildly, crying out "Cok-cok! Cok-cok!", and turned to run.

"My good sir, please wait!" the fox said, with the utmost courtesy.

He wriggled out from under the cabbages, cleared his throat, and spoke in a smooth, pleasant voice. "Are you afraid of me? I am your friend!" The little tufts of fur above his eyes rose, and his mouth stretched into a gleaming smile. "I've only come to hear you sing," he said.

Chanticleer settled his wings into place and tried to pretend he had not been going to run. He fluffed his feathers a little. "To hear me sing, you say?"

"I do say," the fox replied. "You have more of a feeling for music than any musician I have ever known. You know, you quite take after your father. Many a morning I sat with utter pleasure and heard him sing. He put all his heart into his songs. And do you know, he had a trick for making his voice even stronger!"

"Oh?" Chanticleer stepped a bit closer to the fox.

"Yes, he would close his eyes as he sang, and stand on tiptoe, stretching his neck with the high notes." The fox closed his own eyes dreamily. "What talent he had! And what wisdom too!" He eyed Chanticleer out of one half-opened eye for a moment; then he opened both eyes wide. "I have a brilliant idea! Let me hear you sing just as your father did, and will you use his special trick? How I long to hear such singing again!"

Chanticleer flapped his wings. "Why, I would be delighted to entertain you, sir," he said eagerly, his chest swelling.

Chanticleer folded his wings and stood on tiptoe. He threw his head back, closed his eyes, and began to sing with all his strength.

No sooner had he begun than that sly fox seized him by the throat and carried him off toward the woods!

The hens immediately set up a loud, frightened clucking. Madam Pertelote clucked louder than them all. "Hurry!" she cried. "The wicked fox has Chanticleer in his teeth!"

The widow and her two daughters bolted from the house with sticks in their hands. The neighbors came running. A dog joined the chase, and the cow and the calf lumbered after him, and even the hogs began running wildly about in their pen.

Chanticleer, pinned tightly in the fox's teeth, had a sudden inspiration. "If I were you, sir," he began, a bit timidly, "I would not run from these fools in such a frenzy. You are almost to the woods and will be able to eat me in safety anyway. I would turn upon the lot of them and frighten them with gruff snarls and growls.

What fun it would be to see them stop in their tracks, turn tail, and run!"

The fox began to chuckle. "I say, I shall do it!" he said. But no sooner had he opened his mouth to speak than Chanticleer broke from his teeth and flew to the branch of a nearby tree.

"Alas!" cried the fox, seeing he had lost his meal. Then his mouth stretched into another sly grin. "My good sir, please come down," he said. "I should never have frightened you by seizing you like that and running. I really had no intention of eating you. Do come down, and I shall explain my behavior."

Chanticleer cocked his head at the fox. "You shall not fool me any more with your flattery," he said. "I have learned never again to close my eyes when I should keep them open."

The fox licked his lips and lowered himself to the ground. He put his head on his paws and sighed. "And I have learned," he said, "never again to open my mouth when I should keep it closed."

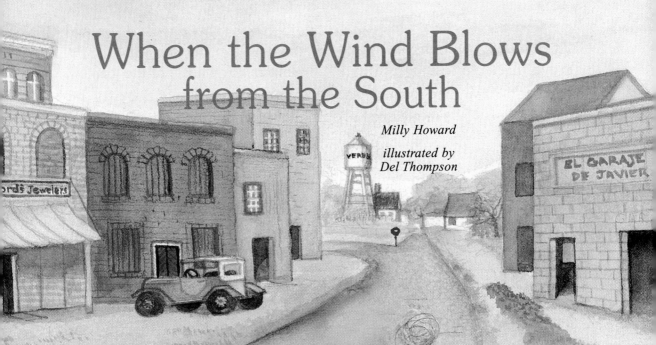

When the Wind Blows from the South

Milly Howard

illustrated by
Del Thompson

In the small Texas town of Las Verdes, colorful shops line the downtown streets. One of the shops is a small jewelry shop owned by a thin young man named Waldo Medford. Waldo is the best watch repairman in Las Verdes—or any other town, for that matter. He is a quiet man, dependable and reliable. That is, until the wind blows from the south.

South Wind Blowing

One spring day, as Waldo unlocked the door of his shop, a gust of hot wind whipped around the corner. Hand on the doorknob, Waldo stopped for a moment. Along the street the oak trees whispered dryly, nodding to each other. In the window boxes of the shops, marigolds and geraniums stretched and bobbed back and forth. Waldo hesitated and then firmly shut the door to the shop and turned the key. As he walked away, he passed the postman.

Holding onto his cap, the postman nodded cheerfully. "Wind's from the south today, Mr. Medford!"

Smiling, Waldo agreed. "Indeed it is, Fred. Time for a vacation."

"Enjoy yourself," Fred called as he walked away.

Humming to himself, Waldo drove back to his house. He parked the car and opened the garage door. The sun gleamed off the vehicle parked inside. Waldo walked around it, carefully dusting off the fenders. He had spent all winter getting the amphibious jeep repaired and in running order. He had purchased supplies and stacked them in the corners of the garage. Everything had been ready for a long time. Ready and waiting.

The next day a sign hung in the window of Waldo's shop.

"Closed!" Mrs. Pennyworth exclaimed as she read the sign. "Don't tell me! Another trip to Mexico, and my watch is locked up inside! Whatever does come over that young man?"

Mr. Pennyworth felt the breeze and nodded. "Wind's from the south," he said. "It's the spirit of adventure that comes over Mr. Medford."

Far down the road to the south, Waldo was humming happily. No, not humming—singing! The strong tenor voice that sang in the church choir rang out cheerfully as the miles spun away beneath the wheels of the jeep.

At the border of Mexico, he inched along with the other cars. Then, custom inspection over, the jeep roared away again, following the south wind. Mexico unfolded its treasures—open bazaars in Nuevo Laredo, a festival in Monterrey, a bullfight in Mexico City. Then, wanting to see the "real" Mexico, Waldo turned toward the coastal plain of the Gulf of Mexico. Leaving the highways, he traveled through small villages. He was delighted with the performance of the little jeep. It roared easily over the roughest roads and took to water like a duck.

In one little village, Waldo stopped to fill the gas tank. The garage had only one pump, old and rusty. Leaning against it, drinking a Coke, was a ten-year-old boy with the brightest eyes Waldo had ever seen.

"*Buenos días, señor.* I am Pepe. Would you require ethel, premium, or diesel?" the boy asked, pushing a faded New York Yankees cap back on his head.

Waldo stared in disbelief at the tank. "All three in one tank? What's really in there?"

The boy grinned. "Whatever Cousin Alfredo can find. Guaranteed to make your car run or your money back."

Waldo grinned back. "As long as you have that much faith, fill it up."

"*Muchachos!*" the boy called. "Feelerup!"

Three little boys spilled from the gaping door of the garage. One pumped gas as the other two attacked the windshield with slightly clean rags. Pepe finished the Coke as he inspected the jeep.

"This jeep, he is funny, *sí?*" he said, running his hands over the bumpers.

"It's an amphibious jeep," Waldo said, counting out his pesos. "It runs in water as well as on land."

"Ay-yi," Pepe said admiringly. "You must be a very rich man. Are you married?"

Startled, Waldo looked up. "Why, no, I'm not. And I'm not rich. I bought the jeep and repaired it myself."

"You have girlfriend? You get married soon?"

Waldo laughed and shook his head.

One of the little boys snapped his rag and stopped beside Waldo's door. "Pepe, he looking for father," he said shyly. "Pepe want to go to America."

"Don't you have parents, Pepe?" Waldo asked, puzzled.

Pepe shook his head. "No parents. I stay with cousins. They're okay, but someday I want to go to America."

"Well, I'm sure you'll make it, Pepe," Waldo said, handing over the change and fumbling for a card with his name on it. He gave the card to Pepe and told him, "If you do, look me up."

"*Gracias, señor,*" Pepe said, beaming. "I will!"

Grinning at the sun-browned little boys, Waldo gunned the motor of the jeep. They laughed and squealed, running for the shelter of the garage. Waldo roared away, leaving a cloud of dust behind him.

what to do. Then one man suggested a kite-flying contest. The engineer offered ten dollars to anyone who could fly a kite from one shore to the other. After trying for more than a day, a young boy landed his kite on the opposite shore. Workmen tied it down and used the string to pull ropes across. Finally they were able to haul across the steel cable. A boy with a kite had helped build a bridge from the United States to Canada!

These days we have helicopters and airplanes to work for us. So we use kites mainly for fun. It's not difficult to design and make your own kites from light wood and paper or plastic. Or you can buy a kite easily. There are over two hundred stores in the United States that sell only kites—all kinds of kites.

If you get tired of flying a kite by yourself, you can join one of many kite clubs around the country. In these clubs you can learn all about kite fighting—using your kite in the air to cut the line of your opponent's kite. You can also learn about hang-gliding—using a kite to glide through the air. You can learn how kites are used for fishing, sailing, and many other things.

So, alone or in a group, for fun or for work—go fly a kite!

The Kite

Harry Behn

How bright on the blue
Is a kite when it's new!

With a dive and a dip
It snaps its tail

Then soars like a ship
With only a sail

As over tides
Of wind it rides,

Climbs to the crest
Of a gust and pulls,

Then seems to rest
As wind falls.

When string goes slack
You wind it back

And run until
A new breeze blows

And its wings fill
And up it goes!

How bright on the blue
Is a kite when it's new!

But a raggeder thing
You never will see

When it flaps on a string
In the top of a tree.

SKILL LESSON:

Prefixes

illustrated by Steve Christopher,
Noelle Snyder and Preston Gravely Jr.

Sometimes in your reading you will come across a big word that you don't quite know the meaning of. Often, if you know what the prefix means, the meaning of the whole word becomes clear. You'll find that it's handy to learn the meanings of some common prefixes.

• *Trans-* **"across"**

If a gardener wants to *transplant* his seedlings, what will he be doing to them? He will actually "plant them across" from small pots to larger ones.

In the 1800s, people cheered when the first transcontinental railroad was finished. Where do you think that railroad went?

The Latin root *port* means "to carry." Can you guess what *transportation* literally means?

And have you ever wondered what a radio transmitter does? If you know that the Latin root *mittere* means "to send," you can get a pretty good idea. The transmitter "sends across" the radio waves to the receiver.

The Latin root *gress* means "to step." When you know that, you can figure out what the word *transgress* means. If you transgress, you "step across" the boundary that God has drawn for you.

• *Inter-* **"between"**

In "Up, Up, and—Way Up," you read about a bridge that goes

an international bridge

United States

Canada

over the Niagara River. This bridge connects the United States and Canada, two separate countries. Why do you suppose we would call this kind of bridge an international bridge?

Have you ever ridden on an interstate highway? Some of them stretch from the Great Lakes to the Gulf of Mexico! Why do you suppose these highways are called interstates?

If you know that the root word *sect* means "to cut," can you figure out what a highway intersection is?

The Latin root *cedere* means "to go." When you know that, you can figure out what it means to intercede. When Christ intercedes for us, He stands between us and God and pleads for us.

NAMING THE STARS

Eileen M. Berry

Not Quite Stellar

Joel sat on the back steps, watching Gramps stroll up the road from the pond. The fishing pole Gramps carried against his shoulder made him look almost like a soldier—a soldier in red plaid flannel and denim. But a real soldier wouldn't be whistling in that slow, shrill way.

The door squeaked open behind Joel. Mom came out, still dressed in the suit and high-heeled shoes she had worn to work. "Supper's ready, Joel," she said. She was smiling, but her eyes looked tired. "Holler at your grandpa to hurry, would you please?"

Joel stood up and cupped his hands around his mouth. "Gramps!" he shouted. "Supper time!"

Gramps saluted and broke into a slight jog. Joel went inside.

"Hey, Mom?" Joel carried two glasses of iced tea to the table. "Could you help me with my homework after supper?"

Mom sat down in her place. "What subject?"

"Science."

She sighed. "That was your dad's specialty. Gramps may be able to help you. Why don't you ask him when he comes in?"

Joel didn't answer.

Gramps sat at the head of the table, where Joel's dad had sat when he was alive. When Gramps prayed, his voice was quiet, but not shaky like some old men's voices. Mom was the first to speak after the prayer.

"Were the fish biting tonight, Dad?"

"Just the little ones," Gramps said. "No big bass tonight." He winked at Joel. "One of these days I'm going to convince this grandson of mine to come with me."

"Fishing's kind of slow," said Joel. He kept his eyes on his plate. "I'd rather play basketball."

Mom's laugh sounded nervous. "Joel's never been much of a fisherman, Dad. Even when Tom was alive, Joel didn't go down to the pond with him much either."

Gramps smiled. "Fishing does take some patience," he said. "Joel's right. But there are a few things about it that you couldn't get playing basketball. Like the look of the sunset in the water. And the bullfrogs and crickets trying to outdo each other with their racket."

"Pass the potatoes, please, Gramps," said Joel.

Mom leaned forward a little. "Dad," she said, "Joel needs some help with his homework tonight. It's science—I was wondering if you'd look at it."

"Be glad to. I'm afraid I wasn't much help last time with that computer stuff."

"It's not computers this time, Gramps," said Joel. "It's stars."

"Stars." Gramps put down his fork and smiled across at Mom. "Well, now. We'll see what we can do."

After supper, Joel helped Mom with the dishes while Gramps went outside to put away his fishing tackle. Mom handed slippery, wet plates to Joel one by one. For a while, the only sound was the gentle sloshing of the soapy water and the clink of the plates as Joel stacked them in the cupboard.

"Speaking of stars, Joel," Mom said finally. She paused with a glass in her hand and looked Joel in the eye. "Your behavior toward your grandpa is not what I'd call stellar."

Joel stared at the soap bubbles inside the glass. He knew that *stellar* was one of Mom's favorite words to describe the brightest and the best things.

Mom turned her attention back to the glass and the dishcloth, but she kept talking to Joel.

"Just the fact that Gramps is much older than you is reason enough for you to treat him with kindness and respect. But there's even more reason. Your grandpa gave up his home in town to come out here and live with us.

He did it for *us*—not for himself. He was perfectly happy on his own. He doesn't have to stay here, and if your unloving attitude toward him continues, he certainly won't want to."

Joel dried the glass Mom handed him without looking at her. He put it in the cupboard. He felt like he should say something, but he could think of nothing to say. When the last glass was dry, he spread the damp towel out on the counter. "I'll go ask Gramps about my science, I guess," he said.

Joel trudged up the stairs to get his science books. He paused on the stairway beside the picture of his father that hung on the wall. Dad had died six months ago. In the photograph, his face looked young and strong. The gray eyes beneath the dark brows were solemn but kind. Joel could remember how Dad used to raise one eyebrow and smile with his lips together whenever someone told a joke. Looking at the picture still brought a tightness to Joel's throat.

Celestial Navigation

In his room, Joel sat on his bed and opened his science notebook. He remembered the conversation he'd had earlier with his friend Bobby on the bus.

"What's it like having your granddad in the house?" Bobby wanted to know. "He's been there a whole month, hasn't he?"

"Yeah. He's nice, and we're glad to have him around. But— he's just *old*."

A sound in the doorway made Joel's head jerk up. Gramps was standing there. "Let's have a look at that homework," he said.

"Sorry, Gramps. I was going to bring it down to you."

Gramps held up a hand. "No harm done. Does these old legs good to climb the stairs once in a while."

Joel cleared his throat and moved over to make room for Gramps. "We're studying the constellations," Joel said. "And our teacher gave us certain ones we have to find. I've gone out to look the last two nights, but there's one I haven't been able to see."

"Which one?" Gramps leaned closer to the book, and Joel wondered if he could see it clearly without his glasses.

"Orion."

Gramps nodded. "Um-hmm. Orion—the great hunter of the sky."

Joel looked over at him, eyebrows raised. "How'd you know that?"

Gramps winked. "Orion's an old friend of mine," he said. "Tell you what. I'll meet you in the front yard around nine—when it's good and dark. Bring your jacket—it'll be chilly out." Without another word, Gramps squeezed Joel's shoulder, stood up, and left the room.

Gramps sat in his chair and read the newspaper as usual that evening. But around eight-thirty he went back to his room. Joel kept glancing at the clock, wondering if he had gone to bed and forgotten about their meeting in the front yard.

When nine o'clock came, Joel peered down the hallway. Gramps's room was dark. Joel frowned. He grabbed his jacket and let himself out the front door.

The porch light gleamed. Two long shadows stretched across the lawn. One was a man's. The other was oddly shaped and seemed to have very long, thin legs.

"Gramps?" Joel called softly.

"Out here, Joel." Gramps's voice came from the dim lawn. "Turn off that porch light and come on out."

Joel flipped the switch, and the shadows disappeared. He stumbled toward the faint outline of Gramps. "What are you doing, Gramps? What's that thing?"

"This," Gramps said, "is a telescope."

Joel realized the long, thin legs he had seen were part of the telescope's wooden stand. "Gramps!" he almost shouted. "I didn't know you had one of these."

Gramps backed away from the eyepiece. In the darkness, Joel could tell he was grinning. "I have some tricks up my sleeve," he said. "During my navy days I learned celestial navigation."

"What's that?"

"Telling your ship's position by the stars. I got so interested in the stars that when I left the navy, I bought a telescope. It's an oldie, but a goodie." He put an arm around Joel's shoulder, drawing him up to the telescope. "Look right through here," he said. "I've got it pointing toward our friend Orion."

Gramps showed Joel how to move and focus the telescope. "Do you see the three stars lined up in a row?" he asked. "That's the belt around Orion's waist."

"I see it now. Wow, Gramps—the stars look so much *bigger* through this thing."

"Bigger and brighter," said Gramps. "And this telescope really isn't even that powerful compared to some."

Joel was quiet, thinking how many thousands of stars those little pinpoints of light represented.

"Just up from the belt and a little to the left is Betelgeuse," said Gramps.

"Our teacher talked about that star," Joel said. "It's a big one, isn't it?"

"A supergiant, to be exact." Gramps chuckled. "Hundreds of times bigger than our sun."

"No kidding." Joel whistled. "It doesn't seem *that* big."

"That's because it's so far away. Now look down on the other side of the belt, Joel. South of Betelgeuse, on a diagonal line. See that other bright star?"

"I think so. Is that another supergiant?"

"You better believe it. That's Rigel—one of the brightest stars known to man."

"How'd you learn so much about the stars, Gramps?"

Gramps rubbed his chin. "Well, Joel, I've had a few more years to study them than you have."

The silence of the night settled around them for a few moments. Joel stepped away from the telescope and threw his head back to look at the stars with his own eyes. How small, how dim, how far away they looked. He shivered suddenly.

Gramps placed a hand on his shoulder. "Joel, do you know what it says in the Psalms about God? It says, 'He telleth the number of the stars; he calleth them all by their names.' There are stars so far away that we can't even see them through this telescope. But God made them. They're His, and He knows their names. Just like He knows ours—yours and mine."

Joel turned to look up at Gramps in the darkness. He had his chin up, his face tilted back to the sky. He seemed suddenly taller. Joel wondered if the profile of Orion, the mighty hunter, would look like that if Orion were a human.

"Hey, Gramps," Joel said. He hesitated for a moment. "Do you think I could have my friend Bobby over sometime to look through your telescope? He would love it."

"Consider it done," said Gramps. "And if you're interested, you boys can take a look at some of my navy stuff. You might like to see the almanacs we used for navigation."

"Almanacs?"

"Books that show where the stars are going to be at different times of the year," said Gramps. "It would make a humdinger of a science project."

Gramps gave Joel's shoulder a playful thump. "Well, it's time we got you and this thing back in the house. I promised your mother I wouldn't keep you up too late."

Joel stood rooted to the spot, watching Gramps pack up the telescope. "You go on in, Gramps," he said. "Tell Mom I'll be there in a minute."

Gramps saluted and marched off toward the house, the telescope on his shoulder.

Joel craned his neck to the stars again. "Rigel. Betelgeuse." He pointed to each one. "God," he said, "it's hard to believe Your stars are so big. They look so small from here." His voice dropped to a whisper. "But I guess the truth is, *I'm* small." Tears turned the stars into bright blurs.

A few minutes later, Joel stepped through the front door of the house. Mom was sitting on the couch with a book. She looked up at him, her eyes full of questions. But all she said was, "How'd it go, honey?"

Joel grinned and gave her a thumbs up. "Stellar," he said.

Look at the Stars

Eileen M. Berry

illustrated by Preston Gravely Jr. and Duane Nichols

Did you know that the closest star to the earth is the one you see during the daytime? Our sun is a star. There are other stars in the sky during the day, but the sun shines so brightly that we cannot see them. When the earth rotates so that we face away from the sun, it is nighttime and the sky fills with little points of light.

On a dark, moonless night, we can see many hundreds of stars. But there are billions more that we cannot see because they are too far away. And we can only see certain stars at certain times of the year because of the rotation of the earth. Some stars that ap-

pear to be one star are really star systems. Two or more small stars may be revolving around each other, creating one bright light that we can see.

We live in a huge star system called the Milky Way *galaxy*. In our galaxy alone there are more than two hundred billion stars. And ours is not the only one. Astronomers estimate that the universe contains one hundred billion other galaxies. Imagine what the psalmist meant when he wrote that God can tell the number of the stars and that He calls them all by their names (Psalm 147:4)!

What are stars made of? A star is composed of dust and gas particles pulled tightly together by gravity into a ball. The temperature of a star's surface ranges from 3,000°F to 60,000°F. The hottest stars are blue-white, and the coolest are a reddish color.

All stars appear to be about the same size when viewed without a telescope. But stars exist in various sizes. The smallest are called *dwarf stars*. Our sun is classified as a dwarf star. Very large stars are called *supergiants*.

Supergiants are often hundreds of times larger than our sun.

What can you see in the stars? Among the stars are shapes and pictures that have fascinated people for centuries. Probably the most commonly known of these shapes, or *constellations,* is the Big Dipper, part of a bigger constellation known as Ursa Major. The Big Dipper is made up of seven bright stars arranged in the shape of a cup with a long handle. The Big Dipper is easy to spot, and once you find it, you can easily trace a path to the North Star, Polaris. Follow an imaginary line straight up from the two Dipper stars farthest from the handle, and the line will lead to Polaris. Polaris is located in the constellation we call the Little Dipper. Polaris appears never to move, but telescopes have shown it makes a very small circle each night. As long as you are facing Polaris, you are facing north.

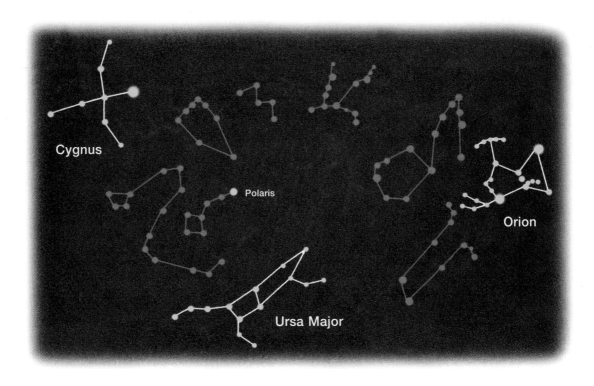

Cygnus

Polaris

Orion

Ursa Major

What other constellations can you find? Orion is a group of stars thought to look like a hunter with a shield in one hand and a raised club in the other. A lopsided rectangle represents the hunter's shoulders and legs, and three bright stars in the center of this rectangle make up his belt. One of the reasons we can see Orion so well is that it contains seven supergiants.

The constellation Leo is shaped like a lion running through the sky with head and tail outstretched. The bright star Regulus, which connects the lion's body to its front leg, is often called "the heart of the Lion."

The Pleiades are one of the most beautiful star clusters in the sky. The Pleiades are also called the Seven Sisters, but there are many more than seven stars in the cluster. Clouds of dust in space surround these stars and reflect their light, making them appear very bright.

Cygnus is a constellation shaped like a long-necked bird in flight. The word *cygnus* means "swan." This group of stars is also called the Northern Cross. At the tail of the swan or the top of the cross, depending on how you look at it, is the constellation's brightest star, Deneb.

Not all of the constellations can be seen from one place at the same time. Some constellations can be seen only from the Northern or Southern Hemisphere. They are higher in the sky at certain times of the year than at other times. In the Northern Hemisphere, Orion and Pleiades are visible in the winter. Leo is a spring constellation. The Dippers are most easily seen in summer. And Cygnus makes its flight in fall. Some constellations, such as the Southern Cross, can be seen only by people in the Southern Hemisphere.

What do you think about when looking at the stars? Their height? Their beauty? Their great number? Knowing facts about the stars is important, but even better is knowing the God who created them. "Seek him that maketh the seven stars and Orion" (Amos 5:8).

Unit 6

HEROES

Friend or Foe

by Milly Howard
illustrated by Steve Mitchell

John Darragh, a fourteen-year-old Quaker boy, lived in Philadelphia during the War for Independence. Though the Quakers preferred to live in peace with their neighbors, the encampment of the British in their city forced the Darraghs to make choices they otherwise might never have faced. This fictionalized account lets us see their struggle.

An Ordinary Button

"Out of the way, boy!"

John Darragh jumped aside as a trio of mounted British officers galloped around the corner. Their swords glinted in the winter sun, their leather boots gleamed and blue cloaks whipped back to reveal red coats. People scattered, muttering and scowling, some shouting as they slipped in the icy mud.

A printer's apprentice snatched his precious handbills from the wet cobblestones. John stopped to help. The boy struck John's hand away angrily. "Away with ye, Quaker!" he said, sneering at John's plain clothes. "Ye're naw

'friend' of mine, nor of America! We need fighters, not the likes of ye!"

As John straightened up slowly his eyes met the steely ones of a baker. "Aye," the baker said slowly. "The lad is right. I've a boy about your age with General Washington. Fourteen, are ye?"

John nodded. The baker motioned abruptly. "On your way, boy. We need no fence straddlers here!"

Anger surged through John. For one heated moment he almost shouted, "My brother is a Lieutenant in the same army!"

Most of the Patriots had joined the army or had fled Philadelphia when Washington moved his troops. The city had been left firmly in the control of the British army. The British soldiers had received a rousing welcome from the Tories of Philadelphia. John held his tongue. He knew that harsh words were the only weapon the few remaining Patriots could use in the occupied city. So instead of speaking his mind, John straightened up and walked away.

By the time he had turned off Spruce Street onto Second Street, the bitter wind had cleared his head and blown away his anger. John's father often reminded him to control his hasty tongue or ruin would fall upon them all. Today, John thought, he had succeeded. As he reached the headquarters of the German ally, Lieutenant General von Knyphausen, he was thankful he had held his peace.

Horses stamped impatiently in the street. The steam rising from their sides told of a hard and fast run. Soldiers, red-faced in the cold, stood guard. British officers hurried in and out of the headquarters. Excitement tingled along John's spine. Something was up, for sure.

John forced himself to walk directly across the street to his house in his usual long stride. He took the steps two at a time and let himself in the door. He tossed his coat and muffler onto the hall tree, and hurried to the kitchen.

His mother and father jumped up and tried to conceal something on the kitchen table. "It's John!" he called.

"John! Thou shouldst say so sooner!" Lydia Darragh said in a shaky voice. "Thou gavest us quite a fright!"

"I'm sorry, Mother," John said. "So much is going on I forgot."

"What did thou see this morning?" Friend Darragh asked, picking up his quill pen again. "Perhaps it can be added to the message we're sending today."

The Irish Darraghs were no ordinary Quakers. Torn between the desire for the peace their Quaker faith demanded and the fight for the independence of their land, they had chosen to fight. "We have freedom to worship here," Friend Darragh had told his family. "It is our right to protect that freedom, as other Patriots are doing. Even the Society of Friends must not stop us from doing what is right."

The Darragh boys had breathed sighs of relief. Their Irish blood had often chafed at the Society of Friends desire to avoid all warlike attitudes or actions. The Darraghs were no Tories and never would be! With the blessing of his family, if not that of the Society, John's oldest brother joined Washington's army. Now a lieutenant, Charles was camped at Whitemarsh, just outside Philadelphia.

In town, the other Darraghs helped in any way they could. Being across the street from the Knyphausens gave them ample opportunity to observe the activities of the British. They kept the fact of Charles's enlistment to themselves. Secretly they gathered information to take to him. Neither the British nor the Philadelphia Patriots suspected the Quaker family. They saw the Darraghs only as the peaceloving "Friends." Both John and his mother gathered important information from the soldiers right across the street and also on their errands around town.

Today John added his latest observations on the movements of the British to what his mother had already recorded. John's father wrote the information down. A lot of information could be written on a tiny scrap of paper if the writer used a shortened version of the words as John's father did. When he finished, Lydia Darragh tucked the paper inside a wooden button mold. She covered it with cloth left over from making John's winter coat.

"Get thy coat, son," John's father said, "and we'll see if the fabric still matches."

After his mother sewed the button onto the coat, he put it on and strode across the kitchen to the window. He watched the soldiers across the street as his parents inspected their handiwork.

Lydia shook her head doubtfully. "I don't know," she said hesitantly. "Stand a little closer to the window, John, so we can see the fabric in the light."

The Darraghs inspected the coat carefully. If John were caught—Lydia shuddered, raising her hand to her throat. . . . No one had forgotten the hanging of Nathan Hale the year before. If a captured spy actually had papers on him, no one could help. John could expect no trial, no mercy because of his age. Everything possible to insure his safety must be considered now.

"It's too new," Friend Darragh told his wife. "It shows up against the old cloth. Perhaps a little soil?"

Lydia agreed. When the cloth button was rubbed gently with a bit of dirt from one of Lydia's winter plants, it blended in with the worn coat. "There," Lydia said, "It doesn't look too new, now."

"I'll be all right," John said, impatient to be on his way. He enjoyed the trip to Whitemarsh. In a way, the trip helped overcome some of the disappointment of not being old enough to enlist. The possibility of capture made John feel an important part of the fight for independence. He straightened and smoothed the coat over his chest. "Mother, thou knowest I'm fourteen years old. I have sense enough not to get caught."

"Others older than thee have been caught," his father said dryly. "Mind thy mother's wishes, son."

When preparations had been finished to his mother's exacting standards, John stood up, ready to go. Warmed by a stomach full of rich, hot soup and bundled into a coat, two mufflers, extra socks and vests, he stepped outdoors. Pausing on the steps, he shook the folds out of a large flour bag. Anyone who happened to be watching only saw a boy on his way to the mill to replenish the family's supply of flour. Frankfort Mill was located well outside British-controlled land. He tucked the flour bag under his arm and turned into the wind. There had been heavy snow this winter, and the wind blew straight from the north. General Howe's men had complained bitterly about the Yankee weather. John smiled at the thought. Let them complain. The worst was yet to come. Then the smile changed to a frown as he remembered the condition of the men at Whitemarsh.

new button and handed it to his brother. Charles extracted the tiny sheet of paper and sat at a folding desk to transcribe his father's shorthand. As he wrote, John sat down on the camp bed and unbuckled his shoes. Quickly he stripped off the extra pairs of woolen socks. Then, standing, he took off his coat and began to strip off two woolen vests.

Charles looked up from his work and laughed.

"Trust Mother!" he said softly. "And thee, John! But won't thou be cold going back?"

John shook his head. "If I can't stand a little cold for a few hours, I'm not fit to be a Patriot!"

"Bless thee, John," Charles said quietly and returned to his

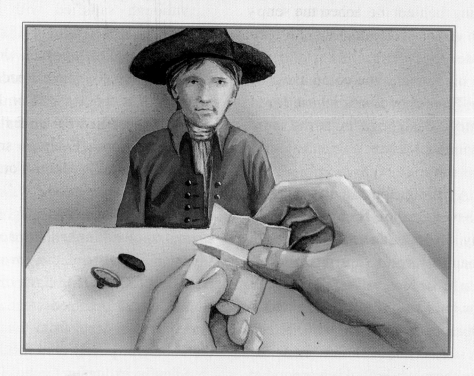

work. When he had finished he had a complete report for General Washington.

Charles's usually easy, cheerful manner changed to the firm, commanding look John had grown to respect.

"I'll take this to General Washington immediately, John," he said. "And I'll see that thy gifts are used wisely."

When John reached the sentry post, he saw Captain McLane waiting for him.

"I thought you could use a lift back," he said, smiling at John's surprised delight. "It's a long walk back to Philadelphia."

John swung up behind him and they galloped across the hill. At the end of Nice Town Lane, Captain McLane halted and John slid off the horse.

"Thank you, sir," he said. "It was kind of you to bring me this far."

"Nay, lad," the Captain replied. "You and folk like you risk your lives to bring us information from behind enemy lines. Without that information many soldiers would never live to see freedom in our country. Nay," he said again, reaching down to shake John's hand, "I thank you, friend!"

John shook his hand and stepped back as Captain McLane turned his horse and galloped back toward camp. Then John started back down the road to Frankfort Mill where he would pick up the filled sack of flour and take it home. Even the snow that had begun to sift down out of the darkening sky could not dispel the warmth John felt from the soldier's praise. The way home might be cold and long, but the job had been done.

Alone over THE ATLANTIC

Richard Barry
illustrated by Preston Gravely Jr.

Before 1927, no one had ever made a solo flight across the Atlantic Ocean. Some men had tried to make the trip, but they had all crashed or disappeared at sea. Other people said it was impossible. But one man, Charles Lindbergh, thought he could do it. Lindbergh's airplane was smaller than the airplanes the others had tried. And Lindbergh wasn't going to take a radio with him as the others had. From the moment he left land, Charles Lindbergh would be alone over the Atlantic.

Only Five Sandwiches

On May 20, 1927, Charles Lindbergh lay in the bed of his New York hotel room. It was after midnight, but he couldn't sleep. He was listening to the rain and thinking. For several years Charles had been an airplane pilot, and he had done some dangerous things. But now he was going to try something more dangerous than ever before. In a few hours, if the weather was good, he would take off in his airplane for Paris, France.

No matter how hard he tried to sleep, Charles kept thinking about the flight. He hoped he hadn't forgotten anything. His airplane, the *Spirit of St. Louis,* was ready and waiting at the airfield. Charles had read about the other men who had tried to fly over the Atlantic. Some of them had died when their planes crashed. Others had simply disappeared over the ocean. Charles rolled over. He had faith in his sturdy little airplane, but he was still nervous.

At two o'clock in the morning he got up. It was still dark outside, but he knew he would never get to sleep. Besides, he wanted to get an early morning start. At least the rain had stopped.

At the airfield Charles found reporters and a crowd of five hundred people waiting to see him take off. Everyone stared at the young pilot. Would he really decide to try it?

While the mechanics fueled up the airplane, Charles examined the dirt runway. It was soft and muddy from the rain. Next he looked at the men filling his airplane with gasoline. He had told the men to fill the *Spirit of St. Louis* with as much gasoline as possible. He didn't want to run

out of fuel over the ocean. But he knew that the overload of fuel would make his airplane very heavy. The weight of that extra fuel would make it hard to get the airplane off the ground. He looked back at the runway. The heavy airplane might even get stuck in the mud.

Charles climbed into the cockpit and warmed up the airplane's engine. He wanted to be sure it was running perfectly.

One of his friends stepped up to the cockpit. "Are you taking only five sandwiches?" he asked.

"Yes, five," Charles answered. "If I get to Paris, I won't need any more. If I don't—well, I won't need any more either."

Mr. Mulligan, Lindbergh's mechanic, walked over. "The engine's doing as well as you can expect in this weather."

Charles paused. "Well, then, I might as well go," he replied.

It was now 7:52 in the morning. The young pilot leaned forward, opened the throttle, and gripped the control stick. The *Spirit of St. Louis* started down the runway, leaving deep wheel marks in the wet dirt.

The crowd held their breath as the airplane picked up speed. Everyone wondered one thing now: could the overloaded airplane get off the ground?

The *Spirit of St. Louis* roared down the runway. The wheels left the dirt strip, but only for a moment. The plane lifted again only to touch down once more. Finally, the wheels left the runway and this time the airplane rose, inching its way skyward. As it rose slowly into the air, it drew closer and closer to the end of the runway. Then with a burst of speed and a lift of the nose, the heavy plane cleared the runway, barely missing the telephone wires at the end of the strip.

A cheer went up from the crowd. Lindbergh was in the air and on his way to France!

During the first part of his flight, Charles flew up the coast of New England and Nova Scotia. Whenever he passed over a town, people ran outside to see his famous airplane. The newspapers carried stories about him that morning, and radio stations told the latest news about his progress.

Many hours later Charles flew over the town of St. John's on the island of Newfoundland. He zoomed over the town and flew out to sea. There would be no more land until he got to Europe.

After Charles disappeared over the horizon, there were no more news reports. He had refused to carry a radio because he didn't want to add more weight to his airplane. No one knew where Charles was or even if he was still alive. All that day people talked about Charles. Could he do it? Would he be the first man to fly across the Atlantic? Was he even still alive?

The young pilot didn't know it at the time, but as he flew along, people all over the world were praying for his safety. That night forty thousand people gathered in New York's Yankee Stadium to see a heavyweight prizefight. But first the announcer asked for a moment of prayer for Mr. Lindbergh. Silently, forty thousand people stood, bowing their heads in prayer.

Which Way Is Ireland?

But Charles was alive and well. He had flown all day and was far out over the Atlantic when night came. All he could see were the stars above him, the clouds around him, and the black ocean below. Sometimes he saw white icebergs floating in the cold water.

The *Spirit of St. Louis* climbed high into the night sky as Charles tried to stay above the storm clouds. For a while he was able to fly over or around these clouds. He didn't want to get caught in a storm now. But at last he came to a huge cloud. It was too high to fly over and too wide to go around without wasting time and gasoline. He decided to risk going through it.

The moment his airplane entered the cloud, Charles lost sight of everything. Blackness was all around him. He used his flashlight to see the instrument panel and continued flying.

A few minutes later he noticed how cold he was. He thrust one hand out the cockpit window.

Little cold pieces of something pelted his hand.

"Ice!" he thought.

He shined his flashlight out the window. Sleet was freezing on his wings! Charles was scared now. He knew that ice could add a lot of extra weight to his airplane. Even worse, ice could change the curve of his wings enough so that they wouldn't work right. That would send him crashing into the ocean below. He had to get out of that cloud—fast!

He carefully circled around and found his way back out of the cloud. He breathed easier again. It would take extra time and fuel to go around the storm cloud, but he didn't dare risk flying through one again.

On and on he flew into the night. After a while he no longer felt cold. He was comfortable. He was so relaxed he could almost sleep . . .

Charles jerked his head up. He had almost fallen asleep. Last night he had been so nervous he could not sleep a wink. Now he was tired. He was so sleepy he could hardly keep his eyes open. Over and over he slapped his cheeks. He must not fall asleep now.

Finally the sun rose, and he felt less sleepy. On he flew over endless water.

The morning passed. The afternoon was passing. Charles hoped he would see land before the sun set again. If he was still on course, he should soon see the island of Ireland.

Charles had been flying for twenty-seven hours when he looked down and saw specks in the water. Fishing boats! Land must be near! He dove down toward one of the boats but saw no one. He circled around another and saw a man put his head out a porthole. Charles slowed the airplane and circled again.

"Which way is Ireland?" he shouted out the window.

The man just stared. He didn't even point. Maybe he didn't speak English. Or maybe he was too surprised to see an airplane from America. Charles gave up and flew away.

An hour later he saw something dark on the horizon. It was land! He opened his map and looked at the coastline. It was Ireland all right. He was on course. It would be easy to get to Paris now.

Charles flew on, skimming over Ireland and England. The sun was going down just as he crossed the English Channel and reached the coast of France. He flew low over a French village and saw people running into the streets. They looked up, pointing and waving at him. It was then that he realized he hadn't eaten anything all day. He pulled out a sandwich and chewed it while he flew on to Paris in the deepening twilight.

The darkness was complete when Charles spotted the glow of light in the distance.

One word came into his thoughts: "Paris!"

Minutes later he flew over the Eiffel Tower and circled around it before heading for the airfield.

Then he saw lots of little lights. It looked as if hundreds of cars jammed the roads around the airfield. What were they doing there?

The *Spirit of St. Louis* circled the airfield several times. Then Charles let the airplane dip, gliding down to the runway. The wheels lightly touched down, and he was back on the ground.

Before Charles had even stopped his engine, he saw a crowd of people running out to meet him. Thousands of voices were crying, "Lindbergh! Lindbergh! Lindbergh!" He didn't even touch the ground when he stepped from the airplane. The crowd picked him up and carried him on their shoulders like a hero.

He had done it. After thirty-three and one-half hours of flying alone, Charles Lindbergh had conquered the Atlantic and set a new record in the history of flying.

Sulphur Springs Challenge

Susan W. Young

Old Enough

"Today's the day," Travis announced. He swung his backpack into the van and climbed in after it. "Chris and Zack and I are going to hike the Sulphur Springs trail by ourselves this year."

"Can I go with you?" Travis's younger brother bounced on the seat in front of him. "I'm old enough."

"You're not old enough because I wasn't old enough until this year and you're younger than I am." Travis gave Kurt a playful shove.

"Settle down, boys." Dad turned the key. "Here comes your mother."

Mom slid into her seat. "We've got the potato salad, the vegetable platter, the lemonade, and the cherry pie. I hope I'm not forgetting anything."

"Sounds like enough to feed the whole Zimmer clan." Dad checked the mirrors and looked over his shoulder. "But I don't think you'll have to worry about filling Travis up this year. He's too excited to eat much."

Travis watched behind them as Dad backed out of the driveway. His stomach did feel small and tight.

"What are you so excited about, Travis?" Travis knew that

436

Mom was just pretending not to know.

"I'll give you three guesses."

Mom turned around in her seat. "Three guesses, huh?" She adjusted her seatbelt. "Well, since you're too excited to eat, I guess it's not the food. And since you're always excited about seeing your cousins, I would say it's probably not that. So, my guess is that it has something to do with hiking."

Travis just smiled.

Every year for as long as Travis could remember, he and his cousins, Chris and Zack, had begged to be allowed to hike the old Sulphur Springs trail that led up the mountain from the picnic area where the Zimmer family reunion was held. Dad and his brothers had always hiked with them, but every year they promised that when the boys were older they could hike it alone.

And this year they were old enough.

The hike had always come after lunch, and this year was no different. Travis endured the cheek pinching, hugs, and pats on the head from all the aunts and uncles. He entered in the games that kept the children occupied while lunch was prepared. He remembered to let the older people go first in line to get food, but it was hard to wait. Finally he and his cousins carried their plates to a table away from everyone to discuss their plans.

"Do you really think they'll let us go?" Zack wiped his mouth on the back of his hand.

"Sure. My dad said we could. Besides, the trail's all marked, so we can't get lost." Travis took a bite of his hamburger.

Chris scooped up a forkful of potato salad. "I hope Mom's forgotten about the old dam and the ruins. She tells dad every year to be sure we don't get hurt."

"Yeah, my mom worries, too." Travis wiped the ketchup off his chin. "But Dad told her not to worry. He said we were smart enough to stay out of trouble."

"It'd be a cinch to walk out on that dam." Zack took a swallow of soda. "You just have to know where to put your feet."

"Don't even think about it. If our parents knew you thought that, they'd never let us go." Travis crumpled his napkin.

"Don't worry, I'm not going to tell them. I'm not stupid, you know."

The boys dumped their plates in the trash cans and wound their way through the tables of adults.

Travis tapped his dad on the shoulder. "We're done."

"And I suppose you want to go for a hike." Dad smiled. "Well, you know the way." Dad looked serious. "But stay away from the dam. It's dangerous."

With a whoop and a holler, the three boys headed out of the shelter.

"Be careful!" The words rose in chorus from the three sets of parents.

Brave Enough

The trail followed a shallow creek that widened and narrowed as it flowed through the trees. The boys stuck to the trail most of the way, stopping occasionally to poke sticks into the water to disturb whatever might be living there. Soon the trail became rough with rocks and tree roots, and the sticks came in handy for climbing up and over the obstacles.

"Look!" Travis pointed through the trees. "There it is." The far end of the dam was just visible through the green boughs of the pine trees.

The boys clambered over the rocks and roots as fast as they could. Just beyond a curve in the trail the trees ended abruptly. The dam stretched out before them. Its rough-hewn rock surface held back the water of a small lake. Along the edge of the lake lay the crumbling walls of an old pump station.

Zack stepped over a pile of rocks. "It seemed a lot bigger last year."

"Yeah." Chris followed him. "The dam doesn't look so big either."

Travis kicked at a crumbling wall. "Maybe it's 'cause we're older."

Chris jumped down into a round rock enclosure. "Here's the old wheel that used to open the dam. Maybe the three of us could turn it."

"Naw, we try that every year. It's rusted tight." Zack headed for the dam. "This year let's walk across the dam."

"I don't think that's such a good idea," Travis said. "It may not look as big as it did last year, but it's still dangerous. Look." Large rocks interlaced with fallen trees lay just below the boys. "If you fell on those, there'd be no saving you."

"And if you fell the other way, you'd probably drown." Chris pointed at the dark, murky water. "They'd never find your body."

"But I'm not going to fall." Zack stood at the edge of the dam. "I'll cross over, and if you two aren't still chicken, you can follow me."

Travis climbed over the wall to stand beside Zack. "You won't make it all the way. It's covered with water out there in the middle."

Zack laughed. "A little water never hurt anyone."

"Maybe not. But there's algae under the water. I can see it from here. You'll slip for sure."

"Oh give up, Travis. You're just afraid 'cause your dad told you it was dangerous. You wouldn't walk across your own front yard if he told you not to."

"And what's wrong with that? My dad says if you recognize danger and steer clear of it, you don't have to regret some dumb mistake." Travis stepped in front of Zack and crossed his arms. "I'm not crossing the dam because I want to get back home in one piece. And maybe that means I'm scared. But you know what Mr. Wentworth said in Sunday school? 'God gives us the common sense to recognize danger so we'll know to walk away from it.' I don't think not walking across the dam makes me a coward."

"Well, since I don't sense any danger, I guess I don't have to walk away, do I?" Zack stepped out onto the dam. "I'll show you there's nothing to be afraid of."

"What if Travis is right, Zack?" Chris pushed his hair back from his forehead.

"He's not, and I'm going to prove it." Zack took another step.

Carefully placing one foot in front of the other, Zack walked out onto the dam. Travis and Chris held their breath as he crossed the

slippery section where the water spilled over.

Zack gave a shout when he reached the other side. "Come on over, it's easy."

"No! You come back." Travis shielded his eyes against the sun. "And be careful."

"I made it over, didn't I?" Zack started back.

When he reached the water, he paused for a moment and then moved forward. One step, two steps. Then it happened. Zack's foot slipped. His body jerked. His arms grabbed at the air. He disappeared into the lake.

Chris grabbed Travis's arm. "What are we going to do? He can't swim!"

Travis shook himself free. Off came his shoes. In three bounds he reached the edge of the water. Keeping his eye on the place where Zack had gone down, he jumped in feet first. The cold water closed around him. One strong kick and he rose to the surface. He could see Zack just a few yards away. With a few quick strokes, he reached him and grabbed him from behind.

"I've got you." Travis grabbed a breath of air before the water closed over their heads. Still holding on, he kicked back to the surface.

Zack's arms flailed. His fist hit Travis in the face.

"Cut it out, Zack. I've got you." Under the water they went again. Travis could feel his grip loosening. When they reached the surface this time, he flipped his hair out of his eyes and spit the lake water out of his mouth. "Give up, Zack, or we're both going to drown." He tightened his grip. Zack quit swinging and relaxed just a little. "Hang on, and I'll get us to shore." Travis was glad to feel Zack help kick as he pulled toward the bank.

Chris pulled Zack up onto the bank. Travis flopped down beside him.

Zack sat up and coughed. "That was close." He leaned his head on his knees. "I thought I was gone for good."

"Yeah, me too." Chris sat down next to them. "If it hadn't been for Travis, you would've been."

Zack lifted his head to look at Travis. "How'd you know what to do?"

"Lifeguard class at the pool. The last thing we learned was lake rescue." Travis pushed his wet hair back from his forehead. "I sure never thought I'd have to use it."

Zack squeezed the water out of his shirt. "If I'd listened to you, you wouldn't have had to use it. Talk about dumb things to do. I never should have done it."

"Yeah, but you sure were brave to try." Chris grinned at Zack.

"I wasn't brave. I was just as scared as you were. I just didn't want you to know it, so I did a stupid thing." Zack threw a stone into the water. "I guess I just don't have any of that common sense Mr. Wentworth was talking about."

"You have it all right. You just didn't listen to it." Travis threw one after it.

"So if I'm afraid to tell my dad what happened, because I decide that telling him is a scary thing to do, does that mean my common sense will tell me to stay away from that too?" Zack pulled himself up to sit on a piece of wall.

Travis laughed. "I don't think so, Zack. I think Mr. Wentworth would say that that kind of fear is the kind you face and overcome because it keeps you from doing the right thing."

"So let me get this straight. If I'm afraid of something dangerous and walk away, it won't make me a coward. But if I'm afraid to do the right thing and I walk away, I will be a coward." Zack ran his fingers through his hair.

"You've got it." Travis held out his hand to Zack. "Now all you have to do is do it."

"Boy, I'm glad I'm not in your shoes, Zack." Chris stood up and brushed off his pants. "I sure wouldn't want to have to tell my dad."

Zack took Travis's hand and pulled himself up. "Well, the punishment my dad gives me won't be anywhere near as bad as falling on those rocks or drowning in that lake would have been." He headed down the trail; then stopped and looked back. "But I will tell you this, telling the truth won't be as easy as falling off that dam."

Travis laughed. "But it won't kill you either."

Mort and the Sour Scheme

Tim Davis
illustrated by Tim Davis
and John Bjerk

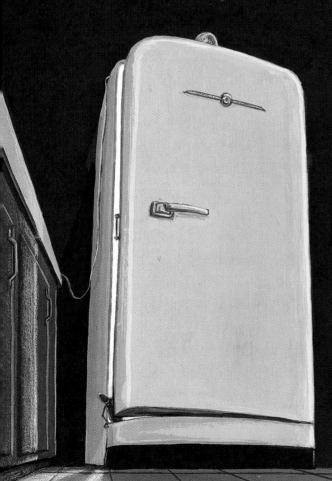

A Puckered Plan

One night, way in the very back of the old refrigerator, in the corner that no one ever cleaned out, someone or something was grumbling. It was the quiet sort of grumbling that people can't hear. It was the grumbling of sour, spoiling, forgotten food.

Now if there's anything that food hates, it's being left to spoil—because when somebody finds it, he just says something nasty about it and throws it away. Food doesn't like that at all. In fact, although it's hard for humans to understand, food likes being eaten by people, and it especially likes to hear a satisfied "mmmm" on its way down somebody's throat.

Way in the back of the refrigerator, Mr. Lemon and his sour friends knew they'd never get a chance to be enjoyed by anybody. They were too spoiled and sour. The more they thought about it, the more sour they got.

"Aww, we'll never get eaten," grumbled Mr. Lemon.

One of the rotten eggs muttered his agreement. "Yeah, that really makes my yolk boil. We didn't ask to be left back here."

"I'll bet sweet little Miss Sugarbowl never got left back in this smelly corner of the refrigerator," sneered Mr. Lemon.

"She gets used every day," grumbled an ill-tempered egg.

"I'd just love to stick her back here for a couple of months," said Mr. Lemon. "She wouldn't be so sweet then."

One of the rotten eggs spoke up. "Why don't we then?"

"Yeah!" a chorus of sour pickles joined in.

So the rotten group huddled together to work out a nasty sort of kidnapping plan.

On the rack just above them, a little mushroom named Mortimer hid and listened.

"Oh, no," he thought. "How could they do such a thing to sweet Miss Sugarbowl? I've got to warn her!"

Mort knew he wasn't strong enough to push open the big refrigerator door by himself, but he had heard about a secret exit up through the freezer far above him. Mortimer could sneak out and warn her that way.

Quickly he started off in that direction. But before he had gone two steps, his foot slipped on a bit of oleo. Mort fell on the rack with a clatter! The noise startled the group below him.

Mr. Lemon looked up at the terrified little mushroom. "Looks like a spy! After him!"

Three sour pickles slid out of their jar and started after him.

Mort quickly shinnied up the cool ketchup bottle to the next rack up. Then he sprinted toward a large bowl of vegetable soup covered with clear plastic wrap. With one tremendous leap, he landed right in the middle of the stretched wrap. Like a trampoline, it bounced him up to the drip tray of the freezer.

The pickles were gaining on him until they reached the bowl of soup. The first one jumped onto the plastic wrap, but he weighed much more than Mort did. Splat! Into the soup he went with the plastic wrap stuck all over him.

"Never mind him—after that spy!" shouted another pickle. They quickly stacked up a few containers and climbed up into the drip tray.

But the little mushroom had reached the other side. He hopped up to the latch of the freezer. It was just a lightweight aluminum door, but it took all of Mort's might to open it just a crack. By then the sour pickles were right behind him. He squeezed into the freezer.

The pickles pushed the freezer door open a crack more and rushed into the frigid compartment.

Mort saw a hole almost covered by frost. The secret exit! He brushed aside the icy crystals and crept through the opening. It led to the back of the refrigerator near the top. He felt the warm kitchen air on his face as he peeked out. The little mushroom climbed a few steps up to the smooth white top of the refrigerator. There was only an electric clock and lots of dust up there.

The cord on the clock ran down the side of the refrigerator to an outlet over the counter. Mort shinnied down toward the counter below. The pickles spotted him and quickly slid down behind him.

Mort dropped onto the counter and ducked behind the cookie jar. A few seconds later the first pickle ran by. Where was the second? Crawling on his hands and knees, Mort peered cautiously around the cookie jar. Right in front of his nose was a pair of slimy green feet. He looked up. Above him stood a pickle wearing a nasty grin. The pickle grabbed at him, but Mort ducked and took off in the other direction.

Mort looked up to see where he was running, and his heart froze. In front of him stood the other pickle, holding a long, sharp knife. The blade alone was bigger than Mort!

The little mushroom looked around. The edge of the counter was on one side, the wall and a toaster on the other side, and the two nasty-looking pickles stood behind and in front of him. Mort was trapped! He scurried to the top of the toaster and jumped into a slot. It was just big enough for him.

"Whew! At least they can't fit in here," Mort thought to himself. But the pickles walked over to the toaster, grinning at each other. One turned the temperature setting all the way to high, while the other pulled down the handle.

Inside, the walls started to glow red-hot. Mort looked below him. Trying to get as skinny as he could, he squeezed through the wires toward the bottom. It was getting mighty hot. He had to hurry. Plop! The mushroom dropped onto a tray full of burnt bread crumbs. It was still pretty warm down here, but at least it was tolerable. Mort waited patiently for his chance to escape.

"I don't hear much sizzling in there," remarked one of the pickles. "Maybe you'd better take a look."

The pickle with the long knife climbed to the top of the toaster and looked down both slots.

"I can't see him, but it's pretty bright." The pickle poked his knife down into the slots.

"Say, uh, I wouldn't do that if I were you," the other pickle warned.

"Why n—" Zzzzzap! A charge of electricity sizzled through the surprised pickle.

Meanwhile, Mort took the opportunity to squeeze out of the bottom of the toaster and run.

"There's the rascal!" cried the last pickle, and he took off alone after Mort.

Mort shinnied up a vase of flowers. Then, like a squirrel in a tree, he jumped from stem to stem, petal to petal, until he got to

rowels. Of course, there was a trick to his pulling out his watch at the end of the story, because he'd always remind me the watch showed it was my bedtime.

As long as I can remember, I have wanted to be a top rider like my Pa. But in my seventeen years on the ranch I had never had a horse of my own. About all the riding I got to do was on the old sorrel mare Pa and I took turns riding when we had work to do up in the hills above the ranch cup, and on Saturdays when I worked over at the Kingman place.

"Some day," Pa always said, "you'll have a horse, Billy boy. When we kind of git caught up on things an' I c'n afford it."

But there never did seem to be money for me to have a horse like other kids who lived on ranches in that part of southern Arizona.

Ours was a small ranch, as ranches go, just a few miles out of Patagonia, the nearest town, and until I got big enough to help him, Pa did the working of it himself. Ma ran a few chickens along with her housework, and we always managed to have enough food, though our clothes were nothing to brag about. And the one pair of boots I owned had to do me for school, church, and chores. They were so thin I finally got a new pair last Christmas. I remember it was Christmas because every year Pa had hoped to get me a horse for Christmas, and every year there would be something else, just like last year it was the boots.

I really never did figure to have a horse of my own till I could earn enough money to somehow buy one. That was why I'd been spending a lot of time working Saturdays over at the Kingman ranch which adjoined ours on the east. Old man Kingman had been a good friend of my Pa's for a long time and it was really Pa who got me the job.

"Course he ain't got no more sense'n a mule," Pa told Mr. Kingman. "But he's strong an' he'll do what you tell him."

Mr. Kingman was a big bull of a man with a forehead like a barn door and a slow grin that made folks like him right off when they met him. He had done well, too, from the way Pa talked.

"Trouble is, I should 'a' done like him," Pa used to say. "He settled down an' got started early raisin' beef an' buyin' up land as fast as he c'd afford it. Me, I spent too much time chasin' rodeos, driftin' from one ranch t'another. Always workin' for somebody else an' never savin' a dime."

Mr. Kingman ran upwards of a thousand head on his place with four cowboys and me to do the work. Not that I could do much, just working Saturdays, but he paid me two dollars every week for my trouble and I saved all of it. I figured if it took me a couple of years or more, I would be willing to work it out in order to buy a colt he had that was just about the prettiest little foal I ever did see.

"He's a Morgan," I told Ma, the first day I had seen the colt over at the Kingman place. "Thoroughbred, I b'lieve, except he's pretty big-boned for a thoroughbred."

Ma had looked at me in that sad way of hers when the family needed things we couldn't afford. "I know Billy," she said, "but we could never buy one of Mr. Kingman's horses. He raises 'em for a hobby an' they're all expensive."

"Doesn't matter," I told her. "I'm going to buy him with my own money. I've been saving right along, and I've got sixteen dollars already."

She just shook her head and said sixteen dollars was probably a long ways from what that foal would cost. So I took it up with Pa that evening.

"Y'mean that little black he's got over there?" Pa asked. I nodded. "May's well ferget about buyin' that hoss," he advised. "Y'got a good eye for hosses, though. I will say that. Trouble is, y'set yer stakes too high. "

"I don't care what he costs," I declared recklessly. "I'll keep savin' till I can buy him. Maybe somehow I can make some money next summer, too."

Pa's leathery old face clouded with worry. "Trouble is, I need y'here durin' the summer, Boy. 'Bout all I c'n do is spare y' on Saturdays."

I knew that was true and it was not any fault of his, so I said no more about the colt. Pa said no more either, except that he knew the way I felt, that I wanted a horse in the worst way and he would still try to get one for me come Christmas.

For the next few weeks I felt pretty glum until I gradually got over the notion of buying the Kingman horse. I reckoned I would keep saving my money and maybe someday I would find a colt like him that I could afford to buy. However it did not keep me from hanging around the corral when I would finish my work at Kingman's, just watching the little rascal grow up. When I would come in from hauling fence or doctoring calves I would pick up a handful of oats and perch on the top rail of the corral, then coax at him. He was the worst one to get spooked by

anything in the corral, and how he would jump when he was startled. Sometimes the wind would whisk a tumbleweed at him, and he would light out like a dust devil on the rampage, kicking and snorting. He did not have a name yet, so I started calling him Sox. That was because his ankles were white.

Sometimes when I was trying to make friends with the little horse, Mr. Kingman would stop around at the corral, and I guess he noticed I was plenty interested in that little foal.

"Sure a mighty fine horse," I told him.

"He ought 'a' be," Mr. Kingman said. "Champion quarterhorse stock, you know."

Some Kind of Present

Mr. Kingman was proud of his horses, just as he was proud of everything else he had. Not that he was the kind to brag about things, but it showed in the way he talked about his house, his car, and his stock.

"What're you going to do with him?" I asked. "Sell him?"

"Probably, one of these days."

I swallowed, wondering when that would be. I hoped it would not be for a couple of years, because perhaps by then I could save enough to buy him.

"Like to get your dad to break him for me," Mr. Kingman observed, looking over the little horse again.

"Pa's getting pretty old for that anymore," I reminded him. Pa was in his sixties and just about every bone in his body had been broken at one time or another. He was not in any shape to ride out a rough horse any more in the way he used to. "Maybe I could break him for you."

Mr. Kingman looked at me in a way that was not encouraging. "I don't know. We'll have to see.

There just isn't anybody anymore, who can ride the kinks out of a bronc as your dad used to."

Right then I remembered a few of the stories Pa had told me about his younger days. "Did you know about the time he won the gold spurs?" I asked.

"Know about it?" Mr. Kingman laughed. "I was there, waiting for my turn to ride. Your dad drew a big, ornery buckskin horse, and I told him he was crazier 'n' a loco longhorn to get in the chute, let alone ride him. I never did see such a horse. Must have weighed thirteen hundred pounds."

"That's what Pa says," I agreed. "Thirteen hundred!"

"He near killed your dad," Mr. Kingman said softly.

"But Pa stayed on for the full ten seconds, raked him and whipped him and gave him a whale of a ride!"

"I'll say he did. And he wouldn't have been hurt, either, if the cinch hadn't let go. That horse just swung up and snapped it."

It had been a bad accident from what Ma told me. Pa had been in the hospital in Cheyenne for weeks afterwards, and his back never did quite get healed. Ma used to tell me that part of the story when I would talk about breaking horses.

Along about Christmastime, school let out for two weeks vacation, and I got a full-time job on the mail truck, helping to deliver packages out of Patagonia. I did not work for Kingman during that time at all, and I missed seeing the little black colt. But I figured I could add to my savings considerably by working through the holi-days and still have enough money to buy some kind of present for Ma and Pa.

When I got my check, the day before Christmas, it was for nineteen dollars and seventy-two cents. That evening we all went in to Tucson to do our Christmas shopping. I got Pa some soft brown bedroom slippers for two dollars and almost ran into him at a little jewelry store where I was headed, looking for something to buy Ma.

"Where you goin'?" Pa asked, startled.

"Thought I'd find somethin' for Ma in here," I told him, and pointed at the shop window full of gadgets.

He fell in step with me, directing me away from the jewelry store and up the street toward a dress shop. "Ma wants a new dress awful bad," he said. "But they're a lot o' money. Want t'go in with me an' get her one?"

It sounded like a good idea until we got to looking at the dresses. The only one that would fit Ma that looked like anything was over twenty dollars. Pa was about to settle on another one that was cheaper when I offered to pay half on the one we wanted if he would buy it. We did that, and I just shut my eyes, trying to forget about saving for a horse. Somehow, after we left the dress shop, though, I felt awfully good inside.

We were sitting around the Christmas tree that night when Ma opened the big box and took out the dress. All she did was make a little gasping sound, and her eyes filled up as though she was going to break right out crying.

"It's beautiful," she said. "Oh, isn't it beautiful?" And she held it up in front of her while she looked in the mirror.

Pa unwrapped his bedroom slippers and put them on as though he was going to wear them for the rest of his life.

"Fit fine," he said. "They're just dandy." Then he took them off and pulled his boots back on.

"Your present's over there on the tree, Billy, with a white string attached to it," said Ma.

The two of them waited while I hunted through the tree for a white package. It was so little I could hold it in one hand. It did not weigh an ounce. I opened it and inside was a piece of paper tied to the end of the string.

"Follow the string," it said.

I followed the string, which led out the back door, across the yard and into the feed barn. Ma and Pa were walking behind me, all of us bundled up in jackets because the frost had already settled and the night was cold. When I opened the door of the feed barn, Pa held up the lantern, and I stood there trying to believe what I saw. In the manger, up to his hocks in straw, was the little black colt, looking at me the way he had so many times over in Kingman's corral.

"Is he mine?" I blubbered.

Pa nodded, and I hugged him and Ma together, wondering how they ever got enough money to buy him. Then somewhere far off, the church bells were ringing midnight, and Pa took out his watch to check the time.

"Merry Christmas," he said. Ma said "Merry Christmas" too, but I could not say anything. I was looking at Pa's watch. And the gold spurs were gone.

Gail Fitzgerald

illustrated by Preston Gravely Jr.

John Wesley: A Fiery Brand

"Fire, Father!"

"Fire! Fire!"

The frightened cries of Hetty Wesley mingled with the shouts of someone in the streets of Epworth, England. The rector jumped from a sound sleep and threw open the bedroom door.

"Susanna, my dear wife, the fire is in our own house!" he shouted over his shoulder. "Rise quickly and get yourself out!"

Then he rushed to the nursery where five of his children and a nurse slept peacefully.

"Nurse! Get the children up and follow me quickly!" he commanded. As he carried the youngest children into the garden, a cry from the upstairs nursery startled him.

"Father, I am up here!"

It was John, age six, who had not heard the commotion. The orange light of flames had finally roused him from his sleep.

"John, I'm coming!" shouted Mr. Wesley. He rushed into the house, but again and again flames forced him out.

"Give me a light man to stand on my shoulders," someone shouted.

John was soon rescued from his fiery loft by two neighbors— and none too soon. Within seconds the thatch roof collapsed. In moments the house was gone.

"John Wesley, surely you are a brand plucked from the burning." Susanna Wesley held her second son close. Her mother's heart whispered that God had a special work for this boy. She would take extra care to raise him for the Lord.

Each morning the family members went to their private prayers before they got their breakfast or came to see the rest of the family. School was conducted by Mrs. Wesley from nine to twelve and from two to five. Mr. Wesley made sure that his children learned Greek and Latin. After school the children paired up for an hour of Bible reading. It's no wonder that John was a good student, an eager reader, and a lover of the Bible. It is a wonder that he had time to become a swimmer and a horseman too.

The Wesley household was busy in other ways. Every year another baby appeared, until nineteen children had been born. At least ten lived to become adults. Ten children meant many mouths to feed, many bodies to be clothed, and many minds to be educated. But Mr. and Mrs. Wesley trusted in God.

There were problems. One dark night, the family's three cows were stabbed. Another night some villagers hacked up the Wesleys' front door. Then the children heard their father say, "All things must be endured with patience. Courage then! Think on eternity!"

When funds were low and clothes were threadbare, Mrs. Wesley said, "It is much easier to be contented without riches than with them. It is so natural for a rich man to make gold his god. I do not know one rich man in the world with whom I would change conditions."

Thus the children learned that real, living faith is tested every step of the way. They also learned that the God of their parents was faithful.

One day when John was nearly twelve years old, his father called him into the study. "Son, your mother and I have tried to give you the best education possible."

"Yes, sir, and I am grateful."

"You have done a good job. So you have been accepted at the Charter House School in London."

John's eyes shone. "And I may really go?"

"As fast as you can pack your bags!"

John studied hard in London for four or five years. He was never idle. His mother's words often rang in his ears: "Idle hands and minds are the devil's workshop."

By the time John was sixteen years old, he was ready to go to Oxford University. Big decisions loomed in front of him. What should he do with his life? Since he had always loved, honored, and obeyed his parents, he wrote to them. Should he go into the ministry?

Samuel Wesley was pleased that his son thought so highly of the ministry. He wrote to John, "You ask me which is the best commentary on the Bible? I answer, the Bible itself. . . . I will help you in every way I can." For the next eight years, John tried to live in a way that pleased the Lord. He got up early and never stayed up late. He never spent money on fancy clothes or foolish things. He visited the poor, the sick, and people in jail. When he found uneducated children on the streets, he taught them to read. He read his Bible often. But John did not have a saving faith in Jesus Christ. He hoped to save his soul himself. After eight years of trying hard, John was ordained into the ministry. He still believed that his good works could save him.

Samuel Wesley was delighted that his son was now a minister. Now his son could take over the church at Epworth. But John had other ideas.

"Father, I must stay in London. Drunkenness, robbery, and slave trading are all too common here. I must try to do as much good as I can." And John did stay in London until he received word that his dear father was dying. Then he quickly hurried to Epworth.

His father's tired old face shone. Over and over he whispered, "The Inward Witness— that is the strongest proof of Christianity."

John was puzzled. What did his father mean? Wasn't it enough to do good? John bent over his father. "Are you not near heaven?"

In a voice that rang with certainty, he answered, "Yes, I am!" After his father's death, John was left with an empty feeling in his heart. He spoke of it to his younger brother. "Charles, what is the proper way to care for one's soul?"

Charles looked at John's troubled eyes. "Come with me to America to preach to the Indians. In that way we can save our own souls and do good."

John readily agreed. Before long their ship left England. John discovered that the ship was also carrying a group of Moravians to America. He became friends with several of them.

On the vast ocean, three terrible storms pounded the tiny ship. At one point the angry waves broke over the ship. The main sail split, and water poured onto the decks.

John clung to a post, his heart beating as wildly as the storm. "Aren't you afraid?" he asked his Moravian friends.

"Of what?"

"Why, the storm threatens to swallow us up! We will die!"

"Then may our blessed Lord Jesus receive us into His arms," was their calm reply.

John didn't understand. They had peace and he did not. Yet he was a minister and they were not. He wrote in his diary, "I was then unwilling to die."

Finally the ship landed safely in America. During his two years there, the young minister tried to work among the Indians. He wept when he saw their sin. He was troubled, too, because he still had problems that had followed him from England. At last John admitted to himself that he was a failure. He boarded a ship and left for England. What would he do now?

John returned to London with a troubled heart. He wrote in his diary, "I went to Georgia to convert the Indians, but oh! who shall convert me?"

Not too many people had answers for John. England was in sad shape. Many churches did not believe that Christ is God. Most churches were nearly empty. There were no Sunday schools, and few of the poor could read.

John turned to the only people he knew could help him—the Moravians. In the spring of 1738, he attended one of their house meetings. There he heard a truth that brought peace to his restless soul. Salvation could never be earned by works. Sinners are saved by faith in the blood of Christ alone.

"Charles," he wrote excitedly, "I have at last found out that the Inward Witness is Christ Himself, dwelling in our hearts by faith. I find my heart strangely warmed by His presence. I have been converted."

This warmth grew into a burning fire, and John began to preach with a zeal that was strange to the English people. Many churches closed their doors to John Wesley. The people who were converted under his preaching were called heretics.

Even John's brother Samuel believed the bad stories about John. He wrote to his mother, "John has become a fanatic." Mrs. Wesley was confused at first. When she learned the truth, however, she wrote, "I have a great and just desire that all your brothers and sisters should be saved." Mrs. Wesley's prayer was answered: sooner or later all her children were saved.

But what was a preacher without a church to do? Why, preach everywhere, of course! In the mornings John preached at the old city jail. Every afternoon he preached in the countryside. The first time he preached in the open air, about three thousand people

came to hear him. He often spoke to crowds of ten to twelve thousand.

Every evening he preached to a room packed full of people with hungry hearts.

These new converts needed to go to church, but there were no good churches for them to attend. John talked it over with his brother Charles and several other men. They decided to form converts into groups. These groups built chapels, and the movement grew and grew. The converts copied their leaders, doing good works and living holy lives after they were saved.

But some people in other churches were angry. Mobs began breaking into the converts' houses. They ruined the houses and stole property. Sometimes they even hurt the people.

One time John himself was seized by a mob. The Lord delivered him and spared his life. Another time a mob brought out a fire engine to spray John with water while he preached. One man hired boys to shout and disturb the preaching. Then he sent in a drunken man to make noise. At last he himself began playing the French horn. John just continued speaking, and the troublemakers disappeared.

John Wesley traveled all over England on horseback in rain, snow, cold, and heat. Nothing could stop him. Even at eighty years of age he was rising at 4:00 A.M., preaching at 5:00, and then traveling thirty to seventy miles to preach several more times. His hours of horseback riding were not spent in idleness. He always had a book in his hand.

During his lifetime, John Wesley preached 40,000 sermons and traveled over 225,000 miles. That's about 15 sermons a week and 5,000 miles a year!

John's life prayer had been, "Lord, let me not live to be useless." When at last he died on March 2, 1791, he left 511 preachers and 120,000 members in his new churches. Everywhere lives were changed for the glory of God. John's native land, England, had been transformed—all because a brand plucked from the burning had been willing to burn for God.

SKILL LESSON:

Bible Study

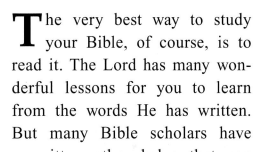

The very best way to study your Bible, of course, is to read it. The Lord has many wonderful lessons for you to learn from the words He has written. But many Bible scholars have written other helps that can make reading and studying God's Word even more of a blessing to you. Some editors have put helps right into the Bible itself in the margins and at the beginnings of chapters. If you understand how to read and use these aids, you can go a long way toward appreciating the Bible even more.

• Page Headings

Look at the sample Bible page on page 479 of your reader and notice the chapter and verse given in the top left and top right corners. The first verse on the page is chapter 5, verse 15. The last verse on the page is chapter 6, verse 16. These verse headings work much the same way as guide words in a dictionary. But Bible page headings also tell the name of the book you are in. What book is this page taken from? If you form the habit of looking at the page headings, you will be able to locate passages in Scripture very quickly.

• Topics

Sometimes you can't remember which chapter a certain story is in. Many Bible scholars have put topic guides throughout the chapters of Scripture to help you find your particular topic quickly and easily. These topic guides are usually in italics. Suppose your Bible has these topic guides and you want to find the story of Joshua and the battle of Jericho. You might notice that right under the heading "Chapter 6" are the words *God gives Jericho into the hands of the Israelites.* Then you would know that you are in the right place.

• Cross-References

The verses given in tiny print in the middle of the sample Bible page are called cross-references. Each one directs you from some word on that page to another place in the Bible that can help explain the passage you are reading. It may tell, for example, the first time something was mentioned in the Bible (references *a* and *d*), who someone was (reference *b*), or somewhere else in Scripture where something is mentioned (reference *c*). Using cross-references can be a great help to you in your Bible study. You may even want to add some cross-references of your own as you study or listen to sermons.

15 And the captain of the LORD's host said unto Joshua, Loose thy shoe from off thy foot; for the place whereon thou standest is holy. And Joshua did so.

Chapter 6

Topic ⟶ *God gives Jericho into the hands of the Israelites*

1 Now ^aJericho was straitly shut up because of the children of Israel: none went out, and none came in.

2 And the LORD said unto ^bJoshua, See, I have given into thine hand Jericho, and the king thereof, and the mighty men of valour.

3 And ye shall compass the city, all ye men of war, and go round about the city once. Thus shalt thou do six days.

4 And seven priests shall bear before the ark seven trumpets of rams' horns: and the seventh day ye shall compass the city seven times, and the priests shall blow with the ^ctrumpets.

5 And it shall come to pass, that when they make a long blast with the ram's horn, and when ye hear the sound of the trumpet, all the people shall shout with a great shout; and the wall of the city shall fall down flat, and the people shall ascend up every man straight before him.

6 And Joshua the son of Nun called the priests, and said unto them, Take up the ark of the ^dcovenant, and let seven priests bear seven trumpets of rams' horns before the ark of the LORD.

7 And he said unto the people, Pass on, and compass the city, and let him that is armed pass on before the ark of the LORD.

^aJosh. 2:1

^bDeut. 3:28

^cJudg. 7:19-22

^dEx. 25:10-22

8 And it came to pass, when Joshua had spoken unto the people, that the seven priests bearing the seven trumpets of rams' horns passed on before the LORD, and blew with the trumpets: and the ark of the covenant of the LORD followed them.

9 And the armed men went before the priests that blew with the trumpets, and the rereward came after the ark, the priests going on, and blowing with the trumpets.

10 And Joshua had commanded the people, saying, Ye shall not shout, nor make any noise with your voice, neither shall any word proceed out of your mouth, until the day I bid you shout; then shall ye shout.

11 So the ark of the LORD compassed the city, going about it once: and they came into the camp, and lodged in the camp.

12 And Joshua rose early in the morning, and the priests took up the ark of the LORD.

13 And seven priests bearing seven trumpets of rams' horns before the ark of the LORD went on continually, and blew with the trumpets: and the armed men went before them; but the rereward came after the ark of the LORD, the priests going on, and blowing with the trumpets.

14 And the second day they compassed the city once, and returned into the camp: so they did six days.

15 And it came to pass on the seventh day, that they rose early about the dawning of the day, and compassed the city after the same manner seven times: only on that day they compassed the city seven times.

16 And it came to pass at the seventh time, when the priests blew with the trumpets, Joshua said unto the people, Shout; for the LORD hath given you the city.

Cross-References

An Old Testament HERO

Joshua and the Battle of Jericho • Joshua 6:1-20
illustrated by Del Thompson and John Bjerk

1 Now Jericho was straitly shut up because of the children of Israel: none went out, and none came in.

2 And the LORD said unto Joshua, See, I have given into thine hand Jericho, and the king thereof, and the mighty men of valour.

3 And ye shall compass the city, all ye men of war, and go round about the city once. Thus shalt thou do six days.

4 And seven priests shall bear before the ark seven trumpets of rams' horns: and the seventh day ye shall compass the city seven times, and the priests shall blow with the trumpets.

5 And it shall come to pass, that when they make a long blast with the ram's horn, and when ye

hear the sound of the trumpet, all the people shall shout with a great shout; and the wall of the city shall fall down flat, and the people shall ascend up every man straight before him.

6 And Joshua the son of Nun called the priests, and said unto them, Take up the ark of the covenant, and let seven priests bear seven trumpets of rams'

horns before the ark of the LORD.

7 And he said unto the people, Pass on, and compass the city, and let him that is armed pass on before the ark of the LORD.

8 And it came to pass, when Joshua had spoken unto the people, that the seven priests bearing the seven trumpets of

rams' horns passed on before the LORD, and blew with the trumpets: and the ark of the covenant of the LORD followed them.

9 And the armed men went before the priests that blew with the trumpets, and the rereward came after the ark, the priests going on, and blowing with the trumpets.

10 And Joshua had commanded the people, saying, Ye shall not shout, nor make any noise with your voice, neither shall any word proceed out of your mouth, until the day I bid you shout; then shall ye shout.

11 So the ark of the LORD compassed the city, going about it once: and they came into the camp, and lodged in the camp.

12 And Joshua rose early in the morning, and the priests took up the ark of the LORD.

13 And seven priests bearing seven trumpets of rams' horns before the ark of the LORD went on continually, and blew with the trumpets: and the armed men went before them; but the rereward came after the ark of the LORD, the priests going on, and blowing with the trumpets.

14 And the second day they compassed the city once, and returned into the camp: so they did six days.

15 And it came to pass on the seventh day, that they rose early about the dawning of the day, and compassed the city after the same manner seven times: only on that day they compassed the city seven times.

16 And it came to pass at the seventh time, when the priests blew with the trumpets, Joshua said unto the people, Shout; for the LORD hath given you the city.

17 And the city shall be accursed, even it, and all that are therein, to the LORD: only Rahab the harlot shall live, she and all that are with her in the house, because she hid the messengers that we sent.

18 And ye, in any wise keep

yourselves from the accursed thing, lest ye make yourselves accursed, when ye take of the accursed thing, and make the camp of Israel a curse, and trouble it.

19 But all the silver, and gold, and vessels of brass and iron, are consecrated unto the LORD: they shall come into the treasury of the LORD.

20 So the people shouted when the priests blew with the trumpets: and it came to pass, when the people heard the sound of the trumpet, and the people shouted with a great shout, that the wall fell down flat, so that the people went up into the city, every man straight before him, and they took the city.

What Is Black?

Mary O'Neill
illustrated by Sam Laterza

Black is the night
When there isn't a star
And you can't tell by looking
Where you are.
Black is a pail of paving tar.
Black is jet
And things you'd like to forget.
Black is a smokestack
Black is a cat,
A leopard, a raven,
A high silk hat.
The sound of black is
"Boom! Boom! Boom!"
Echoing in
An empty room.
Black is kind——
It covers up

The run-down street,
The broken cup.
Black is charcoal
And patio grill,
The soot spots on
The window sill.
Black is a feeling
Hard to explain
Like suffering but
Without the pain.
Black is licorice
And patent leather shoes
Black is the print
In the news.
Black is beauty
In its deepest form,
The darkest cloud
In a thunderstorm.
Think of what starlight
And lamplight would lack
Diamonds and fireflies
If they couldn't lean against
Black. . . .

The Genuine Spring-Operated, Brass-Handled, Black
UMBRELLA

Milly Howard
illustrated by Del Thompson and Noelle Snyder

In the early twentieth century, inventors were constantly trying to think of new gadgets to make life easier. Many of their inventions are things that we take for granted now. But when the girl in this story borrows an umbrella, it is the first of its kind in her neighborhood.

As you read, you'll notice that Amelia lives at a time when apartment buildings still have doormen and elevator operators. Many city children during this time go to school on city buses. Have fun stepping back in time and watching Amelia with her newfangled umbrella.

First of Its Kind

"Good-bye, Mom," Amelia called as she opened the front door of the apartment. "I'm off for school!"

"Better take your . . ." The slamming of the door cut off Mrs. Widener's reply. She stopped in the kitchen doorway, wiping her hands and shaking her head. "That Amelia," she said to herself, "always in a hurry. Now there's her umbrella still here, and it's pouring outside."

At the end of the hallway, Amelia jabbed the elevator button again. She chewed impatiently on the end of a pigtail as she watched the indicator light above the elevator. "One . . . two . . . three . . . Oh, it's stopped again, and if I'm late, Elise will leave without me," she muttered to herself. "I'll just have to take the stairs!"

Amelia opened the door to the service stairs and hurried down, taking two steps at a time. When

486

she reached the lobby floor, she was out of breath. Panting, she crossed the carpet just as the elevator bell rang and the door opened. Jimmy, the elevator operator, grinned at her cheerfully. "Racing me again, Miss Amelia?" he asked as the other passengers got off.

Amelia grinned back, unable to answer. She waved her hand and followed the others to the lobby doors. Simmons, the doorman, held the door open for the children and businessmen. Morning greetings were exchanged as umbrellas were unfurled. Whish! Snap! Bright colors unfolded above the children's heads. Then the children splashed out from under the apartment building's canopy, looking like yellow and red elves under multicolored mushrooms. Whish! Snap! Black umbrellas unfolded above the men's heads. Then they all strode away, dark shadows on the wet, shining pavement. Only Amelia remained under the canopy, hesitating.

Simmons looked down. "No umbrella, Miss Amelia?"

"I forgot it," Amelia replied mournfully, staring at the pouring rain. "Even if I run, I'll get soaked, and if I go back upstairs, I'll be late."

"I have an extra one," Simmons said. He reached behind him and pulled a long black umbrella from the umbrella rack. "A salesman left me this one for me to try out. Said it was the coming thing."

"But it's a man's umbrella," Amelia said in dismay.

"Oh, but it's a special one," Simmons said, his eyes twinkling. "The salesman said it was a genuine spring-operated umbrella. Just watch."

Simmons held the umbrella aloft and pressed a button on the brass handle. With a satisfying whump! the umbrella opened above Amelia's head. She stared up at the black silk stretched tight over shining brass ribs and reached up to touch the gleaming brass handle.

"How did you do that?" Amelia asked.

"Here," he answered, touching a tiny knob on the brass handle. "You just push this little knob."

"How do I close the thing?" Amelia asked.

"Just like other umbrellas, only pull a little harder," Simmons replied. "Make sure you hear a snap. That way you know the umbrella has locked into place."

"Oh, thank you," Amelia said happily. "I really appreciate this."

"No problem, Miss Amelia," Simmons replied, "but you will have a problem if you don't hurry now."

Amelia splashed out into the rain, sliding her boots to send water flying ahead of her. She tilted the umbrella so she could see ahead of her. Past the bookstore, past the pharmacy, past the card shop she hurried, bumping into other people. At last she got her bearings, realizing that she had to allow more room for the big umbrella.

At the next building she saw Elise waiting under the overhanging roof. As Amelia approached, Elise's eyes widened in surprise. Then she giggled.

"Is that you, Amelia?" she called.

Amelia tilted the umbrella farther back. "Leave your umbrella," she said. "This one's big enough for both of us."

"It certainly is," Elise said as she placed her umbrella in the rack and stepped under the black one with Amelia. "It's big enough for you, me, and a whole lot of other people!"

Amelia grinned. "Wait till you see it open! It's a genuine spring-operated, brass-handled umbrella."

"Oh, my father's been wanting one of these," Elise said. "Won't he be surprised when he hears you have one!"

"It isn't mine; it's the doorman's," Amelia answered. "I just borrowed it."

The girls hurried down the street. "If we run, we'll have time to look into Mr. Jenkins's window again," Amelia said. "This is almost April. He may have put the diamonds in the window already."

Mr. Jenkins owned Cara's, the best jewelry store in town. Each month he had one window devoted to that month's birthstone. He always chose his most beautiful necklace for the centerpiece of the window. On a card placed beside the necklace he would write a girl's name. Amelia and Elise had talked Mr. Jenkins into using their names. September had been Elise's month, and both girls had been thrilled to see "For Elise" written on a card below a sapphire necklace, with the sheet music by Beethoven below it. April sixteenth was Amelia's birthday, and her birthstone was the diamond. She could hardly wait to see the new display.

They reached Cara's and stopped beside the display window. "He hasn't changed it yet," Amelia said in disappointment. She started to turn away.

"Wait," Elise said, excitedly. "He's changing it now!"

The girls watched breathlessly as a hand appeared and whisked away aquamarines and white silk. It reappeared with black velvet and smoothed the soft folds over the display case.

"Oh, look," Amelia squealed, bouncing the black umbrella above them as a diamond necklace was coiled into the case. In the center of the coil was placed a black card. On the front was written in silver letters, "For Amelia." The hand disappeared, and a face appeared in its place. Mr. Jenkins peered out at the girls and solemnly winked. Then the curtain closed, and the girls were alone with the display.

"It's beautiful!" Amelia said happily as they began to walk again. "Let's stop on our way home and really take a good look at it!"

"All right," Elise agreed as they turned the corner, "but right now we'd better run! There's the bus!"

The girls splashed past the grocery store and hurried to the end of the line of waiting people. As each person climbed onto the

bus, he snapped shut his umbrella. When Amelia's turn came, she sent Elise on up the steps and turned to snap the black umbrella shut. It didn't budge. Amelia tugged again. Elise was already in a seat and looking back for Amelia.

"Come on, Amelia, let's go!" called one of the boys in the front seat. "You're letting rain in!"

Amelia gave one last, hard pull, and the black umbrella

closed with a soft whoosh. Amelia gave a sigh of relief and clambered aboard the bus. She hurried back to slide into the seat behind Mr. Tidwell, the banker. The umbrella bumped against Elise's ribs as Amelia sat down.

"Ooh, it's wet," Elise said. "Put it on the floor, Amelia."

"I hate to get it dirty," Amelia thought. She tried propping the umbrella against the seat in front. It was too long to hook over the back of the seat, and it kept prodding Mr. Tidwell on the head. After a few cross looks from him, Amelia let the black umbrella slide to the floor.

It Was the Umbrella!

At the next stop, several boys got on the bus and headed for the back. The black umbrella got kicked twice. Unnoticed by Amelia, it now lay halfway into the aisle.

As the bus stopped at the corner across from the school yard, there was the usual scuffle in the back to avoid being the last one off the bus. Across the aisle from the girls, William McCauley put a foot out to claim his place. His boot brushed the black umbrella.

Whump! The black silk umbrella sprang open. William snatched his foot back. The boys and girls at the back of the bus stared at the silk and brass that had wedged itself between the seats.

"Hey, what's this!"

"Mr. Wheatley!"

"We can't get out!"

"Whose umbrella?"

The last voice belonged to Mr. Wheatley, the bus driver, who was looking sternly over the edge of the umbrella.

"Mine," a red-faced Amelia answered. "At least it is right now."

"Amelia, I'm surprised at you. You know better than to block the aisles," Mr. Wheatley said, frowning at her.

"But I didn't . . . at least I . . . it was the umbrella," Amelia stammered.

"Sure," William said scornfully. "The umbrella just opened itself."

When Amelia nodded, he laughed. "So show us how."

"I can't get it loose," Amelia replied, tugging at the handle.

"Come on, I'm going to be late to work," someone shouted from behind them.

"I'll get it loose," William boasted, grabbing a handful of black silk and squeezing the brass ribs.

"Stop! You'll break it!" Amelia demanded. "I borrowed it, and I have to return it."

"Wait a minute!" Mr. Wheatley said firmly.

"William, I can close it from here with Amelia's help. Amelia, you pull when I tell you."

Amelia nodded as Mr. Wheatley gently freed the protruding points of the ribs from the back of the seats. "Now pull," he said, squeezing the umbrella from behind. It folded neatly into Amelia's hand.

"There," Mr. Wheatley said, turning to inspect the wooden seat backs. He shook his head as the children filed past. "Amelia, you know I'll have to report this," he said. "But at least there was no damage."

Amelia nodded and followed Elise off the bus. "Genuine spring-operated umbrella!" she said disgustedly. "Now I'll probably have to stay after school!"

"Don't worry, Amelia," Elise said. "I'll wait for you if you do. We can walk home."

Amelia sighed. "But we won't have time to look at the window again. Dumb old umbrella!"

The two girls hurried into the building. Ahead of them the other children fanned out, disappearing into the classrooms on either side of the hallway. Amelia and Elise walked quickly past the hall clock on their way to the last classroom.

"We're not going to make it," Elise said. "We have only thirty seconds! "

"Run," Amelia gasped.

Holding their books tightly, the two girls began to run. They flew past the fifth-grade classrooms and up two steps. Amelia's boot caught on the edge of the top step, and her books went skidding down the hall—along with the black umbrella. Amelia raised her head in time to see the umbrella spin slowly outside the principal's office. The door to the office opened.

Whump!

"Oh, no!" Amelia cried.

The bell rang just as the principal's foot caught the rim of the open umbrella. Amelia and Elise watched wide-eyed as he tumbled into the black silk. Papers scattered over the hall as he clutched at the brass handle.

When the umbrella stopped revolving, the principal looked at Amelia and Elise. "Girls," he said quietly. "Could I see you for a moment in my office?"

The Genuine Spring-Operated, Brass-Handled, Black Umbrella

"Yes, sir!" Elise and Amelia helped pick up the scattered books and papers. Then they followed him into the office. He kept a firm hold on the now-folded black umbrella.

When everything was finally sorted out, the principal suggested that he keep the umbrella until school was out. Amelia and Elise could pick it up after school and never, never, never bring it to school again.

"As a matter of fact, I'd be glad to lend you an umbrella to use on the way home," he said. "It would be a lot less trouble than letting you take this one home on the bus."

But as it turned out, it wasn't even raining that afternoon. Amelia was allowed to take the umbrella home, provided she held it carefully all the way and kept it closed.

Even William kept out of Amelia's way that afternoon, teasing her from a distance about her new weapon. Amelia just tossed her head and got off at her stop with Elise.

"Come on," she said. "Since we didn't have to stay after school, we'll have time to look in Mr. Jenkins's window!"

The girls ran down the street. They had just reached the grocery store when they heard an alarm.

"Mr. Jenkins's alarm!" someone shouted.

"The jewelry shop's been robbed! "

"My necklace!" Amelia said indignantly. "Someone's taken my necklace!"

From around the corner the two girls heard the sound of running feet, then the shrill of a policeman's whistle.

"He's coming this way!" Elise squealed. She grabbed Amelia's free hand and pulled her toward the grocery store.

"Just a minute," Amelia said, pulling back. "I have an idea!" She listened as the steps came pounding closer, then pointed the genuine spring-operated, black umbrella toward the corner of the building. Amelia pressed the spring and turned the umbrella loose.

Whump!

The umbrella opened and sailed away from Amelia, right into the path of the thief. Amelia dodged into the store with Elise

as the thief stumbled over the black umbrella and went down. The handful of jewels he carried scattered over the pavement. A policeman raced around the corner and tripped over the thief and the umbrella.

Amelia and Elise watched the capture from inside the store, pressed against the window with the other customers.

"Did you see that?" Mrs. Hadley exclaimed. "They fell over Amelia's umbrella!"

"That was quick thinking, Amelia," congratulated the grocer. "Whatever made you think of opening the umbrella?"

Amelia and Elise looked at each other and giggled. "Well," Amelia said. "It's a special umbrella."

When the customers looked puzzled, she explained. "It's a genuine spring-operated, brass-handled, black umbrella—and people-catching is what it seems to do best!"

THE OMNIBUS

Milly Howard
illustrated by Roger Bruckner and Bob Reynolds

In France in 1662, lavish coaches were a major means of transportation. These coaches were very expensive, and poor people couldn't afford to ride in them. For this reason, the *voiture omnibus,* or "vehicle for all," was invented. Each coach had eight seats, and the passengers paid five sous, a very small sum, to ride. The rich people also became interested in the *voiture omnibus.*

Even the king and his friends made several trips in the coaches. The fare, however, was still more than most of the poor could pay. As a result, the *voiture omnibus* failed and disappeared.

It took over a hundred years for someone to try using the voiture omnibus again. This time, though, it was a success. Its name was shortened to *omnibus.* In 1829 a man named Abraham

Brower introduced the omnibus to America. His New York omnibus looked like a stagecoach. It had four rows of seats, each wide enough for three passengers. That same year he built another omnibus. This one, which he named the Sociable, had a rear entrance, steps, and a handrail. The Sociable was also the first omnibus with two rows of seats facing the aisle. The aisle space became "standing room" for extra customers.

At first fares were collected by a boy who stood on the rear step. Soon, though, the boy collector was replaced by the fare box. The driver, from his seat on the roof, would lower the fare box through a hole in the ceiling of the omnibus. He would wait for each passenger to deposit his fare in the box. Then he would draw it back up.

When a passenger needed to stop the bus to get off, he tugged on a cord or strap attached to the driver's leg. Immediately the driver would pull the omnibus to a sudden halt, often to the dismay of standing passengers.

The drivers loved their power. They raced up and down the streets in a manner described in the newspapers of the day as "brutal and dangerous in the highest degree." The newspapers also described them as "of a ferocious spirit, defiant of the law, delighting in destruction." Evidently they earned their reputation. Rival omnibus drivers raced to the corner to pick up passengers. Pedestrians ran for their lives. Sometimes two racing omnibuses would crush carriages that got trapped between them.

Such wild races made the passengers very angry. The sight delighted the onlookers, however. They often cheered their favorite drivers. In spite of the danger—or perhaps because of it—small boys especially liked sitting beside the dashing drivers. Most children and adults preferred the upper deck. There they could ride perched above the street scene.

Rail omnibuses were first introduced in 1832. In the beginning they were not very popular, but by the 1850s, riders were getting tired of reckless drivers.

They started to notice the rail omnibuses. These vehicles couldn't leave the rails on which they ran. So the ride was much safer and smoother. By the 1880s, 100,000 horses and mules pulled rail omnibuses. But the rail omnibuses also had problems. Many cities wouldn't let the railways add snowplows to their omnibuses. Instead, the snow stayed on the streets for the people who drove sleighs. So some street railways started using sleighs as their "omnibuses." But even with the sleigh omnibuses, winter caused problems. Small heaters were installed underneath the cars. The heaters had pipes to carry the warmth upward. Often the pipes set the cars on fire. But spring always came, and the fresh air brought many passengers out. Although horse-drawn omnibuses continued their routes, the horse-drawn railway cars were well established.

Steam-powered omnibuses became popular for a little while during the 1830s. But steam gave way to petrol, or gas. With the popularity of the new gas-powered cars came the motorbus. By this time the name omnibus had been shortened to bus. The new motorbus kept much of the style of the old omnibus. With its rear steps, upper deck, and interior wooden seats, it was a familiar sight by the 1900s. In 1910, the motorbuses outnumbered the old horse-drawn buses. Six years after that the last horse-drawn buses went out of service and into history.

DANGER
at Milner School

Doris Moose
illustrated by Stephanie True

Milner Memorial Academy is a real school for missionary children in the Central African Republic. Miss Rachel Larson was a real missionary teacher there. This true story tells of the Lord's provision for her in a time of need.

On her first shopping trip into the town of Kaga Bandoro in the Central African Republic, the young missionary lady saw the man. He wore dirty short pants and a T-shirt. His hair was uncombed and matted with grime. He waved wildly to the passing carload of missionaries, but he did not approach the car as it moved slowly along the dirt road. He could not move more than fifteen feet from the tree under which he stood, for he was chained to the tree!

Moved with pity, Miss Larson asked, "Why is that man chained to that tree?"

"His family doesn't know what else to do with him," the senior missionary, Mr. Baker, explained. "The man is mentally ill, and there are no hospitals or centers for the care of mentally disturbed or insane people here."

"Everyone knows him from seeing him under his tree," Mrs. Baker added. "They call him 'the town crazy man.' Sometimes he gets loose and wanders off. The gendarmes find him and put him in jail until his family comes. It's sad. The family doesn't even take him into their house to bathe him before they put the shackle back around his ankle."

"He can be dangerous," Mr. Baker said. "If he gets angry when he's loose, there's almost no stopping him. Once he fought off four gendarmes. He nearly killed one of them with his bare hands. Some people think it's only a matter of time before he gets loose and does kill someone." He shook his head. "Poor man."

Miss Larson spent the rest of the trip in quiet thought. "There are so many needs on this mission field. So many people need Christ to save them. So many have physical and mental needs."

Then her mind settled on a group of twenty-one children—her students—with special needs of their own. They were all missionary children, and some were as far as two or three days' journey from their parents. The students lived at the school with house parents for eight months of every year.

Each morning the children simply walked down a hill on a path that wound through tall grass, and there was their school. Two red brick buildings housed all the classrooms. Inside the class-rooms there were regular school desks and chalkboards. The window openings were screened, and the shutters opened and closed on the inside.

Everyone hoped for sunny school days so that there would be enough classroom light. Electricity came on only when the mission dentist needed it for his drill. Also on sunny days everyone could hear the teacher. But when rain pounded on the metal roof, Miss Larson had to shout every word.

The young missionary teacher believed that most, or perhaps all, of her students had accepted Christ as Savior. What she longed for most was to teach them more than just math and history. She wanted to teach them how to know God and His Word and to trust Him completely.

A time for such teaching came unexpectedly one cloudy afternoon. Miss Larson sat at the front of the room in the corner at the study table with her third-grade Heritage Studies class. The older children worked quietly at their desks.

Miss Larson was looking through Mr. Baker's notes on the Sango language. She understood many of the words, but she still could not speak it in sentences. Every time she tried to talk to the African children in their language, they crinkled up their noses and laughed at her.

Suddenly a man burst through the back door.

"Baloa! Baloa!" he shouted. Miss Larson understood that this was a hello. But she had to be sure who the intruder was. In English she asked the children quickly, "Do you know who this is?"

"The town crazy man!"

Miss Larson looked at him quickly. He carried a red toy truck.

"My brother's truck!" Eric Baker cried out.

In his other hand the man carried a long iron file on a leather thong. It would have been a useful tool in the carpenter's shop, but it could now become a deadly weapon. Miss Larson knew that if the man had roamed freely in Mr. Baker's yard and in the carpenter's shop to pick up the file, the mission station was not protected. There was no point in screaming.

Instead, a silent prayer left Miss Larson's unmoving lips. "God, give me wisdom and the right Sango words."

"What do you want?" she asked calmly in Sango. She was a little startled at how quickly she thought of the sentence.

"I came to see children," he replied.

He seemed calm. But he swung the iron file in a wide circle

above his head as he walked around and talked.

He moved close to Miss Larson and leaned over her shoulder to look at the pages of the book she held. The swish of the iron file above her head caused her to shiver.

"You can see we are all here." She spoke to him gently in Sango.

Seeing the fear in the children's eyes, the teacher ignored the dangerous iron file. In English she spoke to them bravely. "Children, God is here with us." She quoted a verse from the Psalms. " 'Though an host should encamp against me, my heart shall not fear . . . for in the time of trouble he shall hide me in his pavilion.' "

Then, looking at the man, she said firmly in Sango, "We are having class. We need to do our work now." The steadiness of her own voice speaking in Sango calmed her. "God is helping me with the language!" she thought.

The crazy man stopped swinging the file. "I think I'll go now," he said. "But I want to shake hands with the children first."

"Do we have to?" one child begged, nearly in tears.

"Yes," Miss Larson answered. "We do not want to make him angry. The Lord wants you to be brave."

Obediently, each child politely took the filthy hand offered to him. Some of the older ones felt sorry for him. They tried to smile when they shook his hand.

"Baloa! Baloa!" the wild man shouted. His greeting was also his good-bye. As he walked out the door, he pushed the red truck up and down his arm. He whistled happily as he walked down the road.

The perfectly still classroom came to life. Miss Larson ran to the back of the room and bolted the door.

"Now we are safe, and God has protected us," she said. "He has surely answered some prayers today. We're going to have a prayer time to thank Him."

Two and a half weeks later, when the mail plane came, Miss Larson learned a wonderful thing.

She discovered that on that frightening day others were praying to the Lord for her protection.

One letter had been written three weeks before from First Baptist Church in Little Falls, Minnesota. It said, "You are our missionary of the week. We are praying especially for your physical safety this week."

Another letter came from one of Miss Larson's former students at Bob Jones Academy. "Today I was in the dorm laundry room at 8:00 A.M. I suddenly felt burdened for you and prayed for your safety."

Miss Larson's sister Karen also wrote from Minnesota. "I was fixing breakfast, and I remember looking at the clock. It was 7:00 A.M. 'I need to pray right now for Rachel' went through my mind. I don't know why."

Miss Larson knew why, even before she sat down to figure out the dates and time differences between the various parts of America and Central Africa. It was true. Her friends and relatives were praying for her safety the

exact week, day, and hour of her danger!

How thankful she was that some of God's people at home were willing to pray whenever God burdened their hearts. The missionary teacher could hardly wait to tell her students what God had done for them.

LITERATURE LESSON:

Foreshadowing

- **Planning the Story**

When a writer thinks of a story, he must carefully plan everything that will happen. The writer of "Champion Stock" has a very good story to tell. He tells you all about the boy who wants a horse and how he receives the horse he wants.

If the author of "Champion Stock" did not mention Pa's gold spurs until the end of the story, you would be surprised to know that Pa has any. Sometimes if you are too surprised at the end of a story, you won't like the story. So a good writer makes sure that you know certain things from the very beginning. The author of "Champion Stock" makes sure you know that Pa has a pair of valuable gold spurs.

• Putting in Clues

Since writers do not want to surprise readers too much, they plant "clues" in their stories. These clues help the readers understand the ending and like it.

In "Champion Stock," you read about Pa's gold spurs from the very beginning. You know the spurs are worth a lot of money. Every time the writer mentions the gold spurs, you remember how valuable they are. Each time you read about them, you receive another clue about the end of the story. Later in the story, the boy sees his father at the jewelry store. This is also a clue. It makes you wonder what the father has been doing. At the end of the story, though, you put the clues together and realize that Pa has sold his gold spurs to buy the horse.

• Foreshadowing

Most stories use clues to prepare the reader for the ending. "The Genuine Spring-Operated, Brass-Handled, Black Umbrella" contains several clues about the ending. Amelia and Elise like to stop at the jewelry store. This clue shows you that there is a jewelry store nearby, filled with valuable gems and money. Amelia's borrowed umbrella gets in the way of other people on the bus and in school. These clues also prepare you for the end, when Amelia uses her umbrella to trip a jewel thief.

"Danger at Milner School" also has clues in it. At the beginning of the story you read about the dangerous man chained to the tree. You know that he sometimes escapes, so you are not too surprised when he shows up at the school.

Authors call these clues "foreshadowing." When a writer uses foreshadowing, he is carefully dropping hints to prepare the reader for what is going to happen later in the story. "Champion Stock," "Danger at Milner School," and "The Genuine Spring-Operated, Brass-Handled, Black Umbrella" are three good examples of stories in which authors use foreshadowing.

Seven at One Blow

adapted by Karen Wilt
illustrated by Bruce Day

Cast

Storyteller	Giant	Peasant man
Tailor	Giant's brother	Peasant woman
Jelly Lady	King	Palace guard
Seven flies	Princess	

Storyteller: Once upon a time, long, long ago, there lived a poor but cheerful tailor. Day after day he sewed and mended, until one day . . .

Tailor: *(singing a happy tune as he works)* Cut and pin, cut and pin, a pretty day to cut and pin.

Jelly Lady: Jams! Preserves and jelly, delicious in your belly!

Tailor: What's that you're shouting?

Jelly Lady: Jelly for sale. Strawberry, raspberry, mulberry, cherry, boysenberry, blackberry, blueberry, and orange marmalade. What would you have on a fine spring morning, sir?

Tailor: Let me look. Such a decision to make. Hmmm. A bit of jelly on bread would be just the thing to set my scissors snipping. I'll take an ounce of each and a half pound of orange marmalade.

Jelly Lady: Thank you, sir. That's two pence and a half penny, if you please.

Tailor: Oh, I'm sure it will please me very much. I have a loaf of bread the baker traded for a new waistcoat. Mmmm. My stomach growled all night, but a few bites of bread with jelly will cure it, I'm sure.

Storyteller: The tailor took a huge mouthful and set the rest by his elbow as he picked up his needle. The sweet smell drifted around the room and slipped out the window, knocking the nose of every fly in the yard.

Flies: Buzz, buzz, buzz, bread. Buzz, buzz, buzz, jelly.

Tailor: Hey! Shoo! Get away from my jelly and leave my bread alone. I'll let you have it, I will. *(He swats at the flies.)* Aha! Seven at one blow. That's

out his cheese and squeezed out the whey. The giant was near-sighted and couldn't tell that the tailor had not squeezed a rock at all.

Giant: Humph! What are a few drops of water squeezed from a rock? Let's see you throw it as high as I can throw. *(He throws it. They watch the rock go far up and then come down.)*

Tailor: You cannot throw very high. Why, your rock even returned. I can throw so far that it will not return. Watch this rock I have here in my shirt pocket. *(in a whisper)* Fly home, whistling sparrow.

Storyteller: The tailor tossed the sparrow into the air, and it sped away on wings of the wind.

Giant: Humph. You shall tarry at my castle for the night. Perhaps my brother will know what should be done to a fellow like you.

Tailor: That is a fine invitation. I thank you with many thanks.

Giant: You shall sleep on my own bed until my brother returns.

Storyteller: When they arrived at the castle, the tailor lay down, but the huge bed seemed to swallow him. Before long he crept into a corner to sleep. At midnight the two giants tiptoed into the room, their steps shaking the tailor awake as if an earthquake had struck. Then they took a great staff and beat the bed, thinking to rid themselves of the tailor. Early the next morning they tramped off, laughing stupidly.

Tailor: Well, time for me to be off too. Seven at one blow, indeed! Hmmm. Looks like a goodly city just the other side of this mountain. I shall see what there is to see when I am able to see from there.

Storyteller: So the tailor set off, following his nose, which always went before him.

Peasant man: Look! "Seven at one blow!" A great hero is come to our city.

Peasant woman: Let us inform the king.

Peasant man: Yes, the king should meet this champion who kills seven at one blow!

Tailor: Show me to his royal palace.

Peasant man: Just ahead where the banners fly and the trumpets blow.

Palace Guard: "Seven at one blow"? Are you come to enter the service of the king? Whether or not, follow me. The king must meet such a brave fellow.

King: And who are you, my fine fellow? An honorable and worthy merchant? A respectable and loyal nobleman?

Tailor: It is written here on my belt for all to read.

King: *(putting his spectacles on his nose)* "Seven at one blow"? Quite extraordinary and highly unbelievable. Are you sure you do not exaggerate the matter?

Tailor: No, sire. 'Tis truth.

King: Droves of delirious dragons! You shall have to prove it completely and entirely. And if you do, I shall reward you with half of my vast kingdom and the hand of my beautiful daughter. If

you fail, I'm certain no one shall hear of you or your fearful fate.

Tailor: What test do you set for me?

King: Two terrible and tyrannical giants are plaguing and paralyzing my kingdom. You must kill them. Do you think you can accomplish that in time for a banquet tonight?

Tailor: I imagine I should be able to.

King: Splendid. Now be off. Farewell.

Storyteller: Of course, the tailor knew exactly the giants to which the king referred. Before the king could say "Notorious knights of Niantic," the tailor had discovered the giants asleep under a tree.

Tailor: *(picking up two rocks)* This will instigate a family quarrel.

Storyteller: From the top of the tree that shaded the giants, the little tailor took careful aim and dropped a rock on the mangy head of the nearest giant.

Giant: Hey, why did you clobber me?

Giant's brother: I didn't touch you. You must be dreaming.

Tailor: *(dropping a second stone)* There . . . that one should get a fight started.

Giant: Humph! I close my eyes for two seconds, and you do it again.

Giant's brother: Did not!

Giant: Did too!

Giant's brother: Did not!

Giant: Take that!

Giant's brother: Hey, get your foot out of my mouth! You take that!

Giant: Ow! My eye!

Giant's brother: Get off me!

Giant: Let go of my leg. Take that!

Giant's brother: Ouch. You take this!

Giant: Owww! Take that!

Storyteller: The giants brawled and wrestled until their blows split open the mountain, and it swallowed them. The tailor merrily returned to the city and wed the king's daughter and, of course, they lived happily ever after.

Who's a Hero?

Alicia Peterson

illustrated by Paula Cheadle, Johanna Berg, Jim Hargis, and John Bjerk

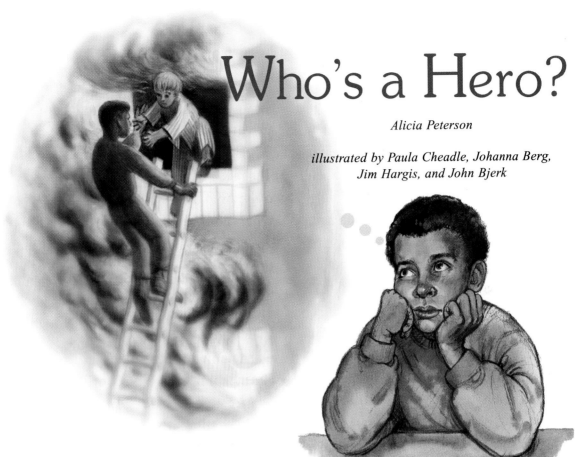

Twin Terrors

Heroes! They were surely the most wonderful people in the world, and their lives were one long, exciting adventure! Jamal thought about heroes a lot. In his imagination he rescued people from burning buildings, snatched a little old lady from the path of a speeding car, or helped the police track a robbery suspect to his hide-out.

Sometimes his teacher broke into Jamal Williams's imaginary adventures. She startled him by asking a question about the lesson. That would remind him to pay attention to what she was saying. Or he might give some answer that didn't fit a question, and his classmates would laugh at him.

Sometimes his dad or mother interrupted his dreams of heroism. One afternoon Jamal had been high in his favorite tree, and his imagination had transformed the tree to a towering peak in Switzerland. He, "Jamal the

Brave," had been struggling steadily upward through a heavy blizzard and a threatening avalanche to rescue a ski party stranded on an outcropping of rock. One of them had a broken leg, and the other . . . At precisely that moment, his mother called, "Jamal . . . Jamal, where are you?"

"I'm up here in the Alps, Mom. I mean the oak tree."

"Climb down and come in for a few minutes, please, Son. I need to talk with you," said his mother.

So Jamal climbed down, leaving his snow-rescue exploits up among the quiet green leaves and sturdy branches of the tree.

Once in the kitchen, the unfinished "Swiss rescue" was made somewhat better by the tall glass of milk and the fresh cookies his mother set on the table for him.

"Jamal, your Aunt Harriet needs help. Your cousin Tasha has to be taken to the clinic for therapy each afternoon, and she can't take Damion and Darnell along on the clinic visits."

Damion and Darnell! They were Jamal's twin cousins—four years old. Jamal thought of them, privately, as twin terrors.

"Aunt Harriet says that Tasha's therapy treatments have only one more month to go. So what your dad and I would like you to do, Jamal, is take care of the twins each afternoon throughout the remaining month of Tasha's therapy."

"Take care of Damion and Darnell? You mean baby-sit!" exclaimed Jamal.

"Yes, Son, I suppose you could call it that, although the boys really aren't babies anymore," his mother replied.

Baby-sitting! What an occupation for a future hero, Jamal thought. But he did want to help his Aunt Harriet and Uncle James. Jamal promised himself that a month surely wouldn't seem too long.

But it was long. From the first day, Jamal's baby-sitting assignment seemed endless. "So much for being a hero," he thought. "I need someone to rescue me!" There were no snow avalanches.

But there were avalanches of books from the bookshelves as the twins climbed up, trying to find exactly the right book for Jamal to read to them. No animals attacked the mission compound—not wild animals at least. But a frantic scramble took place the day Damion and Darnell let two neighborhood dogs in to play. They chased Aunt Harriet's big Persian cat up the drapes. Then they knocked the birdcage over, and Tweet flew out to add to the confusion!

Jamal didn't even have time to daydream! He had to watch the twins every minute. If he didn't, they would be swinging on the refrigerator door or sliding gleefully across the kitchen floor on "ice" made of peanut butter and jelly.

Jamal learned to keep the boys outside as much as possible. In fact, he earnestly prayed every night that the next afternoon would be sunny. But even outside, Jamal had to put up with sneak water attacks with the garden hose and long hide-and-seek games.

One Friday afternoon, the twins and their caretaker were out in the back yard. Darnell and Damion asked for a game of hide-and-seek. Jamal agreed. He was sure that he knew all the places the little boys could possibly hide. He would just pretend to hunt for them in several wrong places before "discovering" their real hiding places.

Jamal went into the kitchen and counted slowly to one hundred to start the game. Then opening the door into the back yard, he called, "Here I come, ready or not!"

Jamal first looked in all the usual places. He made loud comments of surprise and disappointment after each try. He figured that the boys could hear him and were giggling. After several min-utes of fruitless searching, Jamal came up to the big empty oil drum kept near the garden.

"Now where could those boys be hiding?" he said dramatically. He peered into the big drum. And there, sure enough, was Darnell, huddled down as close to the bottom of the barrel as he could get. Jamal lifted his little cousin from the hiding place.

"Aw, why'd you have to find me first, Jamal?" Darnell complained. "It should be Damion's turn to be found first!"

"Well," Jamal answered, "if you'll help me look for Damion, we'll all go inside for a snack. How's that?"

"No sirree! I'm not gonna help you find Damion! That's no fun," he said. "You have to find him all by yourself!" Darnell sat down on the top step of the kitchen porch and propped his chin in his hands to watch.

Finally, Jamal had looked in every hiding place he could re-member. Where, then, could one small, chubby four-year-old still be hiding?

Hometown Hero

Jamal went back over to Darnell. "Darnell, it's time to stop playing hide-and-seek now. We have to eat our snack so I can get the kitchen cleaned up for your mama."

Darnell shook his head.

"You don't have to tell me. I'll hide my eyes—back in the kitchen where I started. You can go get Damion from wherever he is, bring him in, and we'll give him the 'championship hider' award for the day. Okay?"

"Mmmmm—I guess that will be okay. Go in the kitchen and hide your eyes."

In the kitchen again, Jamal began setting things out for the boys' snack. But Darnell burst into the kitchen, his eyes huge with fright. "Jamal," he panted. "Damion won't come out—I think he's hurt."

Jamal and Darnell ran out into the back yard and around the back of the house. Jamal stopped stock-still. There, just past the corner of the house, close to the fence, was a dark, gaping hole. The question raced through his mind: why hadn't he ever seen that hole before? The answer came just as quickly: because it hadn't been there before! The cellar door was supposed to be there.

Jamal tried to calm his pounding heart as he ran toward the open space. Darnell was already on his hands and knees beside the opening, looking down into the dimness. Then he called, "Come out now! Jamal says you win."

Jamal looked into the cellar's gloom too. And his heart pounded. Damion lay in a crumpled heap at the bottom of the rickety set of steps. It was easy to see what had happened. Damion had thought he had found a perfect hiding place. But the wooden steps, badly rotted from the dampness, had been unable to bear his weight. The second step down was swinging by a single nail in the dimness.

"Darnell," Jamal said, "run into the kitchen. Look in the broom closet. The flashlight is there. Bring it to me quickly." Darnell raced back to the kitchen.

Slowly and cautiously, Jamal edged into the cellar. His foot felt for the third step. Then, keeping his weight far to the side of each step and gripping the rails, he moved down from step to step. At last he was at the bottom. He knelt beside Damion's strangely twisted form.

Darnell returned with the flashlight. "Good boy!" Jamal called up to him. "Now stay up there at the door and shine the flashlight straight down on your brother."

Darnell pointed the flashlight beam into the cellar.

"Great. Hold it just like that," Jamal said.

He turned his attention to Damion. "Damion. Damion?" he said softly. There was only a groan of pain in response. The way Damion's arm was twisted, Jamal was fairly sure it was broken.

Darnell's crying broke into Jamal's thoughts. Keeping his voice calm, Jamal said, "Damion has bumped his head, Darnell."

"Well, carry him up, Jamal!" the little boy sobbed.

"Darnell, listen to me. Damion has been hurt by his fall. If I move him even a little bit, I might hurt him more."

"I don't want Damion to be hurt!" the other twin wailed.

"Neither do I, Darnell. That's why you and I have to work hard together to help him. Set the flashlight down. Then go into the house and find me a blanket," Jamal said. "We have to keep him warm."

Darnell just stood there for a minute, ready to cry again.

"Brrrrr!" Jamal said. He hugged himself to try to help explain. "Damion needs a blanket until we can move him. It's cold down here."

Darnell set down the flashlight and headed away toward the house. Running his hands over Damion's skin, Jamal discovered it was cold and clammy. "Oh, hurry, Darnell!" he thought. And Darnell did hurry. Jamal heard his running steps coming back. "This will keep Damion warm." Darnell said. He shoved the heavy bedspread from his parents' king-sized bed over the edge into the cellar.

"Great job!" Jamal said. "That's fine, Darnell," Jamal said. "Now shine the light on us again. Good."

Jamal covered his little cousin with the spread and his thoughts raced. "Now what should I do? It's still ages till Aunt Harriet will get home. Mom! That's it— I'll call Mom!" Carefully climbing out of the cellar, Jamal explained the plan to Darnell. "I have to get some grownups to help. Sit right here and keep the flashlight shining down on Damion."

That night, as Jamal wearily slid into his chair at dinner, his father and mother smiled proudly at him. "You did a great job today, Jamal," said Mr. Williams. "The emergency crew couldn't say enough good things about the way you stayed calm, made the right decision, and got help."

"You've been a real hero today, Jamal!" exclaimed his mother.

"Aw, Mom—heroes are in the Swiss Alps. Or rescuing someone from drowning in the Atlantic Ocean! All I was doing was baby-sitting!"

"Heroes are normal people who forget about themselves long enough to help others," his dad replied. "Sometimes they're in faraway countries, but other times they're right in your own town."

Jamal was silent for a moment. "I never thought about it like that."

Mr. Williams laid his hand on Jamal's shoulder. "Let's eat dinner, hero, or you might have to rescue a starving father right in your own kitchen!"

Glossary

This glossary has information about selected words found in this reader. You can find meanings of words as they are used in the stories. Certain unusual words such as foreign names are included so that you can pronounce them correctly when you read.

The pronunciation symbols below show how to pronounce each vowel and several of the less-familiar consonants.

ă	pat	ĕ	pet	îr	fierce
ā	pay	ē	be	ŏ	pot
âr	care	ĭ	pit	ō	go
ä	father	ī	pie	ô	paw, for, ball

oi	oil	ŭ	cut	zh	vision
ŏŏ	book	ûr	fur	ə	ago, item,
ōō	boot	*th*	the		pencil, atom,
yōō	abuse	th	thin		circus
ou	out	hw	which	ər	butter

A

a·bound | ə **bound′** | —*verb* To be plentiful or to have plenty of.

ac·cel·er·a·tor | ăk **sĕl′** ə rā′ tər | —*noun* Anything that increases speed. In a car the accelerator is a pedal the driver steps on to make the car go faster.

ac·count | ə **kount′** | —*noun* A written or spoken description; a report.

ad·join | ə **join′** | —*verb* To be next to; be side by side.

ad·mis·sion | ăd **mĭsh′** ən | —*noun* A price charged or paid to enter a place.

ad·mon·ish | ăd **mŏn′** ĭsh | —*verb* To kindly correct or instruct against a certain action.

a·do·be | ə **dō′** bē | —*noun* A house built with bricks made of clay and straw that dry and harden in the sun.

adobe

ad·vance | ăd **văns′** | —*verb* To move forward, onward, or upward.

a·feared or **a·feard** | ə **fîrd′** | —*adjective* Afraid; frightened; scared.

al·bi·no | ăl **bī′** nō | —*noun* An animal or person that is white because it or he has no skin pigmentation.

al·le·giance | ə **lē′** jəns | —*noun* Loyal and faithful devotion to someone or something.

am·bu·lance | ăm′ byə ləns | —*noun* A large vehicle that is used to rush people who are sick or hurt to a hospital. An ambulance has special medical equipment and trained people to help on the way to the hospital.

am·mu·ni·tion | ăm′ yə **nĭsh′** ən | —*noun* Bullets, explosives, bombs, grenades, or anything else that can be fired from a gun or weapon or can explode and cause damage.

am·phib·i·ous | ăm **fĭb′** ē əs | —*adjective* Able to travel on land or in water.

an·noy | ə **noi′** | —*verb* To bother; irritate; pester.

an·ten·na | ăn **tĕn′** ə | —*noun* One of a pair of long, thin feelers on the head of some animals.

an·tic | ăn′ tĭk | —*noun* A game, prank, or stunt.

anx·ious·ly | **ăngk′** shəs lē | or | **ăng′** shəs lē | —*adverb* With worry.

a·pol·o·gize | ə **pŏl′** ə jīz | —*verb* To say one is sorry; make an apology.

ap·prov·al | ə **prōō′** vəl | —*noun* A favorable opinion; praise.

aq·ua·ma·rine | ăk wə mə **rēn′** | or | ä kwə mə **rēn′** | —*noun* A blue-green gemstone.

ă pat	ĕ pet
ā pay	ē be
âr care	ĭ pit
ä father	ī pie
îr fierce	oi oil
ŏ pot	ōō book
ō go	ōō boot
ô paw,	yōō abuse
for	ou out
ŭ cut	ə ago,
ûr fur	item,
th the	pencil,
th thin	atom,
hw which	circus
zh vision	ər butter

530

a·quar·i·um | ə **kwâr´** ē əm |
—*noun* A water-filled tank in
which sea life is kept and observed.

arc·tic | **ärk´** tĭk | or | **är´** tĭk |
—*noun* The north polar region.

as·cend | ə **sĕnd´** | —*verb* To go or
move upward; rise.

as·cen·sion | ə **sĕn´** shən | —*noun*
A going up.

as·pen | **ăs´** pən | —*noun* A poplar
tree with leaves that flutter in
even the slightest breeze.

a·ston·ished | ə **stŏn´** ĭshd | —*ad-
jective* Extremely surprised.

a·stound | ə **stound´** | —*verb* To
fill or strike with surprise or sudden wonder; astonish.

as·tro·naut | **ăs´** trə nôt | —*noun*
A person who is trained to fly in a
spacecraft.

at·tain·able | ə **tān´** ə bəl | —*adjec-
tive* Capable of being gained or
accomplished.

at·tempt | ə **tĕmpt´** | —*noun* An
effort or try.

at·ten·tion | ə **tĕn´** shən | —*noun*
Mental concentration; thinking,
watching, or listening carefully to
or about someone or something.

au·di·tion | ô **dĭsh´** ən | —*verb* To
perform on a trial basis; to show
one's skill in acting or singing.

au·thor | **ô´** thər | —*noun* A per-
son who writes a book, story, article, play, or other work.

av·a·lanche | **ăv´** ə lănch | or | **ăv´** ə
lănch | —*noun* A large mass of
material that falls or slides down
the side of a mountain. An avalanche is usually made up of
snow, ice, earth, or rocks.

awe | ô | —*noun* A feeling of won-
der, fear, or respect about something that is mighty or majestic.

awed | ôd | —*adjective* Full of
wonder.

az·ure | **ăzh´** ər | —*adjective* A
light to medium blue, like that of
the sky on a clear day.

aspen

B

balk | bôk | —*verb* To stop short
and refuse to go on.

ban·is·ter | **băn´** ĭ stər | —*noun* A
handrail.

bar·ren | **băr´** ən | —*adjective* Not
producing anything.

bar·ter | **bär´** tər | —*verb* To trade
one thing for another without
using money.

base | bās | —*noun* The lowest
part; the bottom.

bash·ful | **băsh´** fəl | —*adjective*
Timid and embarrassed with
other people; shy.

astronaut

birthstone

ă	pat	ĕ	pet
ā	pay	ē	be
âr	care	ĭ	pit
ä	father	ī	pie
îr	fierce	oi	oil
ŏ	pot	o͞o	book
ō	go	o͞o	boot
ô	paw,	yo͞o	abuse
	for	ou	out
ŭ	cut	ə	ago,
ûr	fur		item,
th	the		pencil,
th	thin		atom,
hw	which		circus
zh	vision	ər	butter

bronc

bay | bā | —*noun* A reddish brown horse.

ba·zaar | bə zär´ | —*noun* A market made up of a street lined with shops and stalls.

bill | bĭl | —*noun* The hard, projecting mouth parts on the head of a bird.

birch | bûrch | —*noun* A tree with smooth bark that peels off easily. There are several kinds of birch trees.

birth·stone | bûrth´ stōn | —*noun* A jewel associated with a certain month, worn by people born in that month.

bit | bĭt | —*noun* A shaped piece of metal that is part of a horse's bridle. The bit goes into the horse's mouth and is used to help control the animal.

bluff | blŭf | —*noun* A steep cliff, hill, or riverbank.

bog | bôg | or | bŏg | —*noun* A soft, wet area of land; marsh; swamp.

bois·ter·ous | boi´ stər əs | or | boi´ strəs | —*adjective* Overactive and noisy.

bored | bôrd | or | bōrd | —*adjective* Made weary by lack of interest.

bot·tle·neck | bŏt´ l nĕk | —*noun* A narrow or blocked section of a river or stream.

bound | bound | —*verb* To run by leaping.

bow out | bou out | —*verb* To gracefully withdraw, usually from a contest or game.

brack·ish | brăk´ ĭsh | —*adjective* Stagnant, sour, or salty.

brand | brănd | —*noun* A piece of burning wood.

bran·dish | brăn´ dĭsh | —*verb* To wave or swing about either as a weapon or as a symbol of triumph.

brawn·y | brô´ nē | —*adjective* Heavily muscled; strong.

bread·board | brĕd´ bôrd | or | brĕd´ bōrd | —*noun* A board on which breads and pastries are prepared.

bronc | brŏngk | —*noun* A wild or partly tamed horse of western North America.

broth | brôth | or | brŏth | —*noun* The water in which meat, fish, or vegetables have been boiled or simmered.

bru·in | bro͞o´ ĭn | —*noun* A bear.

bush·el bas·ket | bo͞osh´ əl băs´ kĭt | —*noun* A basket capable of holding a bushel of grain.

bus·tle[1] | bŭs´ əl | —*noun* A frame used to fill out the back of a skirt or dress.

bus·tle[2] | bŭs´ əl | —*verb* To hurry and move around in a busy and excited way.

ca·ble | kā´ bəl | —*noun* A thick, strong rope made of twisted wire or fiber.

cai·man | kā´ mən | —*noun* An animal that looks like an alligator but is a little smaller.

calm | käm | —*verb* To make or become peacefully quiet.

cam·o·mile or **cham·o·mile** | kăm´ ə mīl | —*noun* An aromatic plant used to make a soothing tea.

can·o·py | kăn´ ə pē | —*noun* A covering like a tent held up over a bed, entrance, or important person.

can·vass | kăn´ vəs | —*verb* To walk door to door for sales purposes or advertising.

car·da·mom | kär´ də məm | or **car·da·mon** | kär´ də mən | —*noun* An edible seed that comes from an Asian plant.

cast | kăst | or | käst | —*verb* To throw or fling.

cau·tious | kô´ shəs | —*adjective* Showing or having caution; careful.

cau·tious·ly | kô´ shəs lē | —*adverb* Showing caution in order to avoid danger or trouble.

cav·al·cade | kăv əl kād´ | or | kăv´ əl kād | —*noun* A loud, colorful parade or procession using horses.

chafe | chāf | —*verb* To feel annoyed or irritated.

chan·nel | chăn´ əl | —*noun* A body of water that connects two larger bodies.

char·ac·ter | kăr´ ĭk tər | —*noun* A person in a book, story, or play.

char·ac·ter·is·tic | kăr ĭk tər ĭs´ tĭk | —*noun* A special feature of a person or thing.

charm | chärm | —*verb* To please or delight.

check[1] | chĕk | —*noun* In chess, the result of a move that places the opponent's king in danger.

check[2] | chĕk | —*interjection* An idiom indicating "yes" or "all set."

chron·i·cle | krŏn´ ĭ kəl | —*noun* A history of events.

cinch | sĭnch | —*noun* A strap for a saddle, usually fastened along a horse's or other animal's belly.

civ·il | sĭv´ əl | —*adjective* Concerning the events happening within a country or community.

clerk | klûrk | —*noun* A person who works in an office and keeps records and other papers in correct order.

cli·ché | klē shā´ | —*noun* A well-known saying or expression.

cable

caiman

canopy

cli·max | **klī´** măks | —*noun* The most exciting part or the turning point in a story.

coax | kōks | —*verb* To try in a gentle or pleasant way to get a person or an animal to do something.

cobblestones

cob·ble·stone | **kŏb´** əl stōn | —*noun* A round stone once used to pave streets.

cock·pit | **kŏk´** pĭt | —*noun* The part of an airplane where the pilot and copilot sit.

col·lide | kə **līd´** | —*verb* To strike or bump together violently; crash.

com·bi·na·tion | kŏm´ bə **nā´** shən | —*noun* The joining of two or more elements.

com·mence | kə **mĕns´** | —*verb* To begin; start.

cockpit

com·men·tar·y | **kŏm´** ən tĕr ē | —*noun* A book containing explanations and illustrations of an important book, play, or poem.

com·mit | kə **mĭt´** | —*verb* To give over to another person or place; give into another's care; entrust to.

com·pass[1] | **kŭm´** pəs | or | **kŏm´** pəs | —*noun* An instrument used to show directions.

com·pass[2] | **kŭm´** pəs | or | **kŏm´** pəs | —*verb* To encircle or surround.

compass

com·pound | **kŏm´** pound | —*noun* A unit of buildings often set apart by a fence, wall, or ditch.

con·ceal | kən **sēl´** | —*verb* To keep from being seen, noticed, or known; hide.

con·duct | kən **dŭkt´** | —*verb* To act as a path for electricity, heat, or other forms of energy.

con·fi·dence | **kŏn´** fĭ dəns | —*noun* Trust or faith in others.

con·fi·dent | **kŏn´** fĭ dənt | —*adjective* Trusting; being certain; assured; especially in oneself.

con·firm | kən **fûrm´** | —*verb* To give or get definite evidence.

con·se·quence | **kŏn´** sĭ kwĕns´ | —*noun* Something that happens as a result of another action or condition.

con·sul | **kŏn´** səl | —*noun* A government representative who lives in a foreign country to ensure fair business and legal practices there for the people of his own citizenship.

con·su·late | **kŏn´** sə lĭt | —*noun* The office or building of a consul.

con·tempt | kən **tĕmpt´** | —*noun* A feeling that someone or something is of little value, worthless, or not wanted; scorn; disdain.

con·tent | kon **tĕnt´** | —*adjective* Pleased with what one has or is; satisfied.

con•ti•nent | **kŏn′** tə nənt | —*noun* One of the main land masses of the earth. The seven continents are Africa, Antarctica, Asia, Australia, Europe, North America, and South America.

con•tri•bute | kən **trĭb′** yo͞ot | —*verb* To give, supply, or donate.

cor•ral | kə **răl′** | —*noun* A pen or place for keeping cattle or horses.

cot | kŏt | —*noun* A narrow bed, usually made of canvas stretched over a folding frame.

coun•sel•or | **koun′** sə lər | or | **koun′** slər | —*noun* A person who advises or guides; advisor.

cou•pon | **ko͞o′** pŏn | or | **kyo͞o′** pŏn | —*noun* A small certificate that can be exchanged for money, food, or other goods.

court•ship | **kôrt′** shĭp | or | **kōrt′** shĭp | —*noun* The period of time when a man tries to persuade a woman to marry him.

crack shot | krăk shot | —*noun* A person who is an excellent marksman with a gun.

crest | krĕst | —*noun* The top of something, such as a mountain or wave.

cross-ref•er•ence | **krôs′ rĕf′** ər əns | —*noun* A reference from one part of a book to related information in another part.

cup | kŭp | —*noun* Any land formation in the shape of a cup.

cu•ri•ous | **kyo͝or′** ē əs | —*adjective* 1. Eager to learn or know. 2. Unusual or remarkable.

cur•rent | **kûr′** ənt | or | **kŭr′** ənt | —*noun* Moving liquid or gas.

cot

cup

D

dash•ing | **dăsh′** ĭng | —*adjective* Brave, bold, and daring.

daze | dāz | —*noun* A state of not realizing what is going on around oneself, a confused condition.

de•bris | də **brē′** | or | **dā′** brē | —*noun* The scattered pieces or remains of something that has been broken, destroyed, or thrown away; rubble.

de•fense | dĭ **fĕns′** | —*noun* The act of defending or protecting.

de•fi•ant | dĭ **fī′** ənt | —*adjective* The attitude of refusing to obey authority.

del•e•ga•tion | **dĕl′** ĭ **gā′** shən | —*noun* A person or group of people who speak in behalf of an organization or government.

de•lir•i•ous | dĭ **lîr′** ē əs | —*adjective* Out of one's senses; raving.

de•pend•a•ble | dĭ **pĕn′** də bəl | —*adjective* Able to be depended upon; reliable.

ă	pat	ĕ	pet
ā	pay	ē	be
âr	care	ĭ	pit
ä	father	ī	pie
îr	fierce	oi	oil
ŏ	pot	o͝o	book
ō	go	o͞o	boot
ô	paw,	yo͞o	abuse
	for	ou	out
ŭ	cut	ə	ago,
ûr	fur		item,
th	the		pencil,
th	thin		atom,
hw	which		circus
zh	vision	ər	butter

disk drive

de·scrip·tion | dĭ **skrĭp´** shən | —*noun* An account in words describing something.

de·sign | dĭ **zīn´** | —*noun* 1. A plan or a specific purpose. 2. An arrangement of lines, figures, or objects into a pattern.

de·ter·mine | dĭ **tûr´** mĭn | —*verb* To decide or settle.

de·vel·oped | dĭ **vĕl´** əpt | —*adjective* Grown; every detail complete.

die·sel | **dē´** zəl | —*noun* A type of fuel high in oil. The oil is burned by hot air in an engine instead of by an electric spark.

dis·ap·point·ed | dĭs ə **poin´** tĭd | —*adjective* Feeling a failure in hopes or wishes.

doorman

dis·card | dĭs **kärd´** | —*verb* To throw away.

dis·con·so·late | dĭs **kŏn´** sə lĭt | —*adjective* Sorrowful; unable to be consoled.

disk drive | dĭsk drīv | —*noun* The device within a computer that operates the diskette in order to store or transmit information.

dis·mal | **dĭz´** məl | —*adjective* Causing gloom or depression; dreary.

dis·may | dĭs **mā´** | —*noun* A sudden loss of courage or confidence in the face of danger or trouble.

drum

dis·suade | dĭ **swād´** | —*verb* To persuade a person against his chosen course of action; convince otherwise.

dis·tress | dĭ **strĕs´** | —*noun* Serious danger or trouble.

di·vine | dĭ **vīn´** | —*adjective* Of or from God.

door·man | **dôr´** măn | —*noun* A man hired by a hotel, apartment, or business to open the door for patrons and provide other small services.

dor·mi·to·ry | **dôr´** mĭ tôr ē | or | **dôr´** mĭ tōr ē | —*noun* A building containing many bedrooms.

dou·blet | **dŭb´** lĭt | —*noun* A jacket, sometimes sleeveless, fitted to the body. Doublets were worn during Shakespeare's time.

doubt·ful | **dout´** fəl | —*adjective* Not sure or certain.

dra·mat·i·cal·ly | drə **măt´** ĭk lē | —*adverb* In a bold, impressive way; showing a strong flair and enthusiasm.

drip tray | drĭp trā | —*noun* The tray for catching condensation at the bottom of an old-fashioned freezer or refrigerator.

drought | drout | —*noun* A long period with little or no rain.

drove | drōv | —*noun* A crowd.

drum | drŭm | —*noun* A container shaped like a barrel.

dust dev·il | dŭst **dĕv´** əl | —*noun* A small whirlwind.

dwin·dle | **dwĭn´** dəl | —*verb* To become smaller or less; diminish.

ec·sta·sy | ĕk´ stə sē | —*noun* A condition of delight, joy, or happiness.

e·di·tion | ĭ dĭsh´ ən | —*noun* One out of a number of copies of a book, all printed at the same time.

Eif·fel Tow·er | ī´ fəl tou´ ər | —*noun* A tourist attraction in Paris, France. The Eiffel Tower is almost 1,000 feet high.

el·e·ment | ĕl´ ə mənt | —*noun* A basic part of something.

em·bank·ment | ĕm băngk´ mənt | —*noun* A mound of earth or stone built up to hold back water or hold up a road.

em·bar·rass | ĕm băr´ əs | —*verb* To cause to feel uncomfortable and nervous.

em·broi·der | ĕm broi´ dər | —*verb* To decorate cloth by sewing on designs.

en·chi·la·da | ĕn chə lä´ də | —*noun* A tortilla stuffed with meat and cheese and served in a hot sauce.

en·coun·ter | ĕn koun´ tər | —*noun* A meeting or confrontation, usually for a purpose.

en·dure | ĕn door´ | or | ĕn dyoor´ | —*verb* To put up with; stand; bear.

en·gi·neer | ĕn jə nîr´ | —*noun* A person who is trained to build such things as bridges, canals, and oil wells.

en·list | ĕn lĭst´ | —*verb* To join or cause to join the armed forces.

er·rand | ĕr´ ənd | —*noun* A short trip taken to perform a task.

et cet·er·a | ĕt sĕt´ ər ə | or | ĕt sĕt´ rə | And other things of the same kind; and so forth. A Latin phrase meaning "and the rest." Used chiefly in abbreviated form: *etc.*

ex·ag·ger·ate | ĭg zăj´ ə rāt´ | —*verb* To describe something as larger or more interesting than it really is.

ex·pense | ĭk spĕns´ | —*noun* Something that requires the spending of money.

ex·per·i·ment | ĭk spĕr´ ə mənt | —*noun* Something done to show a fact, test a theory, or find out what might happen.

ex·ploit | ĕk´ sploit´ | —*noun* A heroic or brave deed.

Eiffel Tower

embroider

ă	pat	ĕ	pet	îr	fierce	oi	oil	ŭ	cut	ə	ago,
ā	pay	ē	be	ŏ	pot	o͝o	book	ûr	fur		item,
âr	care	ĭ	pit	ō	go	o͞o	boot	*th*	the		pencil,
ä	father	ī	pie	ô	paw,	yo͞o	abuse	th	thin		atom,
					for	ou	out	hw	which		circus
								zh	vision	ər	butter

flank

ă	pat	ĕ	pet
ā	pay	ē	be
âr	care	ĭ	pit
ä	father	ī	pie
îr	fierce	oi	oil
ŏ	pot	o͞o	book
ō	go	o͞o	boot
ô	paw,	yo͞o	abuse
	for	ou	out
ŭ	cut	ə	ago,
ûr	fur		item,
th	the		pencil,
th	thin		atom,
hw	which		circus
zh	vision	ər	butter

foal

fab·ric | **făb´** rĭk | —*noun* A piece of cloth.

fal·ter | **fôl´** tər | —*verb* To move unsteadily; stumble.

fa·nat·ic | fə **năt´** ĭk | —*noun* A person who believes in or loves something so much that he does foolish things for it.

fare | fâr | —*noun* The price of a ride on a bus, train, or other vehicle.

fas·ci·nate | **făs´** ə nāt´ | —*verb* To attract and interest very strongly.

fas·ci·nat·ed | **făs´** ə nāt´ əd | —*adjective* Attracted and interested very strongly.

fate·ful | **fāt´** fəl | —*adjective* Life-changing; unavoidable.

feat | fēt | —*noun* An act or deed, especially a skillful one.

fend | fĕnd | —*verb* To provide for oneself; survive.

fidg·et | **fĭj´** ĭt | —*verb* To move some part of the body restlessly.

fig·ure | **fĭg´** yər | —*verb* To work out by using numbers.

file | fīl | —*noun* A tool with a rough surface, used for smoothing, scraping, and cutting.

fit[1] | fĭt | —*noun* A sudden onset of a strong emotional or physical reaction.

fit[2] | fĭt | —*adjective* To be in the proper condition for a task; physically fit.

flank | flăngk | —*noun* The part between the hip and the ribs on either side of the body of an animal or person; the side.

flan·nel | **flăn´** əl | —*noun* A soft cloth made of cotton or wool.

floun·der | **floun´** dər | —*verb* To move in a clumsy way or with difficulty; struggle.

flus·tered | **flŭs´** tərd | —*adjective* Nervous, excited, confused.

foal | fōl | —*noun* A young horse, zebra, or donkey.

fore·shad·ow | fôr **shăd´** ō | or | fōr **shăd´** ō | —*verb* To hint at or suggest in advance.

for·lorn | fôr **lôrn´** | —*adjective* Sad; without hope.

for·sake | fôr **sāk´** | —*verb* To give up; leave; abandon.

for·tune | **fôr´** chən | —*noun* A person's life's work and social standing; success; wealth.

frame | frām | —*noun* A form that holds something; a supporting structure.

fraz·zle | **frăz´** əl | —*verb* To fluster.

fret | frĕt | —*verb* To worry; usually to worry out loud or to show by restlessness that one is worried.

fruit·less | **frŏŏt´** lĭs | —*adjective* Without success or results.

fu·gi·tive | **fyŏŏ´** jĭ tĭv | —*noun* A person running away, especially from the law.

gadg·et | **găj´** ĭt | —*noun* A small, unusual tool or mechanical device.

gal·le·on | **găl´** ē ən | or | **găl´** yən | —*noun* A large sailing ship with three masts that was used mainly during the sixteenth century.

gap·ing | **gā´** pĭng | —*adjective* Wide open, exposing depth.

gar·ret | **găr´** ĭt | —*noun* An attic or loft at the top of a house.

gen·darme | **zhän´** därm´ | —*noun* A French policeman.

ge·ra·ni·um | jĭ **rā´** nē əm | —*noun* A plant with rounded clusters of red, pink, or white flowers. Geraniums are often grown in flowerpots.

girth | gûrth | —*noun* A strap that encircles a horse's belly.

glare | glâr | —*verb* To stare angrily.

glaze | glāz | —*noun* A thin, shiny coating.

gloat | glōt | —*verb* To feel or show great satisfaction.

gloom | glŏŏm | —*noun* Sadness; low spirits.

gor·geous | **gôr´** jəs | —*adjective* Extremely beautiful; magnificent.

gra·cious | **grā´** shəs | —*adjective* Courteous and kind; well-mannered.

grant | grănt | —*verb* To give or allow.

grin·go | **grĭng´** gō | —*noun* A foreigner.

guf·faw | gə **fô´** | —*noun* Hoarse laughter; a short, sudden laugh.

guild | gĭld | —*noun* A union of merchants or craftsmen in the Middle Ages. Guilds set standards of workmanship and looked after the welfare of their members.

guild chap·el | gĭld **chăp´** əl | —*noun* (Medieval) A chapel owned by a guild and used for its religious ceremonies.

guise | gīz | —*noun* A disguise.

galleon

geranium

herald

husk

hal·ter | hôl´ tər | —*noun* A set of ropes or straps for leading or tying an animal. A halter fits around an animal's nose and its neck just behind the ears.

har·mon·i·ca | här **mŏn´** ĭ kə | —*noun* A small rectangular musical instrument containing one or more rows of metal reeds. It is played by blowing in and out through a set of holes.

haugh·ty | hô´ tē | —*adjective* Too proud of oneself; superior in one's own mind; arrogant.

hav·oc | **hăv´** ək | —*noun* Destruction or terrible waste.

heed | hēd | —*noun* Close attention or consideration.

her·ald | **hĕr´** əld | —*noun* A crier or messenger who reads official declarations.

her·e·tic | **hĕr´** ĭ tĭk | —*noun* One who holds false religious beliefs.

hes·i·tate | **hĕz´** ĭ tāt´ | —*verb* To stop or wait because one is not sure.

hoist | hoist | —*verb* To raise up or lift, often with the help of a machine.

hum·ding·er | **hŭm´ dĭng´** ər | —*noun* Something that is very special or amazing.

hu·mil·i·ate | hyōō **mĭl´** ē āt´ | —*verb* To hurt the pride or self-respect of; make ashamed.

husk | hŭsk | —*noun* The dry outer covering of an ear of corn and of some other seeds and fruits.

ă	pat	ĕ	pet
ā	pay	ē	be
âr	care	ĭ	pit
ä	father	ī	pie
îr	fierce	oi	oil
ŏ	pot	ōō	book
ō	go	ōō	boot
ô	paw,	yōō	abuse
	for	ou	out
ŭ	cut	ə	ago,
ûr	fur		item,
th	the		pencil,
th	thin		atom,
hw	which		circus
zh	vision	ər	butter

i·dle | īd´ l | —*adjective* Not working or busy; doing nothing.

il·lus·tra·tor | **ĭl´** ə strāt ər | —*noun* A person who makes pictures or diagrams for printed and other visual material.

im·pact | **ĭm´** păkt | —*noun* The action of one object striking against another; collision.

im·pres·sion | ĭm **prĕsh´** ən | —*noun* An effect, image, or feeling that stays in the mind.

in·dig·nant | ĭn **dĭg´** nənt | —*adjective* Feeling or showing anger about something that is unfair, mean, or bad.

in·di·vis·i·ble | ĭn də **vĭz´** ə bəl | —*adjective* Not capable of being divided.

in·hab·it·ed | ĭn **hăb´** ĭ tĭd | —*adjective* Lived in; made to be home.

in·quis·i·tive | ĭn **kwĭz´** ĭ tĭv | —*adjective* Eager to learn.

in·sane | ĭn **sān´** | —*adjective* Of, showing, or affected by a serious mental illness; crazy; mad.

in·stinc·tive·ly | ĭn **stĭngk´** tĭv lē | —*adverb* Automatically; without thought.

in·stru·ment pan·el | ĭn´ strə mənt **păn´** əl | —*noun* A board of controlling devices and scales used to operate a complicated machine.

in·ter·cede | ĭn´ tər **sēd´** | —*verb* To plead on behalf of another.

in·ter·mis·sion | ĭn´ tər **mĭsh´** ən | —*noun* An interruption or recess in activity; a break.

in·ter·na·tion·al | ĭn´ tər **năsh´** ə nəl | —*adjective* Of or between two or more nations or their people.

in·ter·state | **ĭn´** tər stāt´ | —*adjective* Between states.

in·va·sion | ĭn **vā´** zhən | —*noun* The act of forcefully entering a country by military power.

in·vent | ĭn **vĕnt´** | —*verb* To think up and make; create something that did not exist before.

i·tal·ic | ĭ **tăl´** ĭk | or | ī **tăl´** ĭk | —*noun* A style of printing with the letters slanting to the right.

italic

jus·ti·fy | **jŭs´** tə fī´ | —*verb* To show or prove to be just, fair, and right.

kit | kĭt | —*noun* Shortened form of *kitten.* The young of certain animals such as foxes or squirrels.

knap·sack | **năp´** săk´ | —*noun* A canvas or leather bag made to be worn on the back. A knapsack is used to carry clothing, equipment, or supplies on a hike or march.

knapsack

la·dle | **lād´** l | —*verb* To dip out a liquid using a cup-shaped spoon that has a long handle; to use a ladle.

la·goon | lə **goon´** | —*noun* A shallow body of water that is usually connected to a larger body of water, such as an ocean. A lagoon is often surrounded by coral reefs.

ladle

lariat

land·ing | **lăn′** dĭng | —*noun* A place where boats can unload; a wharf or pier.

lar·i·at | **lăr′** ē ət | —*noun* A long rope with a sliding noose at one end, used especially to catch horses or cattle.

lar·va | **lär′** və | —*noun* An insect in an early form, when it has just hatched from an egg. A larva has a soft body and looks like a worm. A caterpillar is a larva.

las·so | **lăs′** ō | or | lă **soo′** | —*verb* To catch with a lasso or lariat.

lav·ish | **lăv′** ĭsh | —*adjective* To give generously.

lay·out | **lā′** out′ | —*noun* The arrangement of furniture or other structures in a room or building.

leath·er | **lĕ*th*′** ər | —*noun* A material made from animal skin or hide that has been cleaned and tanned.

leg·end | **lĕj′** ənd | —*noun* A story that has been handed down from earlier times.

lever

lev·er | **lĕv′** ər | or | **lē′** vər | —*noun* A simple machine made up of a strong, stiff bar that rests on a fixed point on which it turns. It is used to lift heavy things.

limb | lĭm | —*noun* One of the larger branches of a tree.

Lim·burg·er cheese | **lĭm′** bûr′ gər chēz | —*noun* A cheese with a strong smell.

lo·co | **lō′** kō | —*adjective* Crazy; insane.

loft | lôft | or | lŏft | —*noun* An open space under a roof; an attic.

loop·hole | **loop′** hōl′ | —*noun* A mistake in a written or verbal contract that allows one party to avoid his obligation.

lope | lōp | —*verb* To run with a rolling stride.

low·er·ing | **lou′** ər ĭng | or | **lour′** ĭng | —*adjective* Dark, with gathering clouds.

lunge | lŭnj | —*verb* A sudden, forceful movement forward.

ă pat	ĕ pet
ā pay	ē be
âr care	ĭ pit
ä father	ī pie
îr fierce	oi oil
ŏ pot	oo book
ō go	oo boot
ô paw,	yoo abuse
for	ou out
ŭ cut	ə ago,
ûr fur	item,
th the	pencil,
th thin	atom,
hw which	circus
zh vision	ər butter

M

mag·net | **măg′** nĭt | —*noun* A piece of metal or rock that attracts iron, steel, and some other substances.

make·shift | **māk′** shĭft′ | —*adjective* A quick substitute, usually invented in an emergency.

male | māl | —*noun* A person who is a man or a boy.

mal·e·mute | **măl′** ə myoot′ | —*noun* An Alaskan sled dog that looks like a husky.

man·gy | **măn′** jē | —*adjective* Having bare or dirty spots; shabby.

man·ta ray | **măn′** tə rā | —*noun* A fish with a long, flat body shaped like wings or like a mantle.

man•u•script | **măn´** yə skrĭpt´ | —*noun* A book written by hand or by typewriter. Often a writer sends a manuscript to a publisher, who makes it into a printed book.

mar•i•gold | **măr´** ĭ gōld | or | **mâr´** ĭ gōld | —*noun* A garden plant that has orange, yellow, or reddish flowers.

mar•ma•lade | **mär´** mə lād´ | —*noun* A jam made from sugar and the pulp and rind of fruits.

mas•sive | **măs´** ĭv | —*adjective* Very large and heavy; huge.

mat•ted | **măt´** ĭd | —*adjective* Thick, tangled, or twisted.

me•chan•ic | mə **kăn´** ĭk | —*noun* A person who is skilled in making, using, or repairing machines.

men•tal | **měn´** tl | —*adjective* Of, in, or done by the mind.

mer•chan•dise | **mûr´** chən dīz´ | or | **mûr´** chən dīs´ | —*noun* Things bought and sold; goods.

mer•chant | **mûr´** chənt | —*noun* A person who makes money by buying and selling goods.

mill•stone | **mĭl´** stōn | —*noun* One of two large, round, flat stones used to grind grain.

min•i•a•ture | **mĭn´** ē ə chər | or | **mĭn´** ə chər | —*adjective* Much smaller than the usual size.

mi•rac•u•lous | mĭ **răk´** yə ləs | —*adjective* Like a miracle.

mi•rage | mĭ **räzh´** | —*noun* An illusion.

mite | mīt | —*noun* An extremely small amount.

mo•chi•la | mō **chē´** lə | —*noun* (Spanish). A leather knapsack, sometimes made to fit over a saddle.

moist | moist | —*adjective* Slightly wet; damp.

mold | mōld | —*noun* A hollow container that is made in a particular shape. A liquid or soft material, such as wax, gelatin, or plaster, is put into a mold. When the material hardens, it takes the shape of the mold.

moor•ing | **mo͞or´** ĭng | —*noun* A stable, secure place where a boat can be tied.

Mo•ra•vi•an | mə **rā´** vē ən | —*noun* A Protestant denomination.

mo•sey | **mō´** zē | —*verb* To move or stroll along.

mount | mount | —*noun* A horse or other animal for riding.

mount•ed | **mount´** əd | —*adjective* Put in a suitable place for display or use.

move•ment | **mo͞ov´** mənt | —*noun* The work, membership, or cause of a group of people who are trying to achieve a social or political goal.

muf•fler | **mŭf´** lər | —*noun* A long scarf worn around the neck.

millstone

mochila

mold

muffler

mush¹ | mŭsh | —*noun* A journey by sled dog; a command to a dog sled to go.

mush² | mŭsh | —*verb* To travel by dogsled.

nurse

N

nar·ra·tor | **năr´** āt ər | —*noun* One who tells a story or makes a report.

ne·glect | nĭ **glĕkt´** | —*verb* To fail to care for or give proper attention to.

ne·go·ti·ate | nĭ **gō´** shē āt | —*verb* To discuss or talk over in order to reach an agreement or settlement.

noose | nōōs | —*noun* A loop formed in a rope with a kind of knot that lets the loop tighten as the rope is pulled.

no·tice | **nō´** tĭs | —*noun* An announcement in a public place or publication.

no·tion | **nō´** shən | —*noun* A sudden idea or desire.

no·to·ri·ous | nō **tôr´** ē əs | or | nō **tōr´** ē əs | —*adjective* Well known for something bad or unpleasant.

nurse | nûrs | —*noun* A woman who is hired to take care of someone else's child or children.

O

o·blige | ə **blīj´** | —*verb* To make grateful or thankful.

o·le·o | **ō´** lē ō´ | —*noun* A food made as a substitute for butter; margarine.

o·pin·ion | ō **pĭn´** yən | —*noun* A judgment based on special knowledge and given by an expert.

o·ral | **ôr´** əl | or | **ōr´** əl | —*adjective* Spoken instead of written.

or·dain | ôr **dān´** | —*verb* To install as a minister, priest, or rabbi by means of a formal ceremony.

or·ner·y | **ôr´** nə rē | —*adjective* Stubborn and high-spirited; mischievous.

or·phan | **ôr´** fən | —*noun* A child whose parents are dead.

ă	pat	ĕ	pet	îr	fierce	oi	oil	ŭ	cut	ə	ago,
ā	pay	ē	be	ŏ	pot	ōō	book	ûr	fur		item,
âr	care	ĭ	pit	ō	go	ōō	boot	*th*	the		pencil,
ä	father	ī	pie	ô	paw,	yōō	abuse	th	thin		atom,
					for	ou	out	hw	which		circus
								zh	vision	ər	butter

pal·met·to | păl **mĕt´** ō | or | päl **mĕt´** ō | —*noun* A palm tree with leaves shaped like fans.

pan | păn | —*verb* To wash dirt or gravel in a pan in search of gold.

par·ka | pär´ kə | —*noun* A warm jacket with a hood. Parkas are often lined with fur.

pars·ley | pär´ slē | —*noun* A plant with feathery or curly leaves that are used to flavor or decorate food.

pas·sage | păs´ ĭj | —*noun* 1. A journey or trip, especially on a ship. 2. A part of a written work.

pas·ture | păs´ chər | or | päs´ chər | —*noun* A piece of land covered with grass and other plants that are eaten by horses, cattle, sheep, or other animals that graze.

pau·per | pô´ pər | —*noun* A common man who is very poor.

peal | pēl | —*noun* A loud ringing of a set of bells.

peas·ant | pĕz´ ənt | —*noun* A person who belongs to the group or class of small farmers and farm workers in Europe.

pe·des·tri·an | pə dĕs´ trē ən | —*noun* A person who travels on foot.

peer | pîr | —*verb* To look closely in order to see something clearly; stare.

per·form·ance | pər fôr´ məns | —*noun* The way in which something or someone works.

Per·sian cat | pûr´ zhən kăt | —*noun* A cat with long, silky fur, often kept as a pet.

pe·so | pā´ sō | —*noun* A Mexican unit of money similar to the American dollar bill but of less value.

phar·ma·cist | fär´ mə sĭst | —*noun* A person who is trained to prepare drugs and medicines; a druggist.

phi·los·o·pher | fĭ lŏs´ ə fər | —*noun* A person who is a scholar; one who prefers to think rather than to resort to force or action.

pi·ty | pĭt´ ē | —*noun* A feeling of sorrow for another's suffering.

play·wright | plā´ rīt | —*noun* A person who writes plays.

plot | plŏt | —*noun* The sequence of events in a story or play.

plumb | plŭm | —*adverb* Totally.

pneu·mo·nia | no͞o mōn´ yə | or | nyo͞o mōn´ yə | —*noun* A serious disease of the lungs.

po·li·o | pō´ lē ō´ | —*noun* Poliomyelitis. A disease that can cause paralysis, damage to the muscles, and sometimes death. Poliomyelitis affects mainly children and young people, but a vaccine can now prevent it.

palmetto

parka

peso

porch

portico

pupa

po·lit·i·cal | pə **lĭt´** ĭ kəl | —*adjective* Concerning the affairs or activities of government.

porch | pôrch | or | pōrch | —*noun* A section with a roof that is attached to the outside of a house.

port | pôrt | or | pōrt | —*noun* A harbor and the area of a harbor where boats are loaded and unloaded.

por·ti·co | **pôr´** tĭ kō | or | **pōr´** tĭ kō | —*noun* A porch or walk whose roof is held up by columns.

post | pōst | —*noun* A straight piece of wood or metal set up in the ground.

post·man | **pōst´** mən | —*noun* A letter carrier; mailman.

pot·pour·ri | pō po͝o **rē´** | —*noun* A collection of pretty or fragrant odds and ends.

pre·mi·um | **prē´** mē əm | —*noun* A high-quality gasoline.

pre·serves | prĭ **zûrvz´** | —*noun* Fruit cooked with sugar to keep it from spoiling.

prim | prĭm | —*adjective* Overly proper.

pri·or·i·ty | prī **ôr´** ĭ tē | —*noun* Something of first importance.

priv·i·lege | **prĭv´** ə lĭj | —*noun* A special right or permission given to a person or group.

pros·per | **prŏs´** pər | —*verb* To be successful; do well; thrive.

prov·ince | **prŏv´** ĭns | —*noun* A big division of a country.

pro·vi·sion | prə **vĭzh´** ən | —*noun* The act of giving what is needful or useful.

pub·lish·er | **pŭb´** lĭ shər | —*noun* A person or company that produces and sells printed materials, such as books, magazines, or newspapers.

pu·pa | **py o͞o´** pə | —*noun* An insect during a resting stage while it is changing from a larva into an adult. A pupa is protected by an outer covering such as a cocoon.

quar·rel | **kwôr´** əl | or | **kwŏr´** əl | —*noun* An angry argument.

quar·ry | **kwôr´** ē | or | **kwŏr´** ē | —*noun* An open place where stone is taken out by cutting or blasting.

quar·ry·men | **kwôr´** ē mĕn | or | **kwŏr´** ē mĕn | —*noun* Laborers who work in a quarry for stone cutting or blasting.

qua·ver | **kwā´** vər | —*verb* To speak in a trembling, unsteady way.

quea·sy | kwē′ zē | —*adjective* Nauseated.

quest | kwĕst | —*noun* A pursuit or search for something greatly desired and worthwhile.

quick·sil·ver | kwĭk′ sĭl′ vər | —*noun* The element mercury or something that looks like it.

quilt | kwĭlt | —*noun* A covering for a bed. A quilt is made of two layers of cloth sewn together with a padding of cotton, feathers, or other material between.

quiv·er | kwĭv′ ər | —*verb* To shake with a slight vibrating motion; tremble.

quilt

rad·ish | răd′ ĭsh | —*noun* A plant with a white root that has a strong, sharp taste. The skin of the root may be red or white.

rake | rāk | —*verb* To scrape with a hard object, such as a spur.

ranch | rănch | —*noun* A large farm on which cattle, sheep, or horses are raised.

ran·som | răn′ səm | —*noun* The amount of money demanded or paid so that a person being held prisoner may be set free.

re·act | rē ăkt′ | —*verb* To act in response to something else or because something else has happened; respond.

read·i·ness | rĕd′ ē nĭs | —*noun* A state of preparation or alertness.

re·cep·tion | rĭ sĕp′ shən | —*noun* A social gathering in honor of someone.

reck·less | rĕk′ lĭs | —*adjective* Without care or caution.

reck·on | rĕk′ ən | —*verb* To consider or to compute.

rec·tor | rĕk′ tər | —*noun* A minister in charge of a church and parish.

reel | rēl | —*verb* To stagger.

re·flec·tion | rĭ flĕk′ shən | —*noun* Serious thought.

re·gret | rĭ grĕt′ | —*verb* To feel sorry about.

re·lay | rē′ lā | —*noun* A crew, group, or team that relieves another; a shift.

re·li·a·ble | rĭ lī′ ə bəl | —*adjective* Able to be relied or depended upon.

re·luc·tant·ly | rĭ lŭk′ tənt lē | —*adverb* Lacking inclination; not willingly.

re·plen·ish | rĭ plĕn′ ĭsh | —*verb* To refill.

rep·tile | rĕp′ tīl | —*noun* Any of a group of animals that are cold-blooded and creep or crawl on the ground. Reptiles have a backbone and are covered with scales or hard plates. Snakes, turtles, and dinosaurs are reptiles.

radish

ă pat	ĕ pet
ā pay	ē be
âr care	ĭ pit
ä father	ī pie
îr fierce	oi oil
ŏ pot	ŏŏ book
ō go	ōō boot
ô paw,	yōō abuse
for	ou out
ŭ cut	ə ago,
ûr fur	item,
th the	pencil,
th thin	atom,
hw which	circus
zh vision	ər butter

sorghum

sorrel

spire

spur

sleigh | slā | —*noun* A light vehicle or carriage on metal runners. It is usually drawn by a horse and used for traveling on ice or snow.

slen·der | **slĕn´** dər | —*adjective* Having little width; thin; slim.

slick·er | **slĭk´** ər | —*noun* A shiny, waterproof raincoat or poncho.

smug·gle | **smŭg´** əl | —*verb* To bring into or take out of a country secretly or illegally.

snout | snout | —*noun* The long nose, jaws, or front part of the head of an animal. Pigs and alligators have snouts.

so·cia·ble | **sō´** shə bəl | —*adjective* Liking other people; liking company; friendly.

sol·emn | **sŏl´** əm | —*adjective* Very serious and grave.

sol·i·tar·y | **sŏl´** ĭ tĕr ē | —*adjective* Existing or living alone.

so·lu·tion | sə **lōō´** shən | —*noun* The solving of a problem.

sor·ghum | **sôr´** gəm | —*noun* A grain often used to make syrup or to feed animals.

sor·rel | **sôr´** əl | —*noun* A horse whose color is slightly orange to light brown.

source | sôrs | or | sōrs | —*noun* A place or thing from which something comes.

sour·dough | **sour´** dō | —*noun* A settler in the Yukon who had to make his bread with sourdough instead of with yeast.

spar·row | **spăr´** ō | —*noun* Any of several small brownish or grayish birds that are very common in cities.

spat | spăt | —*noun* A short quarrel.

spire | spīr | —*noun* The highest part of a building that tapers upward above a steeple or other structure.

spoil | spoil | —*verb* To become rotten or damaged so as to be bad to use.

spook | spōōk | —*verb* To startle or make nervous.

sprint | sprĭnt | —*verb* To run at top speed.

spur | spûr | —*noun* A sharp metal piece in the shape of a small wheel with spikes, worn on the heel of a person's boot. It is used to make a horse go faster.

stake | stāk | —*noun* A stick or post with a sharp end for driving into the ground as a marker, support, or part of a fence.

star·tle | **stär´** tl | —*verb* 1. To cause to jump in surprise or fright. 2. To cause to be afraid; to cause wonder.

stead | stĕd | —*noun* A position or purpose held by one person as an exchange or replacement for another.

sten·cil | **stĕn´** səl | —*noun* A sheet of paper or other material in which letters or figures have been cut so that when ink is applied to the sheet, the patterns will appear on the surface beneath.

still | stĭl | —*adjective* Without noise; quiet; silent.

stout | stout | —*adjective* Strong; firm; sturdy.

strad·dle | **străd´** l | —*verb* To sit or stand so that each leg is on either side of something, as when sitting on a horse.

strait | strāt | —*adjective* (Archaic) Tight, confined.

strut | strŭt | —*verb* To walk in a proud manner.

stud | stŭd | —*verb* To dot onto a surface; sprinkle about.

stud·y | **stŭd´** ē | —*noun* A room used for studying, reading, or working.

stu·por | **stoo´** pər | —*noun* A daze; a state of confused inactivity.

sub·merged | səb **mûrjd´** | —*adjective* Covered with water.

sub·mit | səb **mĭt´** | —*verb* To yield to the control, influence, or authority of another.

sub·ti·tle | **sŭb´** tīt l | —*noun* A second title used to explain a heading.

sul·len | **sŭl´** ən | —*adjective* Showing bad humor; silent or angry; glum.

sul·try | **sŭl´** trē —*adjective* Very hot and humid.

sure·foot·ed | **shoor´** foot´ ĭd | —*adjective* Able to walk on steep surfaces without stumbling.

surf | sûrf | —*noun* The waves of the sea as they break upon the shore or the white foam that is on the beach.

sus·pend | sə **spĕnd´** | —*verb* To halt any action for a period of time.

sus·pi·cious | sə **spĭsh´** əs | —*adjective* Causing lack of trust or doubt in others.

swap | swŏp | —*verb* To trade items.

sym·bol·ize | **sĭm´** bə līz | —*verb* To be a symbol of; represent; stand for.

sym·pa·thet·ic | sĭm pə **thĕt´** ĭk | —*adjective* Showing or feeling understanding, pity, or kindness toward others.

syn·a·gogue | **sĭn´** ə gŏg | or | **sĭn´** ə gôg | —*noun* A building or place used by Jews for worship and religious instruction.

stencil

ă	pat	ĕ	pet
ā	pay	ē	be
âr	care	ĭ	pit
ä	father	ī	pie
îr	fierce	oi	oil
ŏ	pot	oo	book
ō	go	oo	boot
ô	paw,	yoo	abuse
	for	ou	out
ŭ	cut	ə	ago,
ûr	fur		item,
th	the		pencil,
th	thin		atom,
hw	which		circus
zh	vision	ər	butter

tadpole

toll

tad·pole | tăd´ pōl | —*noun* A frog or toad when it has just been hatched and lives underwater. In this stage it has gills, a tail, and no legs. The gills and tail disappear as the legs develop and the frog or toad becomes fully grown.

tai·lor | tā´ lər | —*noun* A person who makes, repairs, or alters clothing.

tal·ent·ed | tăl´ ən tĭd | —*adjective* Having a natural ability to do something well.

tan·gled | tăng´ gəld | —*adjective* Mixed together in a confused or twisted mass.

ta·per | tā´ pər | —*verb* To make or become gradually thinner at one end.

taunt | tônt | —*verb* To ridicule.

taw·ny | tô´ nē | —*noun* The color of tanned leather; a light shade of brown.

tel·e·graph | tĕl´ ə grăf | —*noun* A system of sending messages over wire or radio to a special receiving station.

ten·or | tĕn´ ər | —*noun* A man's singing voice, higher than a baritone and lower than an alto.

ter·ror | tĕr´ ər | —*noun* 1. Great or intense fear.　2. A person or thing that causes such fear.

Thames Riv·er | tĕmz rĭv´ ər | —*noun* A large river in England that flows through London.

ther·a·py | thĕr´ ə pē | —*noun* A sustained treatment of a disability or injury to bring about a cure.

thick·et | thĭk´ ĭt | —*noun* A dense growth of shrubs or small trees.

thong | thông | or | thŏng | —*noun* A thin strip of leather used to fasten something, such as a sandal.

thor·ough·bred | thûr´ ō brĕd | or | thər´ ə brĕd | —*noun* A purebred animal.

thread·bare | thrĕd´ bâr | —*adjective* Frayed or worn.

til·ler | tĭl´ ər | —*noun* A lever or handle used to turn a rudder or steer a boat.

tol·er·ate | tŏl´ ə rāt | —*verb* To put up with; endure.

toll | tōl | —*verb* (archaic) To pull something.

top·ic | tŏp´ ĭk | —*noun* A single subject or theme within a larger work.

tow | tō | —*verb* To pull along behind with a chain, rope, or cable.

trade lan·guage | trād lăng´ gwĭj | —*noun* A well-known language from one set of people used by other nations, tribes, or races because it has been spread through the market industry of a certain large area.

tra·di·tion | trə dĭsh´ ən | —*noun* The practice of passing down ideas, customs, and beliefs from one generation to the next.

trag·e·dy | trăj´ ĭ dē | —*noun* A serious play that ends badly for the main character or characters.

tramp | trămp | —*verb* To go on foot.

tram·po·line | trăm´ pə lēn´ | or | trăm´ pə lĭn | —*noun* A sheet of canvas stretched across a metal frame and fastened with springs. Trampolines are used for jumping and other gymnastics.

trans·con·ti·nen·tal | trăns kŏn tə nĕn´ tl | —*adjective* Across the continent.

tran·scribe | trăn skrīb´ | —*verb* To write out completely.

trans·form | trăns fôrm´ | —*verb* To change very much in appearance or characteristics.

trans·gress | trăns grĕs´ | or | trănz grĕs´ | —*verb* To disobey a law or command; sin; do what God forbids.

trans·mit·ter | trăns mĭt´ ər | or | trănz mĭt´ ər | —*noun* A device that sends out electrical, radio, or television signals.

treach·er·ous | trĕch´ ər əs | —*adjective* Not dependable; dangerous.

trel·lis | trĕl´ ĭs | —*noun* A framework used for training climbing plants.

tri·al run | trī´ əl rŭn | —*noun* A preliminary test of a machine or vehicle that simulates actual use.

trop·i·cal | trŏp´ ĭ kəl | —*adjective* Of, like, or found in the very hot regions of the earth that are near the equator.

trampoline

trun·dling | trŭn´ dlĭng | —*verb* Moving or pulling along on wheels.

tum·ble·weed | tŭm´ bəl wēd | —*noun* A plant that, when it dies, breaks free and is blown about by the wind.

tun·dra | tŭn´ drə | —*noun* A large plain without trees in arctic regions. Mosses and small shrubs are the only kinds of plant life that grow on it. The ground beneath the surface of tundra remains frozen all year round.

ty·ran·ni·cal | tĭ răn´ ĭ kəl | or | tī răn´ ĭ kəl | —*adjective* Cruel or unjust.

tumbleweed

ă	pat	ĕ	pet	îr	fierce	oi	oil	ŭ	cut	ə	ago,
ā	pay	ē	be	ŏ	pot	ŏŏ	book	ûr	fur		item,
âr	care	ĭ	pit	ō	go	ōō	boot	*th*	the		pencil,
ä	father	ī	pie	ô	paw,	yōō	abuse	th	thin		atom,
					for	ou	out	hw	which		circus
								zh	vision	ər	butter

U

vehicles

un·der·brush | ŭn´ dər brŭsh | —*noun* Small trees, shrubs, and other plants that grow thickly beneath tall trees in a forest or wooded area.

un·in·tel·li·gi·ble | ŭn ĭn tĕl´ ĭ jə bəl | —*adjective* Not able to be understood.

un·tame | ŭn tām´ | —*adjective* Not able to be subjected; not gentle.

ur·chin | ûr´ chĭn | —*noun* A small, playful child; a child with no money or home.

V

veranda

val·our or **val·or** | văl´ ər | —*noun* Courage and strength in battle.

val·u·a·ble | văl´ yōō ə bəl | or | văl´ yə bəl | —*adjective* Worth much money.

ve·hi·cle | vē´ ĭ kəl | —*noun* Anything used for moving people or goods; a means of transportation. Cars, trucks, trains, wagons, bicycles, airplanes, rockets, sleds, and ships are all vehicles.

ven·i·son | vĕn´ ĭ sən | —*noun* Deer or elk when used for food.

ven·ture | vĕn´ chər | —*verb* To take a risk with; expose to possible loss or danger.

ve·ran·da | və răn´ də | —*noun* A porch or balcony with a roof.

ver·sion | vər´ zhən | or | vər´ shən | —*noun* A new form of something, based on an original model.

ves·ti·bule | vĕs´ tə byōol | —*noun* The area immediately inside the doorway of a building; a lobby.

vol·ume | vŏl´ yōōm | or | vŏl´ yəm | —*noun* One book of a set.

vol·un·teer | vŏl ən tîr´ | —*verb* To give or offer, usually without being asked.

W

waistcoat

waist·coat | wĕs´ kĭt | or | wāst´ kōt | —*noun* A vest.

walk | wôk | —*noun* A place set apart or designated for walking.

wal·low | wŏl´ ō | —*verb* To move in a rolling manner.

war·i·ly | wâr´ ĭ lē | —*adverb* Carefully; cautiously.

watch | wŏch | —*noun* Someone who guards or protects.

wharf | hwôrf | or | wôrf | —*noun* A landing place or pier at which ships may tie up and load or unload.

whey | hwā | or | wā | —*noun* The watery part of milk that separates from the curds when milk turns sour.

whirl•wind | **hwûrl´** wĭnd | or | **wûrl´** wĭnd | —*noun* A wind or current of air that turns round and round, often violently, as a tornado.

whoop | ho͞op | or | hwo͞op | or | wo͞op | —*noun* A loud cry or shout.

wid•owed | **wĭd´** ōd | —*adjective* Left without a husband or wife because of death.

wield | wēld | —*verb* To handle or swing a weapon or tool with great skill and power.

wince | wĭns | —*verb* To move or pull back quickly from something that is painful, dangerous, or frightening.

won•der•ful | **wŭn´** dər fəl | —*adjective* Causing wonder; marvelous; impressive.

work•out | **wûrk´** out | —*noun* Exercise or practice, especially in athletics.

yarn | yärn | —*noun* A long tale; a story, often adventurous or funny.

year•ling | **yîr´** lĭng | —*noun* An animal whose age is between one and two years.

Yu•kon | **yo͞o´** kŏn | —*noun* A northern territory of Canada next to Alaska.

whirlwind

ă	pat	ĕ	pet	îr	fierce	oi	oil	ŭ	cut	ə	ago,
ā	pay	ē	be	ŏ	pot	o͝o	book	ûr	fur		item,
âr	care	ĭ	pit	ō	go	o͞o	boot	*th*	the		pencil,
ä	father	ī	pie	ô	paw,	yo͞o	abuse	th	thin		atom,
					for	ou	out	hw	which		circus
								zh	vision	ər	butter